Decisive Battles, Strategic Leaders

DECISIVE BATTLES, STRATEGIC LEADERS

J. P. Alexander

With a Foreword by
Lt. General Thomas Mathew, *PVSM, AVSM* (Retd)
Former Adjutant General, Indian Army

PARTRIDGE
A Penguin Random House Company

To order additional copies of this book, contact
Partridge India
000 800 10062 62
orders.india@partridgepublishing.com

www.partridgepublishing.com/india

CONTENTS

Front Cover "Wellington at Waterloo"

MAPS

ABOUT THE AUTHOR

J P Alexander is an alumnus of St Xavier's School and Wilson College (Bombay); College of Engineering (Poona); Dept. of Management (University of Leeds, UK).

He has participated in Management programmes at IIM (Ahm); NITIE (Powai); Tata Mgt. Training Centre (Poona); and trained in Total Quality Mgt. at AOTS (Osaka, Japan). He has also attended the International Purchasing Managers Conference (Venice) and Milan Trade Fair and interned with GEC-Elliot (Rochester); Davidson (Belfast); Stothert&Pitt (Bath), besides making business study visits to leading companies—Philips (Holland), Mercedes Benz (Stuttgart), Toto and Mazda Motors (Japan) etc. He was a Sir Dorabji Tata Scholar; British Council Scholar; Wilson College First Scholar and recipient of the Scholarship of AOTS (Japan). After lecturing in Civil Engineering (College of Engg., Poona), he worked in the public sector FACT Ltd, in the areas of Marketing, Materials and Management Development.

He has been Hon. Secretary of the Kerala Management Association; President, FACT Sports Association and represented Kerala State in the Inter-State Tennis Tournament at Hyderabad in 1976. J P Alexander teaches Management at DePaul Institute of Science and Technology and conducts Corporate programmes for managers at middle and senior levels. He has written articles and reviewed books of different genres. In the field of Military History, he has studied and surveyed, over the years, many of the sites of battlefields, castles, fortifications and terrain, which are referred to in this work, and has interacted with senior service personnel, geostrategic theorists and management experts on aspects of Strategy and Leadership. A special tribute must be paid to the strategic guru, K.Subramahmanyam of IDSA, whose clarity of ideas influenced a whole generation of thinkers and policy-makers and shaped the course of India's geopolitics for over 40 tumultuous years. Contact, albeit fleeting, with this profound thinker greatly influenced the writer's geopolitical concepts, particularly his theory of "Multi-polar" versus the prevalent "Bi-Polar" world of the 1970s.

Lt Gen Thomas Mathew, PVSM, AVSM, (Retd)
Former Adjutant General, Indian Army

"Decisive Battles, Strategic Leaders" is fascinating not only for the wide span of time it has covered, but also for the details of battles fought in different continents. Authors have struggled to put together one battle or campaign. It is indeed praiseworthy that a non-military person has researched and analyzed major battles from the time of Alexander the Great to the present in one book. A commander must handle three basic elements—men, material and ground. Success comes to the general who is adept at the art of applying the first two elements to the last, in the most effective way.

As a professional soldier, I have studied many of the battles described and read about some of the others. The book puts together the evolution of land warfare over the ages in a concise and interesting manner. I enjoyed reading it and it has enriched my awareness of these battles and wars, including the geo-political aspects of the conflicts. It will indeed be an asset and treasured possession of soldiers and armed forces libraries in India and abroad.

(Lt. General Mathew saw action with the Rajput Regiment in the victorious Bangladesh campaign in 1971. A career soldier and expert on strategy, he participated in counter-insurgency operations in J & K and the Northeast. He served as Military Attache in the Indian Embassy in Paris and has visited and surveyed many of the battlesites studied in the book.)

Introduction by Rear Admiral (Retd.), B.R. Menon, VSM, IN

This book is akin to an exquisite Arabian carpet woven with silk, cotton and wool into a magnificent tapestry of Man's ambitions. Its vast spread encompasses a broad spectrum of battles and wars, ancient and modern, based on detailed research on the ambience of the period, emergence of strategic leaders and the compulsions of religion, ideology and personal ambition.

Can an introduction be given to Veda Vyas' "Mahabharatha", Valmiki's "Ramayana" or the Bible or the Koran? Sri Alexander's magnum opus has adequate material for a doctoral programme on anyone of the chapters. In this masterly effort, he has vividly brought forth the elements of varying strategic leadership over a span of 3500 years in a logical manner. He has culled from military history not only the development of weaponry, but also cited instances of the strengths/weaknesses of logistics and lines of supply. The description of battles is uniformly incisive but I was particularly enthralled by the siege of Constantinople, including the naval engagements, the Turkish land assault with innovative siege engines and the desperate defence by the scanty garrison. The role of religion including the schism between the Latin and Greek churches and the symbiotic relationship between the Patriarch and the Emperor are lucidly explained.

Battles are dreamt and conceived in the minds of men, and the strategic mindset is all important when two great commanders face off—Napoleon vs. Wellington or Rommel vs. Montgomery. I must however, caution readers that this book is not meant for light reading. Its understanding demands concentration, a fair knowledge of history and an interest in dissecting the art of war, its leadership and strategies at various crossroads of human history.

(Admiral B.R. Menon was Chairman of major public enterprises including Goa Shipyard Ltd. and Advisor to the Govt of Kerala. An alumnus of Royal Naval College, (Greenwich) and National Defence College (Delhi), he was technical attaché to the Indian High Commission (UK), Director of Marine Engineering at Naval HQ (Delhi) and recipient of the Visishta Seva Medal.)

PRE-PUBLICATION REVIEWS

T T Thomas, Board of Governors, Indian Institute of Management (Kozhikode) and past President, All-India Management Association

An amazing book for its width and depth in analyzing the strategies of the great generals and drawing parallels with modern business operations like the frontal assault by IBM on Apple in the computer market or the David vs Goliath confrontation between Nirma and Unilever in the Indian detergent market. The author observes that leadership (in war, peace and business) is largely about communication. He links modern management theories of Fayol, Drucker and Maslow to the motivational and leadership practices of Alexander, Hannibal and Napoleon. The lucid description of the battles, the human interest aspects of the fall of Constantimople, Vijaynagar and Delhi and the tragic fate of Rani Lakshmibai, Tantia Tope and Yamashita will fascinate the lay reader.

CP Thomas (Author and Retd. Member, Postal Services Board)

"There are not many Indian books on Military History and this is one among the few good studies on the subject. The author takes a bird's eye view of some of the most decisive battles in world history. Though there may be different opinions about the omission of certain battles which had great historical importance, the ones recorded are all very significant. The book will be of great interest to aficionados of military history. Very well written and the maps and battle plans enhance its value."

"Intelligentsia" (Magazine)

Covering major battles and sieges from Armagedon (1479 BC) to Dacca (1971), the author analyses the strategies and leadership styles of Alexander, Hannibal and Caesar down to Napoleon, Rommel, Giap and Manekshaw. Detailed battle plans make the descriptions clear and interesting. The theories of Sun Tzu, Clausewitz, Liddell Hart and Mao are examined. An analogy is drawn between Business and War, comparing the principles and practices in both. An array of human interest stories unfolds—Hannibal, Rani Lakshmibai, Tantyia Tope, Yamashita The realistic narration of the fall of the cities of Constantinople (1453) and Delhi (1857) and the slaughter at Panipat (1761) makes history come alive. Makes excellent reading even for the lay reader with an interest in the past because of the lessons we can draw from it in our own tumultuous times.

Rev. Dr. Alex Chalangady Counsellor(Education & Media), Vincentian Congregation.

In the new knowledge economy, strategic leadership is a requisite to lead a nation or to establish a business. 'Decisive Battles, Strategic Leaders' deals comprehensively with leadership styles and strategies and covers major battles and sieges during the period from 1479 BC to 1971 AD. Classical references which reveal the author's eclectic knowledge, are used to explain the concepts of strategic leadership. Going beyond mere theories to illustrate the practice of leadership with fascinating real-life events, makes it different from others of the same genre The book is an invaluable resource and will be tremendously influential in shaping the approach of future leaders.

Dr. (Capt.) C.M. Chitale, Professor, Depertent of Managment Sciences (PUMBA), University of Pune

The book written by Prof. J.P. Alexander contains in-depth analysis of various battles in the past and the learning thereof. The Author has shown the similarily between "Principles of War" expounded by Sun Tsu and the 14 Management Principles contributed by Henry Fayol. Achieving surprise over the enemy was the main strategy to win the battle. The innovative creativity is essential to achieve success in the business world. While discussing the guerrilla warfare techniques, the point regarding flexibility of forces has been highlighted. It is seen that the "Principle of Survival" is applicable to war and business as well. While describing various personalities, the Author has categorically analysed different situations. Detailed analysis of the 1971 war between India & Pakistan talked much about the leadership of "Sam" Manekshaw. This book will be invaluable for practising managers which will help them understand the strategic approach for survival and success.

C Babu Rajeev, IAS (Rtd), former Director General, Archaeological Survey of India

This is a brilliantly researched treatise on the major battles in history from Megiddo to Dacca and leadership styles of some of the great generals who fought them. In many ways military science was born as a result of the experiences of these battles. While the entire book makes very interesting reading I was particularly fascinated by the chapters on the fall of Constantinople, the destruction of Vijaynagar, Waterloo and the fall of Delhi. The detailed maps and well-drawn diagrams on the plan and course of the battles supplement the lucid description. Anyone with a sense of history would find this book most compelling to read.

K E Mammen, Freedom Fighter

I was thrilled to read chapter 18 on the fall of Delhi (1857) and was much enlightened about the current Indian Ocean situation, described in the Epilogue. But it was Chapter 1 which I found most interesting with its clear ideas on Leadership. As a Gandhian, I could appreciate the qualities of the Mahatma's great team, but I also recall with nostalgia my meeting with the Forgotten Hero Netaji Subash, at Madras. Can we forget the wonderful group he led in the INA—Gen. Shah Nawas Khan, Col. Prem Sahgal, Col. G S Dhillon, Capt. Lakshmi Sahgal, Capt. Krishnan Nair?

Gautam Patel (Technocrat, Grandson of Sardar Patel)

Highly readable and well organized, the book gives an authentic overview of four millennia of human conflict. It not only describes battles but also gives the geopolitical background and the raison d'etre for the confrontations, the strategies and tactics involved and the traits and skills of the protagonists. I was fascinated by the chronology of the development of weaponry from the chariot to the longbow, siege engines, cannons, muskets and the battle tank, in parallel with the evolution of appropriate strategy/ tactics. More would be better!

Jaishree Misra, Author of "Rani Lakshmibai"

Best wishes for launch of your book "Decisive Battles. Strategic Leaders"

INFLUENCES AND ACKNOWLEDGEMENTS

"Each of us owes the deepest thanks to those who have rekindled our inner light"

—Albert Shweitzer

Recently, Indira Nooyi quoted Malcom Gladwell's *Outliers* to emphasize that whatever she is today is because of where she came from. At 70, I am truly grateful to the Almighty for the many positive influences in my life. My family (nuclear and extended) provided me with a truly eclectic ambience. My father, J. Alexander who did his doctorate in Crystallography from Durham (U.K.) mentored several generations of students at Wilson College, Bombay and Catholicate College, Kerala. My mother, who studied history at Womens Christian College (Madras), was a walking encyclopaedia on royal (and family!) genealogical trees. My only sister was focussed on English literature, in which she did her Masters. My uncle, K.E. Mammen is a freedom fighter whose uncompromising idealism rubbed off on all those he interacted with. Cousin Abraham George fresh out of Vellore Medical College, joined the Army to fight India's enemies. He was my companion during youthful trekking expeditions to Shivaji's hill forts around Poona. The wonders of Bijapur, Golconda and Vijayanagar were first revealed to me by my uncle, Dr. John George with whom I spent Diwali vacations at Bidar. I also recall the delightful holidays in Bombay and Kottayam with the K.M. Mathew family. Mrs Mathew (Annammakochama) possessed unsurpassed culinary skills and extraordinary patience in dealing with boisterous boys (including her own). Their guest bathroom had a mini-library with a choice selection of books and magazines. Expectedly, I spent much of my time there or at the dining table where the quality of the wide ranging discussions matched the delectable food.

My father's colleagues at Wilson College were exceptionally erudite and I benefited from my close interaction with Dr. Donald Kennedy, Dr. H.J. Taylor, Dr. Cherian, Dr. Augustine Borde, Dr Zachariah and Prof. Esther Kurian (whose husband vainly tried to teach me his energetic "serve & volley" style of tennis) and unlimited access to the huge library. Later, when I joined the college, I was fortunate to receive the First Rank college scholarship and was also the tennis singles champion. The college marker Lakia, who was a practitioner of error-free tennis and endless rallies on the cow dung courts at Kennedy Seaface, reshaped my hitherto erratic game.

Ten years at St. Xavier's School was a cosmopolitan experience with boys from diverse linguistic, ethnic, financial, religious and cultural backgrounds—Parsis, Goans, Bohras, Khojas, Sindhis, Punjabis, Bengalis, South Indians, Maharashtrians and Gujaratis—animatedly arguing (in English) about every topic under the sun. Contemporaries included Sunil Gavaskar, Milind Rege, Ramesh Sippy, Rohinton Mistry, Adi Godrej and Deepak Parekh. Gautam Patel became a lifelong friend. The dedicated Jesuit Fathers were of different nationalities and were led by the dynamic principal Rev. Fr. Britto, who personally coached and accompanied us to participate in debates, quiz programmes and elocution competitions. Our learned lay mentors, notably soft-spoken Miss Ghadiali and masters "Lamboo" Thomas (Maths), "Laski" Mathias (History) and Paul Frank (French) opened multiple gateways of knowledge to our young minds. My years as student and lecturer at the century old College of Engineering (*alma mater* of Sir M Visweswaraya) enabled me to imbibe the very special Pune culture, history and music. Interaction with the denizens of this knowledge-oriented city was truly elevating. My Department Head, the strict disciplinarian Prof. Sathe, constantly emphasized the need to focus on the 'Fundas' (basics/fundamentals') of any subject, a very valuable piece of advice which stood me in good stead whatever I studied later. The many congenial hours on the college tennis courts and boat club and the great Pune libraries were real stress busters.

Joining the executive cadre of FACT Ltd., I came to Kerala practically as an outsider, but was warmly received into the fold and the kinship continues. The many-splendoured Managing Director, M.K.K. Nair, M. Dandapani and N. Gopalakrishnan Nair—all belonging to the IAS cadre, mentored me during my initial working years. The innovative marketing chief, R.N Warrier was instrumental in deputing me to the Marketing Executives course at IIM (Ahmedabad) before he himself left FACT to head the Marketing Department at IIM (Bangalore).

As Regional Manager in Trichy, I began to unravel the intricacies of rural marketing through implementation of FACT's integrated fertiliser sales policy at the grass-roots. I was also fortunate to enjoy the friendship of some very special people like G Parthasarathy and K Unnikrishnan, even after their careers took them to Delhi and beyond. N. Haribhaskar, then District Collector, whose remarkable intellectual attainments catapulted him to into the highest administrative echelons continues to be a mentor and gave several valuable ideas for improving this book. Back in Kochi, as Secretary and Jt Secretary of the Kerala Management Association, I was privileged to interact with visionaries of the calibre of Varghese Kurien and M S Swaminathan.

As one gets on in years, the less influence other people have. But Prof. Madhukar Rao, who passed away recently, was an exception. I spent many an hour at the Lotus Club listening attentively as he waxed eloquent on the Romantics, Victorians and Modern poets or recalled a Gavasker or Tendulkar innings unerringly from the depths of his inexhaustible memory. He was rather pleased with the first draft of this book and noted down several suggestions for improvement. RIP, learned professor! Living next to PK Balasubramanian, the doyen of the Ernakulam Bar was another learning experience as he expounded on the intricacies of the law to my untutored self. He moved on, after elevation to the Supreme Court but one important thing I understood was that law and justice are not always congruent. The proximity and example of this family of legal eagles perhaps prompted my wife, Jaya, and sons, Arjun and Arvind to pursue legal studies!

My six decade long affair with Tennis enriched me with many friends and provided valuable insights into human nature. In 1976, playing for Kerala in the South Zone Inter-State on the cowdung courts at Fateh Maidan, (Hyderabad), we were confronted by the likes of Shankar Krishnan, Royappa, Priyadarshi, Raghuram, S.P. and S.N. Misra. After each 5-0 whitewash, we held (serious!) post-mortem strategy meetings to figure out what had gone wrong and how to do better in the next rubber. I recall that my inscrutable teammate, M.R. Ramesh, continued to be remarkably unperturbed and optimistic right up till our last drubbing. But that is what tennis is about—fighting gamely against heavy odds, always expecting to snatch victory from the jaws of defeat. Leander Paes often beat higher ranked players whenever he played for his country. At the amateur level, G.Padmanabhan, labouring with a physical handicap, inspired us by his self-motivation and never-say-die spirit while playing for University and State. I admired the racquet skills of former Davis Cupper, A.J. Uday Kumar and the strategic thinking of S.Krishnakumar who both partnered me in several tournaments. But I miss most the equanimity and amiability of the late A.M. Habeeb who partnered me in many a victory (and defeat}. Dear departed friend, I hope you are continuing to flummox opponents with your amazing overhead in the Elysian Wimbledon.

I express my gratitude to the Sir Dorab Tata Trust whose funding enabled me to indulge early on in my passion for books and travel. The honour was very special for me since my father too had been a Tata scholar. I cannot forget the empathy and concern of Mrs. Vesugar and Dinshaw Malegamwala who administered the Trust and the tea/dinner meetings they set up with the Tata greats—JRD Tata, Nani Palkiwalla and Freddie Mehta.

I studied management at the University of Leeds thanks to the generosity of the British Council, a very caring organisation which permitted me to intern with industrial units at Glasgow, Belfast (at the height of the IRA activity), Bath and Rochester. I really saw the UK holistically—cathedrals, castles, battlefields, the Scottish lochs, Wordsworth's beloved Lake District, great houses like Blenheim and Chatsworth, Stonehenge and mystical Glastonbury. Delayering historical London meant going back to the bloody legends of the Tower (the Princes, Anne of a Thousand Days, Sir Walter Raleigh, Monmouth), the pubs and theatres of Marlowe and Shakespeare, the intellectual coffee houses of the 17th century, the Dickensian reality of Oliver Twist and David Copperfield and the grim ambience of the Rippper's Whitechapel Road The teaching style at Leeds was informal with easy access to the treasures of the Brotherton library. We were privileged to interact with pioneering thinkers like Reg Revans (the guru of Action Learning), practicing managers like Graham Pound and a host of editors, diplomats and opinion-makers. Stints at the Harrogate Police Academy, GEC Dunchurch and visits to Oxford and Cambridge Universities were part of the well-planned itinerary. Professors Butterworth and Kirkman took me around Yorkshire and Wales and I also spent week-ends with some of my father's former colleagues. I was able to observe the thrilling 1979 {Callaghan vs. Thatcher} elections at close quarters and watch Borg, Connors, McEnroe and Vijay Amritraj live at Wimbledon. All in all, my stay was as much about understanding cross cultural aspects as it was about management studies.

I am grateful to the AOTS and the Japanese government for enabling me to study TQM in Osaka in 1997 and visit Japanese industrial units. The distinguished faculty included Prof. Yoshio Kondo, whose Theory of

Business/Games Analogy has been referred to in this book. Sensing my interest, he was pleased to give me an autographed copy of his *"Human Motivation"*. Osaka Castle and the ancient capitals of Nara and Kyoto were nearby. Having read James Clavell's *"Shogun"* (and seen the movie) I was interested in the rise of Iesu Tokugawa and his historic victory at Sekigahara in 1600. On my return journey, I was able to visit the sites of Yamashita's assault on Singapore island (9th to14th February, 1942}. Both these battles are described in my book.

Teaching management at De Paul Instiute of Science & Technology, was to be young again, as I interacted with the young, both students and colleagues. I learnt practical lessons in empathy from Fr Daison, who is everybody's friend My extensive discussions with Fr Alex Chalangady (whose doctoral thesis was on Leadership) were valuable in formulating the first chapter. Profs Jacob and Stalin helped with software aspects of the book. I am especially grateful to my student, Shajahan Shamsu, for meticulously creating the images, maps and battle-plans and to Mini Thomas, our long time live-in housekeeper for keeping us all well-fed.

My wife Jaya and sons Arjun and Arvind enthusiastically accompanied me on many of my later rambles through exotic Smyrna, Halicarnussus, Nicea, Istanbul, Gallipoli, Troy, Pergamon, Ephesus, Sigriya, Anuradapura. We were pilgrims not tourists or travellers as we traversed a plethora of sites across India and they sportingly humoured my craving for visiting (and revisiting) forts, battlesites and ruins of all kinds! I cannot even begin to explain the innumerable ways in which the trio helped—checking the text, touching up maps, playing Devil's Advocate on the relevance/validity of sections, copyright/licence for cover etc. The journey through life has often been difficult but always meaningful and interesting. As T.S. Eliot wrote in *Little Gidding*—*"...*
And the end of all our exploring, will be to arrive where we started...
and we know the place for the first time..."

J P Alexander

1

2014 AD: STRATEGIC LEADERSHIP— THE SHAPE OF THINGS TO COME

The world today is in deep crisis, with 3 deadly bombs just waiting to explode—Nuclear, Financial and Climate. Every nation is seeking leaders with Vision to guide us through these hazardous times and is groping in the dark to understand the essence of true Leadership. The most logical method would be to study the lives, traits, skills and achievements of those who have already proved themselves as leaders in different fields—prophets, statesmen, entrepreneurs and military commanders. Surprisingly, it is in War that leadership qualities are best displayed, since results are known immediately and any shortcomings of mediocre generals are quickly exposed in action.

Innumerable biographies have been written on the great captains— from Cyrus, Alexander, Hannibal and Caesar, down to Marlborough, Frederick, Napoleon, Lee and the commanders of the post World War II conflicts. Different though they from each other, there are common traits that separate them from ordinary generals. This book seeks to study them in action to identify the qualities that made them special—Physical Traits, Charisma, Motivation, Intelligence, Intuition, Creativity, Courage, Team Building, Emotional skills, Perseverance, Decision-making and Commonsense. Geo-political, Strategic, Tactical and Technical Skills which pertain to their chosen field of expertise, are also best revealed in critical battlefield situations. An understanding of their own (and the enemy's) Strengths, Weaknesses, Opportunities, Threats (SWOT) was also a vital factor in their mental makeup.

Secondly, the validity of the truism that "Those who forget History are condemned to relive it" has been repeatedly proved down the ages. For example, the current happenings in the Swat Valley in Pakistan are an exact replication of what **Sir Winston Churchill** describes in his eye-witness account, *"The Malakand Field Force—1897."* "Contact with civilization assails the credulity on which the influence of the mad Mullah depends. The tribesmen believed that a mighty man had come to lead Islam". Undoubtedly, a study of the past could eliminate human blunders, particularly in the field of geopolitics. Sadly, no useful lessons have been learned, from previous failed attempts to "pacify" the turbulent tribes of Waziristan and Afghanistan, though it is clear that this is the route to the "Eurasian Heartland of the World", control of which is considered the key to global domination. The "**Heartland**" theory, first propounded in Sir Halford McKinder's influential lecture to the Royal Geographical Society in 1904, is even more significant today, with the discovery of extensive hydrocarbon resources in the region. Unfortunately, the USA has not yet learnt how to deal with the "Heartland imbroglio", complicating the situation with an inept choice of alliances and options, around the peripheral regions of Iran, Iraq and Afghanistan.

Learning the right lessons from the past is not easy. Even the great **Napoleon** (in 1812) failed to learn from the wintry defeat of the eccentric Swedish genius Charles XII[th'] who invaded Peter the Great's **Russia** in 1707; or Hitler whose foray into the same sub-zero expanse, ended in total defeat. Forgetting Chernobyl we have landed ourselves in the Fukushima predicament! Human history is indeed replete with such instances of man's inability or unwillingness to read the past, and to apply the obvious lessons of the past to the present.

Looking at the shape of things to come, the eminent futurologist, John Naisbitt observed that the future has never before been so difficult to predict, because it will be so radically different from events in the past on which we usually base our predictions. Karl Popper's *Black Swan* theory now popularized by Nissim Nicholas Taleb propounds the impossibility of predicting *"extreme/outlier outcomes"*. The very nature of conflict between nations, changed totally after the double nuclear holocaust of August 1945. Only the mutual threat of thermonuclear destruction ensured that the visceral confrontation between the Soviet Union and the USA remained just a "cold war" for 40 years. The US is reduced to issuing economic sanctions against those who do not toe its line! The 10 nuke-armed nations have voluntarily abjured nuclear "first strike" because even the enemy's retaliatory strike could prove unbearably costly. But can we totally rule out pre-emptive strikes or major conventional conflicts between such powers? The controversy about whether India had successfully tested a thermo-nuclear (fusion) bomb in 1998, assumes importance in this context—do we really possess sufficient nuclear deterrent to prevent a nuclear strike from China and/or Pakistan? A Pakistan ruled in the future by fanatic *jihadis,* may not worry about the horrific consequences of any retaliatory counterstrike by India on their own country!

The nature of post-World War II conflicts—the Korean War, Arab-Israeli Wars, Indo-Pak Wars, Viet Nam Wars etc—indicate that there is always a conventional war just waiting to happen, apart from incessant ongoing guerilla action and terrorist strikes. This war could be about Resources (energy, water, precious ores), Regional hegemony, Jihad or even be triggered accidentally. But God forbid, if such a conflict does turn nuclear, it could literally be the war to end all wars! Considering the terminal nature of this Armageddon, it is imperative that we have in place leaders and decision-makers equipped with a sense of history, endowed with a sound knowledge of geopolitics and fully capable of diplomatically defusing complex international conflict situations. For India, multiple internal threats have also to be identified, assessed and suitably dealt with.

Ignorance in high places can lead to disaster in an increasingly complex world. It is unrealistic to believe that the latest gizmos (high-powered satellites, sensors, drones and super-computers) can penetrate the fog of war without the support of traditional (and hazardous) grass-roots espionage, spy-craft and intelligence work to ascertain the happenings *"on the other side of the hill!"*

Anyone living in the 1930s and knowing European history of the previous 300 years should have been wary of the looming Teutonic threat. The terrible 30 Years War (1618-48) mostly fought in Germany, closed with the depredations of Turenne's French soldiers, and were quickly followed by the predatory Wars of Louis XIV (1661-1715). The desperate survival strategies of **Frederick the Great** and the imposition of the Napoleonic order, further augmented the German tragedy. Despite the aspirations of the people, Germany remained hopelessly fragmented, even after Prussia participated in the victorious Waterloo campaign (against Napoleon) and the Congress of Vienna (1815). The inevitable German unification and the violent reaction in 1870, led by the aggressive Prussian troika of Kaiser Wilhelm, **Count Bismarck** and Field Marshal von Moltke, simply blew away the French army, toppled Emperor Napoleon III and prised away the province of Alsace-Lorraine from the French fold. But World War I totally reversed the situation, and Germans were left seething with anger at the loss of territory, payment of reparations and the imposition of degrading conditions by the victorious

Allies. After this national humiliation, **Hitler** was a *"situational"* leader just waiting to make his entry, with his populist appeal to militarism since memories of the past were alive in every German mind. A cursory reading of Hitler's *"Mein Kampf"*, (a study in megalomania!), would have revealed the man and his agenda, but British Prime Minister Chamberlain naively walked into the *"appeasement"* trap at Munich with his eyes wide open. To quote from A L Rowse's *"The Use of History"*, *"Britain was to pay a terrible price for the ignorance of her leaders"*. Sir Winston Churchill, had personally participated in various conflicts—the River war in Sudan, the military action in the Swat Valley, the Boer War in South Africa—and had been War Minister during World War I. With his acute sense of history, Churchill vainly continued making Cassandra-like prophecies of doom. It seemed truly like divine coincidence that Churchill took charge as Prime Minister on 10th May1940, the very day on which the Germany launched its irresistible *Blitzkrieg* westward across the Meuse River (Ch21). Incredibly, he accomplished against Nazi Germany, what his illustrious ancestor John Churchill, 1st Duke of **Marlborough,** had achieved 250 years previously by cobbling together a Grand European Alliance to rein in the aggressive **Louis XIV** of France (Ch.15).

Though the national roles had changed, the two situations were basically similar, **Churchill,** the self-taught historian (who later won the Nobel Prize for Literature and authored a brilliant biography of his ancestor Marlborough), clearly recognized the parallels with the past and acted accordingly. He opened up new theatres of war and built up alliances e.g. his Yalta meeting with Stalin and Roosevelt—to counter the Axis powers. Interestingly, despite its location outside mainland Europe, England has consistently helped to maintain the continental Balance of Power, allying itself with France, Spain, Austria, Holland, Belgium, or individual German States, as the occasion demanded, over centuries of conflict.

Alvin Toffler understood the *Shock of Change* and suggests that the very unpredictability of the Future makes studies into the past all the more necessary. Trends can be understood, however nebulously, only by deep knowledge and intense analysis of the past.

Perhaps the only sure-fire prescription against the Armageddon, lies in *World Citizenship*, as visualized by **Prof. Arnold Toynbee** in his Azad Memorial Lecture (1960) in Delhi—*"The new danger to which our race is now exposed—the danger of our being destroyed by our own hands—ought to inspire in us a new patriotism for Mankind as a whole; and this ought to take* *precedence in our hearts and minds over traditional attachments to this or that fraction of Mankind".*

A fascinating array of human interest stories unfolds as we study the great captains. On reading the Duke of Wellington's *"Dispatches from Spain—1811"*, the great mystic and poet **Cardinal Newman** wrote, *"it makes me burn to be a soldier".* Years ago, I was privileged to read Henty's *"the Young Carthaginian"*, from the St. Xavier's school library. It stimulated a fascination for military history in general and **Hannibal** in particular. Fr. John Arago S.J, who taught us French, hailed from Spain from where Hannibal started his epic journey to Italy in 218 BC. I learnt more about this audacious young commander who crossed the Pyrenees and the Rhone River and traversed the formidable Alps with his elephants, to boldly attack Rome itself, over 2200 years ago (Ch.4). Who really was 'the man' behind this legend—strategic genius, charismatic leader and tragic figure? **Gustave Flaubert** describes the adolescent Hannibal, "as *already clothed in the indefinable splendour of those who are destined for great enterprises*"; **Leonard Cottrell** in his eulogic *"Enemy of Rome"* admires *"his political foresight, his capacity for planning and execution plus the ability to change plans quickly"*; and the ancient Roman historian Polybius observes, *"his body could not be exhausted, nor his mind subdued, by any toil."* Studies of other great commanders—**Alexander, Caesar, Napoleon**—reveal that they too possessed the same qualities in ample measure. Though the individuals come in all shapes and sizes, these leadership qualities and traits are the same across all the fields of human endeavour—business, sports, politics, war—and an examination of leadership in battle will provide clues and keys to leadership *per se*, besides unfolding for us, many a fascinating human story.

Wellington, the general who never lost a battle, wrote home after defeating **Napoleon** at Waterloo (1815), *"nothing except a battle lost, can be as melancholy as a battle won"*. Despite this caveat, nothing is as fascinating as war, bloody and tragic though it may be. As **Homer** pithily put it:

"Men grow tired of sleep, love
Singing and dancing
Sooner than of war"

Shakespeare's great tragedies focus on heroes who were destroyed by a *single fatal flaw*—Hamlet (indecision), Othello (suspicion), Macbeth (ambition), and King Lear (gullibility). Karna and Duryodhana in the **"Mahabharata"** exhibit strong negative traits of *'status-seeking'* and *'envy'*, which eventually led to their destruction. Even the dashing Arjuna, is all the more fascinating because he initially questions Krishna about the validity of his mission at Kurukshetra. His feminine streak, showcased in his role as Brihanala, dance teacher to the princess Uttara, makes him appear more human!

Hannibal at Zama (202 BC), Napoleon at Waterloo (1815) and Harold at Hastings (1066) are all poignant figures. Scottish "Braveheart" **William Wallace, Joan of Arc, Gen. Yamashita** (the victor of Singapore), and **Rani Lakshmibai,** touch a special chord in us, because of the pathetic and unfortunate circumstances connected with their tragic deaths.

The cataclysmic fall of the great cities of **Constantinople (1453), Vijayanagar (1565)** and **Delhi (1857),** rivet our attention even more than the splendid victories of Alexander, Caesar and Genghis Khan. **Nietzsche** called war *"an opportunity to display honour and heroism".* Such opportunities present themselves equally in defeat and victory. The pursuit of war enthralls men more than any other sphere of human endeavour. Much of the **Old Testament** is devoted to narratives of war— Joshua's victories against the Amorites, Moabites and Medianites; Saul and Jonathan dying desperately at Mt. Gilboa; David triumphant over the Philistines; or the battles of the Hasmonean Maccabees. Studies on 'kingship' or 'leadership' like **Chanakya's** *'Arthasastra'* or **Machiavelli's** *'The Prince'* are based on the meteoric careers of Chandragupta Maurya and Caesar Borgia, respectively. In *"Glimpses of World History"* the pacifist **Nehru** wondered at his own strange fascination for the bloody career of the monstrous conqueror **Genghis Khan!**

The selection of particular "battles and leaders" in this book is subjective, being based on personal reading and opportunities to visit the actual sites of battles and sieges. Such biases are discernible even in the great historians—Herodotus, Thucydides, Arian, Polybius, Tacitus, Josephus, Gibbon, Clausewitz, Froude, Perroy, Macaulay, H G Wells, Trevelyan, Toynbee, Mazumdar or Thapar.

B) BUSINESS-WAR ANALOGY:

At the top end of Japanese management hierarchy, the complex *Samurai spirit* still pervades all aspects of leadership style and strategy.

In his 17th century *"Book of the 5 Rings"*, samurai **Miyamoto Musashi** succinctly spells out the strategic principles which enabled him to emerge victorious in over 60 duels with different weapons—long-*sword*, *katana* and *naginata*. Consisting of five brief studies titled "Chi" (earth), "Mizu" (water), "Hi" (fire), "Kaze" (wind) and "Ku" (emptiness), his treatise is widely read by managers to glean the secrets of the *Bushido Code*. "Body-Mind together", "Sixth Sense" (intuition), "Short-arm Monkey" (balance), "Release the 4 Hands" (negotiate), "Defensive Pheasant vs. Offensive Hawk", "Rats head-Ox's neck" (seeing the big picture) are some of the techniques explained by Musashi. A contemporary of the Great Shogun Ieyasu, who established the 250-year **Tokugawa** hegemony after his victory at **Sekigahara** (Chapter 13), Musashi was skilled in calligraphy (like Steve Jobs!). According to W.S Wilson's *The Lone Samurai,* Musashi who founded the 2-sword style drew ideas from *Zen* philosophy. To explain "**Emptiness**", Musashi uses the simple-complex example of an ordinary cup designed to hold water.

> *"**Advantage** is had from whatever is there,*
> ***Usefulness** arises from whatever is not."*—**Tao**

The conduct of war is an exact image of **business operations**, particularly **marketing**, where you can clearly identify **competitors** with whom you build alliances or wage war, using principles almost identical to those applied by military leaders. **Barrie James** spells out this analogy in his *'Business War Games'* with examples. **Prof. Yoshio Kondo** elucidates Business-Sports Analogy in his book *"Human Motivation"*. Anyone who has observed inspirational football coaches Sir Alex Ferguson, Avram Grant, Rafael Benitez, Arsene Wenger, Jose Mourinho, Cesar Menotti, Pepe Guardiola; or admired the onfield leadership of Johan Cruyff, Michel Platini, Maradona, Ruud Gullitt or Zidane, will agree. Attacking prongs along the flanks or centre; smothering the enemy assault in midfield; counter-attacking with the opponent off balance; these are all tactics common to war, games and marketing!

LEADERSHIP:

"*Action learning*" theory, as propounded by **Reg Revans**, further moots the practicability of *transposing leadership skills* across totally different professions, through creative **cross-training.**, It has long before been implemented in the field of sports, with cricketers playing football or tennis stars, basketball. It is clear that the study of leadership as practiced in war, will certainly yield valuable lessons on leadership in other fields. **Count Maurice De Saxe** the veteran 18th century general commented about incompetent generals, *"they are totally ignorant and in default of what should be done, they do what they know."* Is this observation not equally applicable to many incompetent managers and bungling business leaders, even in the 21st century? There have been extensive studies on various types of human "*intelligence*" and it is pertinent to examine leadership patterns in terms of **IQ**, and the recently defined **EQ** (emotional quotient). While the concept of IQ is widely known, Emotional Intelligence (as described by **Daniel Goleman**) can better explain the personal traits and skills, possession of which enables a leader to attract, organize, enthuse and direct *teams* of able and willing deputies; and to maintain the team's '*esprit de corps*' unimpaired, in defeat as well as in victory!

Alexander's team of generals: Parmenio, Aristobalus, Lysimachus, Hephaestion, Ptolemy (Ch.03); **Hannibal** supported by Maharbal, Mago, Gisco and Hasdrubal (Ch. 04); **Napoleon** directing his brilliant array of Marshals-Soult, Massena, Desaix, Murat, Macdonald, Davout, Ney, Bernadotte, Junot (Ch.17)—are classic examples of this. The high rate of "*officer casualty*" in Napoleon's armies (1796-1815) is a clear indicator of high motivation and total commitment, since every French soldier "*carried a field-marshal's baton in his knapsack*" and had ample opportunities to win the "*Legion of Honour*", a dukedom or even a kingdom. The Indian Army's high *officer casualty rate* is a pointer to officers' commitment and *morale*. In his non-violent freedom struggle, **Gandhiji** was not only able to inspire the ordinary millions of Indians but could also win the unquestioning loyalty of extraordinary men like Nehru, Patel, Prasad, Azad and Rajaji, through long years of unrequited struggle. To what else can we attribute this amazing *charisma*, but to the high level of *emotional intelligence* attained by the supreme leader.

What it is that makes a **leader**, has been the subject of innumerable studies down the ages. **Thomas Carlyle's** *"Heroes and Hero-worship"* attributes the success of Oliver Cromwell and Frederick the Great to their distinctive *"traits"*, talents, skills and physical characteristics. Carlyle theorized that a *"great man"* helped to change, and perhaps, actually *create history.* **Fiedler** on the contrary, maintained that different *"situations"* gave rise to appropriate leaders. **David McClelland** cited *"behavioural"* factors like a strong personality, coupled with a positive ego and *"need for achievement";* while **Blake's Grid Model** set off *"concern for people"* against *"concern for the task",* to understand leadership patterns. *"Path-goal"* and *"Transactional"* leadership involved *"reciprocity of behaviour"* between leaders and the led, according to TA guru **Eric Berne,** and analysts **Kenneth Blanchard** and **VictorVroom.** **Burns'** *"Transformational"* leadership was based on *"communication"* for goal achievement, with the leader providing the big picture and *vision*; whereas **Carmazzi's** *"environmental"* leaders were naturally thrown up by *group dynamics.*

Looking further, what are the actual *tasks* that a leader performs that exalt him above the level of the merely competent manager? **Drucker, Mintzberg** and **Bossidy** assert that a leader provides *Vision, Values, Culture and Strategy* and takes *Responsibility*, particularly for failure. According to **McClelland**, *Leadership Potential* can be assessed through psychometric testing and can be consciously developed by *Mentoring and Coaching.*

Most of these latter-day leadership theories are seen to be applicable, retrospectively, to the great captains of the past. When **Kurt Lewin** lists *leadership styles*, we immediately have appropriate names to put against each category—Dictatorial (Napoleon), Autocratic (Caesar), Participative (Hannibal) and Laissez-faire (Robert Lee);with most military leaders naturally tending towards the Dictator-Autocrat style and mode! Can we not apply **Maslow's** *"Hierarchy of Needs"* and **Vroom's** *'Expectancy Theory"* to determine what *motivated* these extraordinary leaders? Studies reveal that Ambition (Caesar), Hatred of Rome (Hannibal), Pride (Frederick the Great), Professionalism (Yamashita, Gustavus Adolphus), Avarice (Genghis Khan, Abdali), Patriotism (Harold, Joan of Arc) and Sense of Destiny (Napoleon, Alexander) were their more obvious motivating factors—all located *close to the summit* of the hierarchical *"needs" pyramid!*

STRATEGIES & TACTICS:

I have also endeavored to delineate the *principles of offensive and defensive warfare,* the development and use of specific **weapons** and **tactics**, the **geopolitical back-ground** of the situations in which these leaders were placed, and constraints relating to *terrain, quality of troops* commanded, and characteristics of the *enemy*. The invention and development of **weapons** down the ages and how *offensive tactics* were modified to use, and *defensive tactics* created to counter, **new weapons**, has been discussed, with actual case studies from the battlefield. The changeover from **bronze to iron,** *the use of* **chariots** and **cavalry,** *the* Welsh **longbow** *(13th century),* **cannon** *(14th century), matchlock/wheel-lock* **muskets** *(16TH/17th century),* **Gatling gun** *(19TH century)* etc changed the face of warfare. The advent of the 20th century ushered in a whole new array of weaponry—planes, tanks, submarines, air-craft carriers, guided missiles, chemical weapons, thermo-nuclear weapons and drone strikes, to name a few.

To appreciate how such **new weapons** were invented and optimally used, an entire chapter (Ch20), has been devoted to the study of the development and use of **tanks**, focusing on the *leadership styles* of field commanders like Guderian, Rommel, von Manstein, Montgomery, Patton and Zhukov. We also acknowledge here, the *thinkers* and pioneers—JFC Fuller, Liddell Hart, de Gaulle, Tukachevsky, Chaffee— who nurtured the idea of tanks in battle and conceived of a **synergised system of warfare** fully **integrating tanks with other arms** like infantry, artillery and air power and applying the **ancient principles** creatively. In the Blitzkrieg of May, 1940, the Germans tactically used Liddell Hart's *"Expanding Torrent"*, originally formulated by **Sun Tzu**, circa 350 BC—an exemplary case of very old wine in a brand new bottle!

Clausewitz, the 19th century military thinker, sagely observed—*"Tactics* is the conduct of troops in battle; *strategy* uses battles to win wars". And *War* itself is a logical *extension of Policy*!

A) OFFENSIVE STRATEGY

1) **Frontal Assault** (as epitomized in **Marlborough's** victory at **Blenheim)** results in heavy casualties for the attackers, often 2:1. Despite the prohibitive human cost, it was successfully carried out in 1703 by the Duke, for political reasons and to relieve pressure on England's ally,

Austria. In Chapter 19, **Pickett's** suicidal frontal charge against strongly entrenched Union forces (which failed) at **Gettysburg** in 1863, was a final throw of the dice by **Robert Lee** in what was, for him, a desperate must-win situation. Similarly, in the nascent PC market, **IBM** attacked well-entrenched **Apple** head-on, using a surfeit of resources, to force an entry, whatever the consequent cost.

2) **Flanking Tactics** (**Frederick** at Rossbach against the Austrians or **Wellesley** at Assaye against the Marathas) called "the essence of war" by Von Schlieffen, whose innovative plan was adopted by Germany in World War I. One wing, considerably reinforced, is advanced, while the other wing avoids engagement or defends itself skillfully against heavy odds till complete victory is achieved on the strengthened flank. Parmenio's brilliant defense on the left enabled **Alexander** on the right wing to drive Darius off the field at Arbela (Ch.3). At Panipat in 1761, Marathas empowered their left wing in an unsuccessful flanking operation against Abdali (Ch 16)

3) **Double Envelopment**, involves strengthening both the wings, at the expense of the centre. The enemy was drawn in, as if by a magnet, surrounded and annihilated. First used by the Athenian *strategos* **Miltiades** against **Darius'** Persians at **Marathon** (Ch.2), this high-risk strategy is epitomized by Hannibal's classic triumph over the Romans at **Cannae** (216 BC) detailed in Chapter 4 and **Khalid ibn al Walid's** decimation of the Persians at **Walaja** (Ch 6) in 633. **Hindenberg** and Ludendorf used this manoeuvre successfully at **Tannenberg** in **World War I** against the Russians. The warrior-king **Shaka** organized the Zulu army and his successor **Cetewayo** in 1879, used his deadly *impis* (regiments) as horns to envelope the Lord Chelmsford's hapless force.

4) **Isolating** enemy forces, was an unconventional offensive strategy adopted by **MacArthur,** as he leap-frogged rapidly across the Pacific, leaving many Japanese-held islands untouched in his rear. In 1971, Gen.J S Arora's multiple prongs pushed deep towards Dacca, without attempting to engage Pakistani strong garrisons en route.

B) IRREGULAR WARFARE

Supplemented by local support, is a game-changing strategy often employed against occupation forces, unfamiliar with the local conditions and terrain. Alexander, Hannibal and Caesar were all confronted by the ubiquitous **guerillas**, as was any invader in a foreign land. **Cyrus the Great** was ambushed and killed by the Scythian irregulars in 528 BC. In 9 AD, **Augustus Caesar** lost the **3 legions** commanded by **Varus** at Teutoburger Wald in a dramatic ambush by the Cheruscan chief **Arminius**, who lured the Romans deep into the wilds of Germania. **Spanish guerillas** contributed greatly to Wellington's stunning victories over Napoleon's marshals. The suicidal bravery of **French partisans** and the underground forces all over occupied Europe was largeiy responsible for **Hitler's** downfall. **Irregular warfare** (as practiced by Mao, Giap, Che Guevara, Shivaji or Tantya Topi) broke up the enemy, albeit in different ways It is even more effective in the 21st century, with the availability of high-tech weapons, powerful remote controlled explosives, long-range guided missiles and the ubiquitous suicide bombers. Liddell Hart's *The Strategy of the Indirect Approach (1967)* analyses the effect of terrorism on the state, explaining how the will of the people can be broken through a thousand cuts, by an elusive enemy. Spectacular indeed were Che' s terror chain in Latin America, IRA's pub bombings, 1972 Munich Olympics Black September attack on Israeli athletes (and Mossad's response}, Mau Mau actions (Kenya), LTTE's Rajiv Gandhi assassination and the 26/11 Mumbai attack.

India & the Maoists: The **Red Corridor** stretching **south from Nepal** (Pasupati to Tirupati) through Bihar, Jharkand, Chattisgarh, W. Bengal, Orissa and Andhra, has now expanded into Maharashtra and Karnataka, covering over **200 districts**! The **roots** of the issue are often local, and traceable to some historical problem or past injustice. For example, the memory of the extra judicial elimination in 1966 of Praveenchandra Bhanjdeo, activist **Maharaja of Bastar**, still rankles in the minds of the local tribals. To ensure permanent results, the solution has to encompass all aspects of *governance*—social, political, employment, equity, food security, health care, education, empowerment, human rights. In the 2013 M K Nambiyar Lecture at the National Law University, Kochi, Prof. Christopher Forsyth redefined the province of *legitimate expectations*, a concept introduced into English Law by Lord Denning. Failure to protect such expectations will lead to abuse of power and serious trust deficit between rulers and ruled. The attitude of *"if you are not with us, you are against us"* is not the answer, especially when we are confronted by our own citizens. *Force,* by itself, cannot provide an answer in such complex situations. But force may have to be used, albeit *judiciously*. Ideally, the Indian army, a strong pan-Indian unifier, should not be employed against our own citizens, howsoever *"savage and dangerous"*. The paramilitary and police forces must be suitably equipped, effectively trained, capably led and fully empowered to handle all *"**law & order**"* issues within the country. For this, they should not only be made adept at *guerilla* and *jungle fighting*, but should also evolve *strategy, logistics, weaponry, training and tactics* most appropriate for different *terrain* and *situations*. Not an easy task, when simultaneously handling **militants** in Kashmir, **insurgents** in the North-East and **Maoist-Naxalites** spread across more than half-a-dozen States, speaking a dozen languages and enjoying support from outside our borders. Operations like *"Green Hunt"* should eschew targeting (and antagonizing) the local people. Run-of-the-mill policing methods like road-patrolling in wheeled vehicles, which did not work even against the poacher Veerappan, will invariably fail against **Maoists**, who are well-equipped, well trained and led by consummate tacticians in the mould of **Giap** and **Mao,** the modern masters of irregular warfare! Maoist strategy across the Red Corridor is better integrated than that of the State and Central Governments and winning against them is not easy, unless government strategy is unified across states. The **LTTE**, never more than 25,000 strong but enjoying ethnic support from the 3 million Sri Lankan Tamils, could have continued to defy the Sri Lankan Forces indefinitely, but for self-destructive manifestations of Prabhakaran's *hubris. Local support* and *reliable intelligence* are critical for success in counter-insurgency measures, which are necessarily long-drawn-out and tedious. The successful strategies of the **"Greyhounds"** of the Andhra Police involve first choking off the *supply routes* of the Maoists (particularly from outside the state/country), instead of taking them head on in their jungle fastnesses through *"territory domination"*.

C) DEFENSIVE STRATEGIES

Include use of *static positions* (medieval castles like Stirling or Harlech, or 20th century fortifications like the French Maginot Line or the Israeli Bar-Lev Line, as force multipliers). *Terrain* (rivers, hills, forests) can be exploited for frontal defense or to protectively abut an army's flank. Alexander was forced to fight all his major battles (Granicus, Issus, Arbela, and Jhelum) after crossing a river in the face of the enemy. Against **Genghis Khan** (1221), **Jallaludin Shah** had his right flank against the swift-flowing Indus and his left was protected by a mountain range (Chapter 10). Fighting the Persian host at **Thermopylae** in 480

BC, **Leonidas' 300 Spartans** were flanked by a mountain range and the Aegean Sea (Ch 2). The 1971 war for Bangladesh was one of obstacles, primarily water bodies and marshes. Defense can also be conducted through *dynamic movement*—Robert Bruce's infantry divisions rapidly forming hedgehog *schiltrons* at Bannockburn in1314- (Ch. 9) to confound the enemy cavalry charges. *Pre-emptive strikes* (Hannibal's daring plunge into the heart of Italy in 218 BC or the Japanese strike on Pearl Harbour on 7th December1941) are bold strategies intended to prevent the enemy from initiating an attack. *Counter-offensive* (Duke William at Hastings in 1066 and Charles Martel at Tours in 732) and *strategic withdrawal* (Lee after Gettysburg in1863), are also basically defensive tactics that enabled the protagonist to recover from off-balance situations.

The Mind of the Strategist: Victory and defeat are determined in the minds of the opposing commanders, in a contest of will-power. We can also try to understand how and why commanders took their instantaneous decisions and the spontaneous moves, conceived and executed, in the heat of battle. **Napoleon**, in particular, was said to possess this *"coup d'oeil"* or *"power of the glance."*, making quick sense of a complex battlefield situation and following it up with a spectacular move. Was this the result of fine-tuning of technical skills or sheer genius in action? Genghis Khan's counter-strike against the exposed flank of Jalaludin's attacking right wing is an example. **Malcolm Gladwell's** *'thin-slicing'* theory in his path-breaking *'Blink'*, provides an apt answer. Real experts in any field can make snap decisions of very high quality, using *rapid cognition by the subconscious mind*. At the other end of the spectrum, large business firms often mull interminably over voluminous data, create imaginary scenarios and worry about the applicability of alternative strategies, often ending up with what is derisively described as *'paralysis by analysis*! Geniuses possess *built-in ERP systems,* which enable them to take in, process and inter-link reams of data instantaneously—and arrive at truly amazing conclusions and decisions. They can also "make do" with scarce resources, or what management guru Prof. Vijay Govindrajan would term *"jugaad"* or "Frugal Engineering" today. *Divergent thinking* is another common characteristic of the great commanders, leading to out-of-the-box solutions to military conundrums.

When we examine the ***principles of war*** expounded by Sun Tzu, Clausewitz, Jomini, Lidell Hart or Fuller, we realize how similar these martial principles are, to what **Kenichi Ohmae** says about the 3 Cs of *business strategy* or the *14 management points* listed by **Henri Fayol**. In a *contrarian* view, **Albert Speer**, architect-friend and Armaments minister of **Adolf Hitler**, debunks the validity of such principles by observing (in his '*Inside the 3rd Reich*') that "the victories of the early years of **Hitler** can literally be attributed to his *ignorance of the rules* of the game and his layman's delight in decision-making. Since his opponents were taught to apply rules which Hitler's self-taught autocratic mind did not know, he achieved stupendous surprises. Audacity coupled with local military superiority was the basis of his success." Hitler was indeed a profoundly uneducated genius. Does not Speer's analysis of the Fuhrer remind us of the clash of **Karsenbhai Patel's** '*Nirma*' with **Unilever's** '*Surf*', in the Indian detergent market? The innovation and creativity of the non-expert Patel pitted against the sophisticated strategies of the marketing box-wallas of the giant MNC. Or going back 3000 years, **David's** primitive '*sling and stone*' vs. the giant **Goliath's** state-of-the-art bronze armour and equipment! The lesson to be learnt herein is that any principle can be turned on its head by an unconventional opponent and not that the principle itself is flawed. Principles should be understood and applied selectively and in the appropriate context, something which requires expertise, intuition, skills and intelligence of a high order.

Are such geniuses born or made? Nature or Nurture? After reading Gladwell's *Outliers*, I have been converted to his theory that superstars *"are products of history and community, of opportunity and legacy."*

A caveat: The focus of the book is on **land warfare** and references to **air/sea** battles are made only as factors affecting the former. Sea power has admittedly been a deciding factor in world dominion, as propounded by Admiral Mahan's classic "*The Influence of Sea Power Upon History*". England's global domination from the defeat of the Spanish Armada (1588) until well into the 20th century was the result of her naval strength. Great Sea Battles like Salamis (Persians vs Greeks), Mylae (Rome vs Carthage), Actium (Octavian vs Antony-Cleopatra), Lepanto (Don John of Austria vs the Turks), Nile (Nelson vs Brueys), Trafalger (Nelson vs Villeneuve), Tsushima (Russians vs Japanese), Jutland (British vs Germans) and Midway (Japan vs US) are as complex and fascinating as any land battle. Air power has proved to be an even more dominant factor in the past century, especially when integrated fully with the other two forces. But "boots on the ground" involving land warfare, still remains the final decisive factor.

2

ANCIENT LEADERS AND BATTLES

Survival and aggression were instincts embedded deeply in homo sapiens. We know today that he hunted down and exterminated the closely related but rival species of **Neanderthals,** 30,000 years ago, finishing off the last remnants in the southern extremity of **Spain**. Primitive man, who was a hunter-gatherer, was naturally warlike, using clubs, flint-head arrows and spears as weapons. In the succeeding generations, those men who turned to more productive agriculture were inclined to peaceful coexistence. However, nomadic tribes continued to be aggressively active with weapons since they had to protect their flocks and herds from predators (animal and human). Naturally, these nomads raided settled agriculturists who were beginning to form large civilizations in the river valleys of the Nile, Euphrates-Tigris, Indus, Hwang Ho, and Yangtze.

Smaller civilizations developed along Oxus-Jaxartes, Jordan (Jericho) and Karun (Elam) river basins. In Crete, the Minoan naval thalassocracy was built at the cross-roads of the Mediterranean Sea trade. Strategies devised to counter external barbarian attacks included creation of the institution of *"kingship",* with the supreme ruler as *war leader,* sometimes *chief priest,* often claiming divinity through descent from the gods—Baal, Marduk or Ra. In southern Mesopotamia (Iraq), **Sargon I** and **Naramsin** of Akkad conquered the rival cities of Ur (where Abraham came from) and Lagash, using infantry and chariots, while the **Pharaoh Menes** and his successors absorbed upper and lower Egypt into their fold in the third millennium BC. *"High barbarism"* resulting from the interplay between civilizations and their nomadic neighbors, altered the balance of power decidedly in favour of the latter, as their organization, weaponry and tactics became more sophisticated, while they retained their pristine savagery and war-like spirit. **Copper** was used by the Egyptians as early as the 4th millennium BC. Copper was later hardened and made more workable by adding tin and **Bronze** was created. **Iron** was first smelted in Asia Minor (Turkey) and iron weapons were extensively used by the

Hittites by 1500 BC. Major clashes between the **nomads** and **settled civilizations** occurred in the 2nd millennium BC when the warlike Indo-European hordes poured out of the Central Asian grasslands around the **Caspian** and **Aral Seas**, in search of *'lebensraum'*. Astride sturdy horses and wielding spears and swords, they swept south-eastwards into India (as **Aryans**) and south-westwards into Iran (as **Medes** and **Persians**).

Much havoc was wrought by the marauding hordes on the peaceful settled populations in their path. Will Durant observes "From barbarism to civilization requires a century; from civilization to barbarism needs but a day". However, Arnold J Toynbee's classic ***"Study of History"*** attributes the very growth of civilizations to a series of challenges by the barbarians on the fringes. He defines the phases of a civilization as Genesis, Growth, Breakdown and Disintegration. The major civilizations recovered from external depredation and by 1600 BC, the Middle East was controlled by 2 great powers: **Egyptians** from the Nile valley and the **Mittani** of North Syria/Iraq.

The first major battle ever recorded was fought at **Megiddo (Armageddon),** south-east of Nazareth in Palestine, on **14th April 1479 BC (?)**. The warrior Pharaoh **Thutmose III** decided to put down a major uprising of the city kings of Palestine and Syria, headed by the rulers of Kadesh and Megiddo, backed by the Mittani. **Thutmose** (Thoth is born) had learnt warfare fighting the Nubians in the south. Having just taken control of Egypt from his stepmother, the female **Pharaoh Hatsheput**, he was eager to enforce suzerainty over the distant northern provinces of the empire. The Egyptian army had light dismantable chariots of wood, copied from those of the **Hyksos** who had invaded and occupied Egypt in the previous century. According to the Karnak inscriptions, Thutmose led his army north through coastal Gaza and further towards the city of **Megiddo** situated on the slope of Mt. Carmel, south of the Galilean Hills. Rejecting the sober advice of his minister Thanuny and the Council he moved unexpectedly (and riskily) through the narrow **Aruna** defile, though two easier routes were available. Thutmose's army suddenly debouched on the Esdraelon plain and attacked the startled enemy in 3 battle columns. The charging Egyptian chariots scattered the Syrians. Only a few managed to find refuge within the walls of **Megiddo**, which surrendered after a 7 month siege. **Thutmose**, throughout the campaign, displayed a sound sense of *logistics*, carefully protecting his *line of supply* through Gaza and Jaffa. But he also showed audacity worthy of a Great Captain at the appropriate time, to surprise and rout the rebel kings. Taking the right risks has always been an important characteristic of dynamic leadership. This was the first of a series of annual forays by Thutmose, who in 15 successful campaigns built a vast empire stretching up to the Euphrates River and established the **Pax Egyptica**. The impact of this battle on the ancient world was so great that the name **Armageddon** is enshrined in the Biblical Book of Revelations (16:14-16) as the ultimate battle of the future. **Thutmose**'s mummy reveals a strong jaw and powerful features and he is rightly called "the **Napoleon of Egypt**". His giant stone *obelisks* can be seen in London (Cleopatra's Needle), Rome, Paris, Washington and Istanbul, where they were transported at different periods over the past 3500 years. Breasted writes *"Two of his Heliopolis obelisks, now rise on opposite shores of the Atlantic, memorials of the world's first empire-builder"*

Towards the end of World War I, General **Allenby** outmaneuvered the German-led Turkish 7th and 8th armies in the same region. Like Thutmose, he fooled the enemy into thinking that he would continue north along the coastal route and then used his Australian Light Horse to cut off the Turks at Beersheba, from their bases—Hebron and Jerusalem. Indian infantry distinguished themselves and are honoured every year during the celebration of Haifa Day. On 11th December 1917, he entered Jerusalem (symbolically on foot through the Jaffa gate), accompanied by the enigmatic **Col. T.E. Lawrence (of Arabia)**. Following the strategy of the great Pharaoh, he then out-generalled the Turks at Megiddo by using the pass of **Aruna**, isolating them in Samaria, for which feat he was created Viscount Allenby of Megiddo. Allenby was helped by the thrashing that the well-drilled Turkish army had received in Arabia earlier, from Lawrence's rag-tag camel-mounted **Bedouin** tribesmen whose endurance, individualism and unconventional tactics were unmatched in desert warfare. The extravagant (unkept) promises then made by the British Government to the Arabs for their valuable support, are largely responsible for the current imbroglio in **Palestine**.

There are also detailed accounts existing of the battle of **Kadesh** (1274 BC) between the Egyptians under Pharaoh **Rameses II (Moses'** contemporary?) and **Muwatalli**, the powerful **Hittite** king of Anatolia (Turkey). The records of both sides claimed total success, but it was probably a devastating battle, resulting in a pyrrhic victory for Rameses who was struggling to reassert Egyptian sovereignty over Canaan. Maces, sickle-shaped swords *(kopesh),* axes, spears, were used along with the composite bow of 300 yards range. **Bronze** armour and wooden shields, completed the accoutrement of the warriors on both sides. Because of poor intelligence gathering, the Ammon division was surprised by the enemy as it advanced ahead of the other 3 divisions, but the Egyptians fought back strongly to make it a bloody draw. With over **5000 chariots** involved, Kadesh saw the largest ever assembly of chariots in battle with the large Hittite chariot engaging the light Egyptian single-axle chariot carrying a single archer or spearman, apart from the charioteer. The latter operated much like an armoured car—fast but vulnerable—and mobile Egyptian tactics were generally developed around it. The clash of empires culminating in the devastating battle of Kadesh left both rivals weak and vulnerable to the barbarian waves that soon crashed in from all sides.

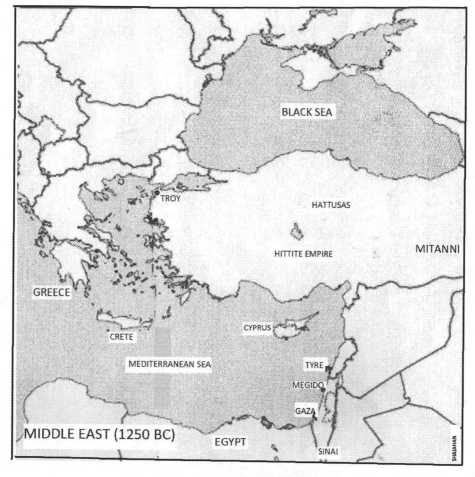

Ancient Middle East—1250 BC

1

By 1250 BC, the region was awash with Hebrews, Philistines, Arameans, Dorians and Chaldeans, all pushing for *lebensraum*. Prof. Oblonsky describes how such chaotic movements could impact settled civilizations, *"Splintered fragments of empires driven by economic want or fear of their neighbours, prospective empire builders fired by dreams, nascent nations emerging out of pastoral nomadism and seeking agricultural lands for a settled life, parasitical hordes craving for richer and warmer lands—"*

The legendary Homeric battles for **Troy** took place around this time, as the bronze-clad Greeks led by **Agamemnon, Achilles** and **Ulysses** invaded Asia Minor, ostensibly to rescue fair **Helen.** Archaeological excavations (pioneered by Schliemann) and recent studies of contemporaneous diplomatic correspondence indicate that the 6th city of Troy (an outpost of the Hittite Empire?) was burnt down *circa* 1250BC, following a long siege. Troy, strategically located on the Asian side of the narrow Dardanelles strait, controlled entry into the Black Sea. The conflict could have been for domination of the Aegean sea and access to the mineral and agricultural wealth of the Black Sea region. In 1915, the disastrous Gallipoli campaign (Churchill's brainwave) was undertaken by the Allies on the European side of the Dardanelles to help Russia by opening access to the Aegean and warm waters of the Mediterranean. The ANZAC dead are still fondly remembered (after 100 years), with crowds of Aussies visiting their well-kept graves. It was sad to observe that the thousands of Indians who also sacrificed their lives in the same campaign are forgotten.

The discovery of the process of iron-making democratized warfare, since iron ore was widely available, unlike copper ore and iron was also harder and better suited for weaponry. With the coming of the **Iron Age**, the familial and tribal units of the nomads soon gave way to larger organizations. The Biblical narrative of the rise of the **Hebrew kingdom** under Saul, David and Solomon (1020-925 BC) provides details of the typical process of this consolidation. Even the resistance to taxation can be seen in the depiction of David's "sin" of numbering the people, as detailed in the '*Book of Samuel*'. Enumeration and classification of the population is a sensitive issue, even in a twenty-first century census, but is an essential feature of the process of organizing smaller units into a nation.

The next great conquerors of the ancient world were the *iron-wielding* **Assyrians of Nineveh** (North Iraq) under **Sargon II**, whose army consisted principally of spearmen and large chariots (designed to carry up to 4 warriors). They were masters of *siege-craft*, using battering rams and towers to capture great cities like Babylon and Tarsus. They over-ran the northern kingdom of **Israel** but Jerusalem was miraculously delivered from their king **Sennacherib (705-681 BC)**, as detailed in the Bible. (II Chronicles Ch.32) by a plague which struck the enemy.

> **Byron's** poem "*The Destruction of Sennacherib*" ends as follows;
> "*The widows of Asshur are loud in their wail,*
> *The idols are broke in the temple of Baal,*
> *And the might of the gentile, unsmote by the sword,*
> *Hath withered like snow, in the glance of the Lord!*"

The Assyrian friezes of hunting and war displayed in the British Museum, depict their awesome military skills, extreme depravity and unbridled cruelty, as do historical records of their huge pyramids of enemy skulls, erected after every victory.

This was an era of scientific warfare, management skills and great dynastic conquests in the Middle East by competing armies. The **Medes** and **Persians**, united under **Cyrus the Great**, conquered Asia Minor (Turkey) defeating the fabulously wealthy **Croesus** of Lydia and the Greeks who had colonized the eastern coast of the Aegean Sea. **Cyrus'** success can be attributed to '*diversity in counsel, unity in command*'. After capturing **Babylon** from **King Nabonides** and his son **Balshazer,** he sent back 40,000 captive Jews, along with their sacred vessels and helped them in rebuilding the **Temple of Solomon** in Jerusalem. The Prophet Daniel considered him a Messiah sent by Yahweh. Cyrus empathized with the Jews because he was an ardent follower of the monotheist **Zoroaster**. Cyrus' 1700 mile Royal Road, running east-west from Susa (Biblical Sushan) to Sardis enabled him to police his vast dominions and he also built a canal from the Nile to the Red Sea, a fore-runner of De Lessep's Suez Canal in 1869. But in his reckless campaign (528 BC), against the fierce **Scythian** barbarians (of Bulgaria), he was ambushed, captured and crucified by their vengeful Queen Tonyris, whose son he had killed. Cyrus' simple tomb at Pasargade bears the inscription '*I am Cyrus who founded the empire of the Persians, Grudge me not therefore, this little earth that covers my body*'

Alexander the Great, an admirer of the Achaemenid empire-builder, visited the sepulchre in 331 BC and inscribed therein, a Greek translation of the above epitaph. Egypt was quickly over-run by Cyrus' son

Cambyses (528-522 BC), but he died mysteriously while campaigning (for whatever reason!) in the arid and inhospitable expanse of the Libyan desert to the west.

Darius I (521-483 BC), organized the vast Persian empire into 20 satrapies, all linked by road to his capital Susa, and stretching all the way from the Indus river to the Aegean Sea. Interfering rashly in the confused politics of the emerging Greek city-states, he was decisively defeated at **Marathon** on the Aegean coast by the Athenians in **490 BC**. Though **Miltiades** was not holding any official position, the war-leaders Callimachus and Themistocles, deferred to his superior military and leadership skills. He deliberately weakened the Athenian centre (4 ranks) and strengthened the wings (8 ranks) to draw the Persian centre into his own line, which became concave under pressure. The strong Athenian wings then wheeled around the Persian flanks and encircled them in a classic "*double envelopment.*" The same ploy was later executed to perfection by **Hannibal** against the Romans at **Cannae** (216 BC), which is the ancient battle most admired by military historians. Marathon gained immortality because of the 26-mile race which commemorates the feat of the **Olympic** champion runner Pheidipides, who brought the news of the victory to Athens. In Byron's elegant words "The mountains look on Marathon and Marathon looks on the sea"

Ten years later, Darius' son **Xerxes** (Biblical Ahasueras), launched a fresh attack on Greece, crossing the Dardanelles to Europe by a bridge of boats. Though the Persians overwhelmed **Leonidas'** heroic "**Spartan 300**" at the **Thermopylae** pass, the Persian navy was decisively beaten at **Salamis** and their army crushed at **Platea** (479 BC) by the **Spartans** who were henceforward rated the best soldiers in the world.

War in ancient **India** is described in **Vyasa's Mahabharata.** In the 6th century BC, **Bimbisara** and his son **Ajathasatru**, using massed armies and systematic spying, subverted and conquered the kingdoms and republics of the **Gangetic plain**—Kashi, Kosala, Vrijes, Anga—to establish a powerful Magadhan empire with its capital at **Rajagriha** (@530 BC. They were the first to use trained war-elephants and conducted *Aswamedham* (ritual Horse sacrifice) to institutionalize their conquests. The parricide Ajatasatru, a contemporary of Gautama Buddha, founded Pataliputra and was the inventor of the destructive *scythed chariot.* After the departure of Alexander 200 years later, **Chanakya** also employed espionage to ensure the success of his master **Chandragupta Maurya**, by ascertaining and exploiting the situation *"on the other side of the hill".* Megasthenes' *Indika* describes the prevailing conditions of the Magadhan empire in great detail. To ensure better control of the realm, the Rajapattra (forerunner of the Grand Trunk Road) passed through Pataliputra all the way to the north-west frontier. Chanakya's *Arthasastra* (Science of Wealth) is an eclectic handbook of politics, economics, administration, rules for kingship, diplomacy and strategy! Unfortunately, the technical side of war did not progress on the Indian subcontinent thereafter. Chariot warfare even survived anachronistically in South India in the wars between the Cholas, Cheras, Pandyas, Pallavas and Chalukyas. Even scientific fortification was not well developed and the siege of Sigriya Rock Fort (Srilanka) in 491 AD appears as a rare occurrence in the history of the region.

Interestingly, the 6th century B.C. provides a contemporaneous galaxy of ethical thinkers—Mahavira, Gautama Buddha, Zoroaster, Lao Tse, Confucius, Pythagoras of Samos and the Hebrew prophets of the Babylonian exile. Intrigued by this amazing coincidence, Jawaharlal **Nehru** devotes a full chapter to this spiritual phenomenon in his *"Glimpses of World History"*, drawing parallels between these philosopher-prophet-teachers of different genres. He observes *"There must have been a wave of thought going through the world, a wave of discontent with existing conditions and of hope and aspiration for something better."*

Meanwhile, the vast **Chinese mass** lay far outside the fulcral area of the other major civilizations, under the Shang and Chou dynasties (till 771 BC) and then the period of the *"warring states"* till 221BC, when they were all unified by the **Chi'ins**. **Sun Tzu** (cica 350 BC) was a successful general of the King of Wu and his perceptive *"Art of War"* was widely studied in China and Japan for his principles of *"creating confusion and friction".* To quote Sun Tzu, *"attack the enemy's strategy, disrupt his alliances"* and *"the primary colours are only 5 in number, but their combinations are infinite. In battle there are only normal and extraordinary forces but their combinations are limitless".* **Sun Tzu's 13 Principles** shaped war in the Far East for 25 centuries.

The aggressive World War II strategies of the Japanese, of **Mao** in China and **Vo Nguyen Giap** in Vietnam were all developed from Sun Tzu's basic theories which raised *irregular warfare* to its apotheosis. **Mao** observes, *"Although flexible dispersion or concentration of forces is the principal method in **guerilla warfare,** we must also know to shift our forces flexibly. Hit-and-run and night action should be constantly employed to mislead, entice and confuse the enemy."* This strategy is currently being unfolded in the broad swathe of land from Pasupati (in Nepal) to Tirupati, to unsettle the Indian security forces and the latter would do well to go back to the old master, **Sun Tzu**, for lessons in counter-insurgency!

But it was undoubtedly the intermittent intercontinental clash of **Persian** and **Greek** armies, between 500 BC and 330 BC, that led to major development of weapons and tactics. **Epaminondas of Thebes** created aggressive new tactics for the *phalanx*, which consisted of heavy infantry *hoplites* wielding long spears called *sarissa*. In 371 BC at **Leuctra**, the Thebans attacked the Spartan *phalanx* in oblique order with the massed left leading and the right wing withdrawn, crushing the Spartan right, killing their king and shattering the Spartan myth of invincibility. *Phalanx tactics* and equipment were perfected by **Philip II of Macedon,** who integrated it with innovative use of his elite *cavalry*. The stage was now set for the advent of one of the most remarkable men of all time— **Alexander the Great**.

3

ALEXANDER THE GREAT, ARBELA (331 BC)

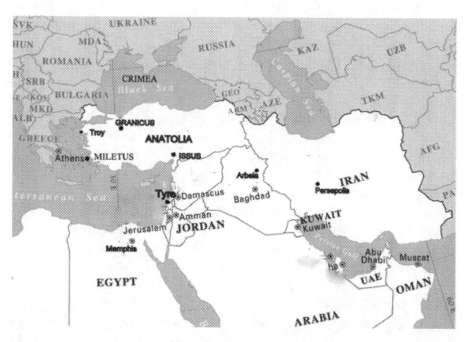

Alexander's Battles—336 to 323 BC

2

Xenophon, boon companion of **Socrates**, fought as a mercenary in the Persian heartland and his narration of his army's successful retreat from Cunaxa (near Babylon) recounted in the *"Retreat of the Ten Thousand"* (400 BC), electrified every adventurous Greek. Prof. Tarn calls it "an epilogue to the invasion of Xerxes and a prologue to Alexander's conquest of Persia"

Alexander's father, Philip, was king of Macedonia on the northern borders of Greece. Born in 382 BC, Philip, spent 3 years as a hostage in Thebes, where he imbibed the essence of creative military strategy,

25

especially the use of the phalanx, observing the brilliant Epaminondas in action. Back home, he created a professional national army from the turbulent Macedonian tribesmen and established his sway in Thrace and the Balkans. He defeated Thebes and Athens at Cheronae (338 BC) and made himself Captain-General of Greece. He was a great military organizer and trainer but was murdered in 336 BC just as he was about to embark on the long-planned invasion of the Persian empire and was succeeded by his 19 year old son, Alexander. Prof. Tarn says—*"the name of Alexander betokens the end of one world epoch and the beginning of another. The whole subsequent course of history—political, economic and cultural—cannot be understood apart from the career of Alexander."*

Descended from the legendary **Hercules** through his father, and the Homeric hero **Achilles,** on his mother's side, Alexander ascended the throne in his 20th year (336 BC). **Philip** had arranged for the philosopher **Aristotle** to mentor him for 4 years, apart from tutoring him personally in the art of war, even allowing him to command the left wing independently at the critical battle of Cheronae. Aristotle, was an outstanding pupil of **Plato**, who had in turn, been mentored by the great thinker **Socrates.**

Aristotle had original ideas on the ***philosophy of war*** and taught his royal pupil to think "outside the box". In his *"Politics",* he classifies the army into *cavalry, heavy infantry* and *light armed troops*, drawn respectively from the wealthy, the well to do and the masses. He opined that an army composed exclusively of the masses, could turn against their masters—oligarchs or monarch—hence the necessity for a heterogeneous force. Philip set up a school for the philosopher at Mieza, where he taught medicine, morals, logic and art to Alexander and his noble companions, who included Ptolemy, Hephaestion, Perdiccas and Cassander, who would later form the core of his officer corps. But the greatest influence on Alexander was his mother, **Olympias**, a beautiful and mysterious necromancer who convinced him of his *divinity*! He was thus fully groomed for his unique transforming role in history. Outstandingly handsome, with a tough and lithe body, he (peculiarly) had one eye blue and the other, brown. The concern he showed for his men inspired intense loyalty and they would follow him, literally, to the ends of the earth. Inheriting a superb army from Philip, his skills as a general and administrator were to be tested soon enough.

As king, Alexander immediately faced and overcame rebellion from the cities of Thebes and Athens. Before crossing over into Asia with 30,000 infantry and 5000 cavalry he left Antipater as Regent and appointed Niarchos, admiral of the fleet. After paying tribute at the grave of his ancestor Achilles at Troy, he used superior tactics to beat the **Persians** under the Greek mercenary Memnon of Rhodes and Satrap Mithridates at the **Granicus** River (334 BC). Traversing Asia Minor (Turkey), he defeated a Persian host personally led by **Great King Darius III** at **Issus** (333 BC) near Tarsus in Cilicia. He systematically occupied Smyrna, Sardes, Ephesus, Miletus and the Mediterranean ports—Halicarnassus, Tarsus, Alexandretta, Byblos and Sidon to ensure the safety of his line of communications. At this juncture, Darius offered him one half of his vast domininions. Parmenio advised,"I would accept were I Alexander" to which our hero replied, "I would accept if I were Parmenio!"

He then captured the magnificent island-city of **Tyre** (Lebanon) after an extraordinary 9 month-long siege (332 BC). Tyre was the mother of the Carthagenian empire and possessed an impressive fleet. An awed prophet Ezekiel had once praised its beauty and power. The Tyrians refused to permit the Macedonian to enter and offer sacrifice at the temple of Melkarte (Hercules, Alexander's mythical ancestor). Tyre, replenished from the sea, had once withstood a long siege by Nebuchadnasar of Babylon, but Alexander first neutralized its fleet with his own, plus "borrowings" from Sidon, Byblos and other ports. The Greeks then built an earthen mole into the sea, despite heavy attack from the Tyrians, thereby converting the island into a peninsula (which it still is). The city walls were breached with engines, before the final assault by shock troops. He then took Gaza, crossed into **Egypt** and proclaimed himself the son of the god **Ammon** at the Siwa Oasis far to the west on the Libyan border.

Darius III, after his defeat at Issus, had not been idle. He collected a huge army near Nineveh (North Iraq), gathering levies from all 20 satrapies of the Persian Empire. It included 25 Indian war-elephants, 80 scythed chariots, cavalry, archers, spearmen, and the elite 10,000 noble-born Persians known as 'Immortals,' in all totaling nearly 3,00,000 soldiers. Having lost Asia Minor (Turkey) and Egypt, his limited aim was to defend the important northern cities of Arbela and Babylon, either of which could be Alexander's next target.

Accepting the challenge, Alexander marched north from Egypt along the Palestinian coast back to Tyre and Antioch and then east across the Euphrates River. Moving north again, he intended to cross the Tigris near

Nineveh (modern Mosul) but instead went further north before crossing, in order to avoid Darius' army, waiting across the river. Then he doubled back southwards along the eastern bank of the **Tigris** river to set up the most epoch making battle in history on the plains of Gaugamela, near **Arbela.** It is interesting that in all 4 of his great battles in Asia (Granicus, Issus, Arbela and Jhelum), Alexander was forced to undertake a difficult river-crossing in the face of the enemy!

According to the records of the Macedonian generals **Ptolemy** and **Aristobalus**, collated by the Roman historian **Arrian** in his authoritative biography of Alexander, 4 days march brought Alexander within striking distance of the Persian host. He rested his men and set up a fortified camp to protect his baggage and stores. Reconnoitering forward with his elite Companion cavalry, he observed that **Darius** had *leveled and prepared the ground* for his destructive *scythed chariots* whose charge could rip up and disorganize any cavalry or infantry formation. Darius, an experienced general, had certainly learned a few lessons from his defeat at Issus, where he had commanded in person. He equipped some of his divisions with the bristling *long pikes* of the Greek phalanx and also planned a charge of his elephants—the first time these pachyderms were used in war, outside India. Behind the elephants and chariots, Darius deployed an entire line of cavalry, of which the Indians and Persians were considered the best, apart from Cappadocians, Turkomans and Kurds. The infantry masses were in the rear and the Persian host outflanked Alexander's army on both wings, apart from outnumbering them nearly 10 to 1.

Alexander had a trained and battle-hardened infantry force 35,000 strong and a highly mobile cavalry force of 7000 horsemen, according to Arrian. The core of his infantry was the **Macedonian *phalanx* of** heavy *hoplites*, arrayed 16 men deep and equipped with the *sarissa* (24 foot pikes). The *phalanx* was a bristling hedgehog whose soldiers had heavy armour and as long as it kept order, it could overcome any opposition. Though essentially cumbersome in movement, these well drilled units were tested in battle and extremely well-disciplined. They were arrayed in close order, with each *phalangite* providing shield-cover to his compatriot on the left, and advanced, when ordered, singing loud *paeans*. There were 3 *phalanx* brigades of 6000 each which were placed at the centre of the formation. Other infantry included Cretan archers, Balearic slingers and javelin-men. The horsemen rode *without stirrups* (which were yet to be invented).

The Macedonian (*Companion*) cavalry and the Thessalian cavalry brigade (3500 each) with long spears were on the right and left wings respectively, ready to sweep up the sides. At Arbela, the centre of the first line was occupied by shield-bearing infantry and most of the 3 phalanx brigades. Since the vast Persian army would overlap and perhaps eventually surround his army, Alexander kept a strong reserve line (including select *phalangites*) so that his whole army could be quickly formed into one vast hollow defensive square, if necessary. In front of the right and centre of the 1st line, light infantry skirmishers (with javelin and bow) were placed to pick off the Persian charioteers.

Alexander, as usual, was conspicuous in shining armor with plumed helmet, and was mounted on his faithful steed **Bucephalus** in the forefront of the right wing, along with his elite Companion cavalry of young Macedonian nobles. The story of how the 8 year old Alexander acquired Bucephalus is well known. The untamed steed refused to let anyone ride him. But the young prince identified the problem—fear of his own shadow—and rode him, facing towards the sun. Horse and rider fought fiercely as one on many a battle-field and several cities were named *"Bucephelia"* in his honour, just as many *"Alexandrias"* and *"Alexandrettas"* were founded to aggrandize his royal master.

Alexander's basic tactics were to focus his attack on one part of the enemy's line to gain a significant advantage there, while refusing to engage elsewhere. He therefore inclined his personally-led attack to the right to enable his right and centre to come into collision with the Persian left-centre. Since this movement was taking the *phalanx* and rightwing cavalry away from the ground specially prepared by Darius for his intended chariot attack, the Great King hastily ordered his leftwing cavalry (fierce Scythians and Bactrians) led by Satrap Bessus, to charge and prevent further rightward movement by Alexander. The Macedonian responded by reinforcing his endangered right with cavalry and infantry from the 2nd line reserves. This reaction broke the Persian left centre, upon which Darius unleashed his deadly scythed chariots at the junction between the Companion cavalry and the solid central infantry *phalanx*. This move was intended to break the *vulnerable hinge* between infantry and cavalry and thereby create a breach in the Macedonian array. But Alexander had anticipated this and the light armed troops screening the Greek army had been specially trained to run between the chariots, wounding horses and drivers and cutting the traces. The *phalanx* then suddenly opened ranks in a planned maneuver to let the charging vehicles through.

This was the decisive moment of the battle, since Darius had been banking on the success of his chariot charge. Intuitively sensing a weakness in the Persian ranks, Alexander led his Companions directly at Darius, who was directing the Persian moves in person from his chariot. With his charioteer struck down, Darius lost his nerve and fled the field on horseback, long before the battle was actually lost!

While this ding-dong battle was taking place on Alexander's right, the depleted left wing, under Parmenio was confronted with a difficult situation.

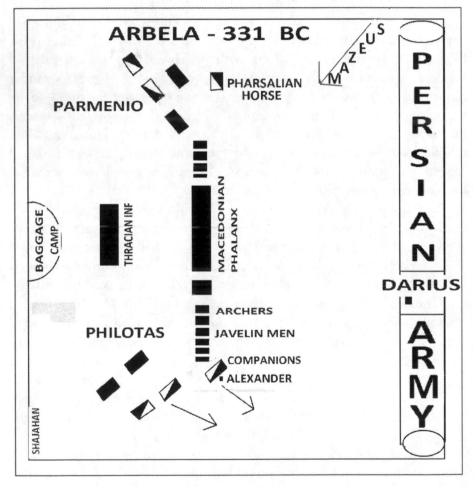

Arbela (Battle Plan)—331 BC

3

Veteran general **Parmenio** skillfully delayed engaging the enemy's overwhelmingly strong right wing. When finally compelled to fight, he dexterously defended his outflanked position against the Cappadocian cavalry brought in by Babylonian Satrap **Mazeus**, who commanded the Persian right wing. Nevertheless, a large column of Indian cavalry and the Persian guards galloped through the 2nd line of the Greek centre. But instead of wheeling back to attack the Parmenio from the rear, they went on to loot the enemy camp which was weakly guarded by a few Thracians. The battle became a confused *melee*, but Alexander's officers were trained to think and act independently and managed to hold on.

The Persian left and centre suddenly lost courage because of the flight of their king and tried to escape in large numbers back to Arbela, across the Lycus River. The still-powerful Persian right made a move to envelope the Macedonian left, trapping Parmenio, who called for urgent assistance. Alexander who was pursuing the fragments of the Persian left, wheeled his Companions sharply around to hit the Parthian, Indian and Persian cavalry successively in the flank. There were no tactics or maneuvering or javelin-throwing; only hard, head-to-head confrontation between the superb cavalry forces, with each man fending for himself. **Hephaestion** was badly wounded and nearly 100 Companions were killed before the Persian right wing forces were driven off.

With the murder of the fugitive king by his Bactrian satrap, **Bessus**, Alexander became undisputed master of the vast Persian Empire and was proclaimed '*King of Kings*'. Though he had another 8 eventful years to live, Arbela was the highpoint of his career. Unceasing in his activity, he occupied Babylon and tried to integrate the Greeks with the Persians, whose noble qualities he greatly admired. Several Persians, including Mazeus, were appointed *Satraps* of various provinces. He then conquered Bactria and put down the wild tribes of Afghanistan.

In the last of his great battles, he defeated the valiant **King Porus**, after crossing the **Jhelum River** (Hydaspes) in tactics similar to those he had employed at Arbela in crossing the Tigris. Leaving a force under Craterus to hold position, he marched north, crossed 20 miles upstream and then marched back. The 7 foot tall Indian king sent a strong chariot force, under his son to confront him. Alexander was hard pressed during this hot contest, but the Indian chariots got stuck in the mud at a critical juncture. Bucephalus was fatally wounded, but the Greeks managed to win. When asked how he should be treated, Porus replied "*Like a King!*"—An appreciative Alexander appointed Raja **Porus**, as client-king of his erstwhile territories, despite completely defeating his army and capturing him and his son.

It was here that the world conqueror heard this interesting discourse from a group of Jain monks, as reported by Arrian and quoted by **Amartya Sen** in *"The Argumentative Indian"*—*"King Alexander, every man can posses only as much of this earth's surface as he is standing on. You are but human like the rest of us, save that you are always busy and up to no good, traveling so many miles from your home, and a real nuisance to yourself and to others! You will soon be dead and then you will own just enough earth as will suffice to bury you".*

His goal was to reach the Ganges and further, to establish the Bay of Bengal as his eastern frontier. Though victorious, the soldiers, battle-weary and homesick refused to go farther east, to the very ends of the earth, as they thought. Acceding reluctantly to their pleas, he turned south, near Pathankot. While making his way down the Indus, to the Arabian Sea, Alexander's recklessness caused him to be isolated and severely wounded during the storming of **Multan**. He then characteristically chose the difficult and arid **Makran** coastal route to return to Pasargadae, while he sent the fleet under Nearchus through the Persian Gulf. He died on 13th June 323 BC in the palace of Nebuchadnasser, at Babylon, allegedly poisoned, at the age of 33. He left an indelible imprint on history, effecting the first serious East-West civilisational interaction.

Despite his sometimes erratic behavior—he burned down **Persepolis** in a drunken fit to avenge the destruction of Athens by the Persians, 150 years before—he was the most remarkable human being the world had known. His persona is truly an enigma. Though attractive to women, he did not strongly reciprocate this feeling and instead formed very close affinities, probably homosexual, with male friends. He left behind only one child, a boy, through the Bactrian princess **Roxanne**, possibly the only woman whom he ever loved—apart from his own mother. His conquests spread across 3 continents, were taken over by the *Diadochi,* his generals **Ptolemy** (Egypt), **Seleucus** (Asia) and **Antigonus** (Macedonia).

In a sense, **Chandragupta Maurya** was also a successor of Alexander the Great, immediately filling the power vacuum in north India left behind by the great conqueror, according to historian **Romila Thapar.** This paved the way for the growth of the Mauryan empire and the rapid spread of **Buddhism** under Chandragupta's grandson, the great **Ashoka** of whom H G Wells wrote in his *Outline of History*—*"The name of Ashoka shone almost alone, like a star".*

4

HANNIBAL AT CANNAE (216 BC) & ZAMA (202 BC)

As Macedonian power declined in the eastern Mediterranean, two superpowers fought for supremacy on the western shores. The rising **Roman republic** had grown from a tiny cluster of Latin villages between the river Tiber, and the Palatine and Capitoline hills, to dominate the whole of Italy by 300 BC, except the Greek colonies on the east coast. In 510 BC, the Romans had expelled the tyrant kings of the Tarquin dynasty and elected 2 Consuls, to jointly govern the state for a tenure of one year—a system which would endure for nearly 500 years.

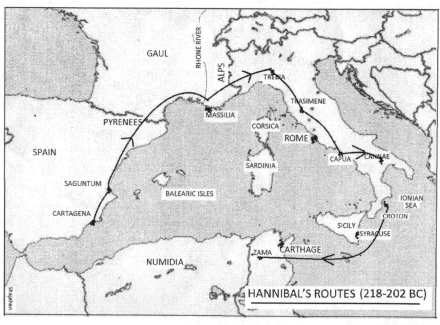

ARJUN A

Hannibals Campaigns—218-202 BC

4

The **Roman** *legion*, like the Greek *phalanx,* relied on shock tactics and this heavy infantry unit was organized in ascending order of age and experience into 3 divisions—*hastati, principes* and *triari* (rear). They were heavily armored and carried cylindrical shields (*scutum)* of composite wood, hide, and metal and the short Roman sword *(gladius).* While the frontline *hastati* had 2 throwing javelins (*pilum),* the 2nd and 3rd lines carried long spears. The cavalry arm was neglected and the horsemen preferred to fight on foot, using horses basically for transportation. Including supporting cavalry (300) and lightly armed velites (1200), the total strength of a legion was around 4500, and it fought under an "eagle standard" as a well-balanced force equally capable of skirmishing, attack, defense or pursuit, according to the situation.

The legion's core consisted of *40 centuries of 80 men* each, under *centurions*, and it was commanded by a *legate.* From the security of the walled cities, the legions went out on their conquests, building transit defensive camps every night, to guard against surprise attacks. They could steadily march 25 kms. daily in full armour and each legion was a self reliant unit with armourers, blacksmiths and medical services. Roman strategy, implemented through the legions, was ideal for conquering and holding on to territory, particularly when the enemy were brave but unorganized barbarians.

Legionaries were citizen-farmers drafted into the army for 20 years service, and were considered veterans if they opted for further service. After retirement, many settled down in distant colonies, which they had helped to conquer. At the time of the fall of **Jerusalem,** in 70 AD, **Vespasian** and his son **Titus** had over *30 legions*, ready to serve anywhere for a yearly salary of **300** *sesterces.* Legionaries did not demur even when led into the wilds of **Dacia** by **Domitian** or into remote **Iraq** by **Trajan** (110AD). Around this period Roman-officered *auxiliary cavalry* supplemented the regular army and these were used mainly for reconnaissance, skirmishing and pursuit. Roman legions were the most disciplined force ever seen, superbly trained like modern commandos, and could even be put to work building the great **Roman** *roads, aqueducts or monuments,* when not actually engaged in battle.

On the African shore of the Mediterranean, **Carthage** (near Tunis) was already a great city, founded by **Phoenician** merchants from Tyre, Byblos and Sidon (in modern Lebanon). Phoenicians were natural seafarers who had fought the Greeks in a fierce struggle for the hegemony of the eastern Mediterranean. This **Afro-Asian** power and the **Indo-European** Romans, both rapidly expanding their spheres of influence, inevitably clashed midway, on the island of Sicily, detonating the **First Punic war** in 264 BC. To keep up the struggle, the Romans tried to emulate the Carthaginian sea power by building a *strong navy* but their new fleet was crushed at Messina in 260 BC. With typical Roman perseverance, they designed and built radically different ships, fitted with wooden boarding bridges and won great sea-battles at Mylae and Heraclea.

In 251 BC, Carthage sent its most distinguished general, **Hamilcar Barca** to Sicily. Since Rome won several naval battles, Hamilcar could not hold on there and the war ended with Sicily becoming the first overseas province of the Roman Empire, followed soon by the island of Sardinia. **Hamilcar Barca** thereupon moved with a Carthaginian force to the colony of **Spain**. He was succeeded there by his son-in law **Hasdrubal** who founded the city of new Carthage (now **Cartagena**) in 228 BC. He made a series of diplomatic alliances with Spanish cities and tribes, using stratagem rather than force to establish total Carthaginian ascendancy in southern Spain.

On Hasdrubal's assassination, **Hannibal** (then 29), son of Hamilcar, assumed command in Spain. His sole objective was to thwart Rome's dream of world empire by initiating the **2nd Punic war.** Described as *the father of strategy*, he is rated in a superclass of commanders with **Alexander** and **Napoleon**, being gifted with a brilliant intellect, fantastic organizational ability, creative tactical skills and a clear grasp of geopolitics. After attacking **Seguntum**, a Spanish city allied to Rome, he realized that his only chance of ultimate success lay, not in Spain, but in boldly striking at the *Italian heartland,* thus forcing Rome to sue for peace by destabilizing her associate cities. **Leonard Cottrell** in his eulogy *"Enemy of Rome"* writes, *"The Romans commanded the sea and would never suspect Hannibal's intentions. To reach Italy by land was an impossibility, involving a journey of 1500 miles through hostile territory, besides crossing the* **Pyrenees**, *the* **Rhone** *and the* **Alps***".* Nevertheless, in early 218 BC, he set out from New Carthage (modern Cartagena) at the head of 50,000 infantry, 12,000 cavalry and 37 elephants, according to the Roman historian Livy. Crossing the Pyrenees, and the broad Rhone River with his elephants on rafts, he dodged the Roman army posted at **Massilia** (Marseilles) under the **Consul Publius Scipio.**

Hannibal's heterogeneous force was drawn largely from North African **Berber** tribes and the **Iberians** of Spain. The former included the superb nomadic **Numidian** horsemen commanded by **Maharbal**, one of the greatest cavalry generals of all time. Phoenicians were also in the ranks and Hannibal's later armies included Greeks, Gauls, Majorcans, and even Italians. The soldiers had nothing in common except a spirit of adventure and were held together for 17 years only by the charismatic leadership of their young commander who was fluent in half-a-dozen languages, including Greek and Latin, and inspired them with his eloquence and personal example. The elephants included some of Indian origin, who were more trainable than the larger African pachyderms and functioned much like tanks in modern war-fare. Apart from Maharbal, Hannibal's principal officers included **Gisgo** and his own brothers **Mago** and **Hanno**, with another sibling, **Hasdrubal**, left behind to hold Spain against the Romans there. And leading them was the 29 year-old **Hannibal** whom Sir Basil Liddel Hart in his *'Greater than Napoleon'* called *"the most original military genius of all time."*

Avoiding the well defended **coastal road** from France into Italy, **Hannibal** headed for the **Little St. Bernard Pass,** miraculously traversing the **Alps** despite the hostility of the mountain tribes, but losing heavily in men, horses and elephants. Five months after leaving Spain, he entered the Italian plains with just **20,000 foot, 6000 horses** and **five elephants**, an amazing achievement based totally on the leadership qualities of one man. **Napoleon**, who himself traversed the Alps for his first major campaign in 1796, observed *"It was Hannibal who crossed the Alps, not the Carthaginians!"*. Thoroughly alarmed, the Roman Senate recalled Consul, **Tiberius Sempronius**, from Sicily and he was soon joined in Northern Italy by **Consul Scipio** who had followed Hannibal from France. Since Consul Scipio was wounded in a skirmish at **Ticinus**, the 40,000-strong Roman army was under the sole command of the impetuous Sempronius. Hannibal, the master of psychological warfare, fully understood his enemy's weakness. He not only scouted the terrain ahead but also personally entered the Roman camp in disguise to ascertain the situation for himself.

In December 218 BC, he won the first of his great Italian battles, luring **Consul Sempronius** to the **Trebbia** river, near Placentia, outflanking and decimating the Roman army by using Maharbal's Numidian horsemen in ambush. Moving south, he trapped another Roman army on the northern shore of **Lake Trasimene** on a misty morning, in 217 BC. As **Livy** describes it, *"the place was formed by nature for an ambuscade, where Lake Trasimenus comes nearest to the mountains* *of Cortona.*" At the entrance to the defile was the town of Passignano, where Hannibal camped. Riding his sole surviving elephant, he then lured the pursuing Romans into the pass between the hills and the lake. Here, 20,000 of his men, waiting in ambush on the hillside, pushed the enemy into the lake, slaughtering the hapless Romans and killing the new Consul Flaminius. This victory opened up the Roman heartland of **Etruria** (modern Tuscany) to the rampaging Carthagenians. But instead of moving directly on Rome as he strategically should have, Hannibal went east to the Adriatic Sea and then deep south to Apulia's rich farmland to replenish supplies for his famished troops, camping around the city of **Bari**. His deficiency in *siege engines*—ballistas, trebuchets, battering-rams—which alone would enable him to take Rome, perhaps prompted this seemingly irrational decision.

The following year, he confronted a powerful Roman army of 4 double legions and auxiliaries (90,000 strong) under the 2 new Consuls—**Aemilius Paulus** and **Terentius Varro**, who held command on alternate days—at **Cannae** (Canossa) in the south. On 2nd August 216 BC, the impetuous **Varro,** who was in charge on that day, was provoked by **Hannibal's Numidian** *skirmishers* to advance precipitately for battle. Hannibal arranged his force of 50,000 in a crescent formation with his Spanish-Gaul infantry in the centre and his powerful African foot-soldiers to their right and left, with his dynamic cavalry posted on the 2 extremities of his line. As the weighty Roman centre pushed forward, Hannibal's deliberately weakened centre was driven back. His African infantry and Numidian cavalry then turned inwards on the two flanks of the 90,000 strong Roman army which was "swallowed up as by an earthquake", according to enemy historian, **Polybius**. To offset the superior numbers of the enemy, Hannibal had tactically shrunk the combat area. **Cannae** is the most imitated battle in history and many generals down the ages have tried to replicate Hannibal's risky tactics of "*double envelopment*". **Will Durant** says about Cannae *"It was a supreme example of generalship and it set the lines of military tactics for over 2000 years"*. The slaughter of 80,000 Romans (including **Consul Paulus**, 2 proconsuls and 80 senators) and 10,000 Carthaginians, is the largest ever death toll on a single day of battle and all within an area of just over one square mile! In the 1st World War, **Count von Schlieffen's** large-scale Cannae-like plan backfired when used against the French. But on the Eastern Front, Germany's **Hindenberg** and **Ludendorff** smashed the Russians at Tannenberg using a similar strategy. Referring to Trebbia,

Trasimene and Cannae, **General J F C Fuller** observes. "*When these 3 battles are examined, there is not the slightest doubt that victory was won by the genius of Hannibal and the mechanical Roman outlook upon war, with the general acting solely as a drill-master*".

Henceforward, the Romans refused to give battle, falling back within Rome and the walled Italian cities whenever Hannibal drew near. These "*Fabian*" tactics were implemented by the new **Consul Quintus Fabius Maximus**, called 'the Delayer', and Rome persisted with this method, despite Hannibal continuing to hold most of Southern Italy, undermining the Roman economy with the allied cities getting increasingly disgruntled. In fact, Fabius was even made sole dictator by the Senate to perpetuate the strategy, despite his growing unpopularity with the plebeians.

Lacking a siege train, Hannibal could not capture the strongly fortified positions in Italy and this altered Roman strategy wore out his army, isolated in a foreign land. **Syracuse** in Sicily, allied to Carthage, fell to the Romans under Marcellus in 212 BC, despite the scientific genius of **Archimedes**, whose military inventions (like molten *Greek fire*) kept the enemy at bay for 2 years. He also perfected ballistic machines based on the principles of "Tension, torsion and leverage". But the city was stormed, nonetheless, and the great man was killed in the massacre which followed. Finally in 207 BC, Hannibal's brother **Hasdrubal**, reached Italy with reinforcements from Spain but was intercepted and killed at **Metaurus,** before he could link up with his elder sibling. This ended Hannibal's last hope of breaking the Roman hold on Italy and he was encircled and isolated in the southern toe of the peninsula.

Publius Scipio, who had been a junior officer under his father the Consul, copying Hannibal's strategy, captured the latter's home base, **New Carthage (Spain)**, in a surprise attack. Since Rome commanded the seas, he next landed in North Africa to threaten mother-city Carthage itself and also successfully wooed the leaders of the **Numidians**, who provided Carthage with its *valuable cavalry*. Carthage, panic stricken, ordered Hannibal to return to Africa in 203 BC. By now, the Numidian king, **Massinisa**, had brought in his horsemen to assist Scipio, giving him a great superiority in the mobile strike force, since only a few Numidians continued to support Hannibal. From his base at **Utica**, Scipio raided the rich Bagradas Valley, luring Hannibal to follow him. Perhaps the latter would have done better to move within the walls of Carthage, since his army was inferior in quantity and even quality, except for the

20,000 veterans he had evacuated from Italy. He kept this elite force in the 3rd line of his formation, as the armies faced each other on the plain of **Zama**, south west of Carthage (Tunis). The first line consisted of Ligurians (from near modern Genoa) and Gauls, mixed with Balearic slingers (from the island of Majorca). The 2nd line was composed of Carthaginian infantry, while he kept his 20,000 battle-hardened veterans in reserve. He posted his 2,000 cavalry (Numidians on the left and Carthaginians on the right) on his flanks and his 80 elephants in front of the 1st line.

Against this formation, **Scipio** maintained the usual legionary organization with 2 lines of maniples (square chequered formation) composed of *hastati* and *principes,* leaving spaces in between, to let Hannibal's charging elephants through. The Roman *triari* of veteran infantry was in reserve in the 3rd line, and the lightly armed *velites* were sprinkled all over. **Massenisa's 5,000 horsemen** on the Roman right wing, faced Hannibal's **1000 Numidians** while the Roman horsemen (under **Laelius)** on the left, faced weak Carthaginian cavalry.

Being sorely deficient in cavalry, Hannibal could not repeat his Cannae tactics of turning the enemy flanks in a double envelopment. According to Livy and Polybius, the battle opened with skirmishing between the Numidian cavalry on the 2 sides, with Massenisa's numbers soon gaining the upper hand. Simultaneously, Hannibal let loose a great 80-elephant charge, designed to break the Roman centre. But the sound of Roman trumpets terrified the untrained pachyderms, many of whom ran back into their own cavalry on the left, allowing a total victory for Massenisa who pursued his defeated countrymen off the field. But some elephants did succeed in breaking through the first two Roman lines. **Laelius' cavalry** on the Roman left also drove off the Carthagenian horsemen, setting up a classic contest of the opposing infantry. Initially, Hannibal had the advantage, with his first 2 lines pushing back the Roman *hastati* and *principes* before meeting the powerful *triari* **veterans** who prevailed in a desperate encounter.

The conflict finally came down to a sustained clash between the **Roman *triari*** and **Hannibal's 3rd line elite infantry,** victors of 16 years of continuous warfare in Italy. **Polybius** writes "Being equal in numbers, spirit, courage and leadership, the battle was long undecided." But Massinisa's Numidians and Laelius' Roman cavalry providentially returned from their pursuit to take Hannibal in the rear, annihilating the Carthaginian army. It was Cannae in reverse. Zama was won by the numerically superior cavalry of Scipio, acting under his strict control. Perhaps out of respect for his great adversary, Scipio offered Carthage extremely generous terms, despite its cataclysmic defeat.

For seven years, Hannibal, as Suffete (President), strove to rebuild Carthage, despite the machinations of petty men both in Carthage and Rome, and he was repeatedly protected by the generous Scipio. Ultimately, in 195 BC, the envious **Consul Cato** sent an embassy to Carthage to arraign him. Fleeing into **Asia**, Hannibal continued his unrelenting mission against Rome. He acted as military advisor to Antiochus III, the Seleucid king, in his war against Rome, then fled to Armenia and to **Bithynia** where he won a great naval victory near Pergamon. Finally betrayed to the Romans, he committed suicide in 193 BC, to avoid capture. So long was his shadow that for centuries, Roman matrons quietened their children with the warning, *'Hannibal ad portas!'* For his great victory at Zama, Scipio was rewarded with the title **'Africanus'** at the age of 35 but later, was forced into exile because of the inevitable petty machinations of his envious peers.

Absurdly, every year the Roman Republic continued to elect **2 Consuls** of equal rank to jointly command its armies. At Cannae, Consul Varro was a *plebeian*, while Consul Paulus belonged to the aristocracy. The latter was a competent general who had been Consul earlier, whereas the former was a butcher by trade and had no command experience. Not surprisingly, their joint command was a total disaster. As **Mommsen** says, *"It was impossible that the question of the leadership of the armies of Rome should be left to be decided by the Pandora's Box of the balloting-urn".* Rome's standard tactics sometimes failed against an **enemy of genius** like **Hannibal**. Later, **Arminius (9AD),** lured Varro's 3 legions into the wilds of Germania and annihilated them in the Teutoberger Wald, during the otherwise successful reign of Augustus Caesar. And only Julius Caesar's innovative tactics saved the Romans at Alesia, in 52 BC, where they faced off against the indomitable Gaulish chieftain **Vercingtorix.** But the **Roman system** had a sound political basis because it was broadly *democratic* and therefore commanded wide popular support, despite some overwhelming defeats. It was the inborn Roman discipline, patriotism and unyielding character that generally won, against all odds.

The triumph of the Romans at Zama ensured that Indo-European **Jupiter**, rather than the dark sacrificial religion of Semitic **Baal**, had hegemony of the Mediterranean, leading to a world empire and establishing a Latin civilization that endured through the ages. **Julius**

Caesar's conquests, **Augustus'** *"Pax Romana"*, **Constantine's** triumph in 312 AD and the rise of a Rome-centered Christianity were all consequences of the clash of arms at Zama in 202 BC. The defeat of the great Carthaginian commander by the brilliant young Scipio, who studied, copied, improved and countered the master strategist, was arguably the most important event of the pre-Christian era.

5

MILVIAN BRIDGE (312)—CONSTANTINE, THE FIRST CHRISTIAN EMPEROR

Such was the deep-rooted Roman antipathy towards her great African rival that not content with the total defeat of Carthage, the call of *"Carthage must be destroyed"* echoed repeatedly in the Roman Senate till the dark deed was eventually done in 146 BC. Rome had no rival left in the western Mediterranean-north Africa, the Iberian peninsula, Gaul, Sicily, Sardinia, Corsica and the Balearic Isles plus total control of Italy. Roman hegemony of the eastern Mediterranean was also soon established with the defeat of Alexander's Macedonian successor state. Despite the distractions of internal class strife and chronic civil wars, Rome took on the barbarians surrounding its territories to expand in all directions. **Sulla,** leader of the patrician faction, won great victories against Rome's external enemies even while successfully carrying on the internal class conflict against his plebian rival, **Marius**. The great revolt led by the *gladiator* **Spartacus** was brutally suppressed by Crassus in 71 BC and 6000 crucified slaves lined the Appian Way, south of Rome.

Unarguably the greatest of Rome's generals, **Julius Caesar** (100-44 BC), subdued the Gauls (of France and Belgium) led by their valiant leader **Vercingtorix**, after initially suffering a severe reverse at Gergovia. Besieging Vercingtorix in his stronghold of **Alesia**, Caesar was himself hemmed in by a vast Gaulish host. His brilliant tactics and the discipline of his legionaries ultimately prevailed over raw courage and desperate resistance and the heavily chained Vercingtorix soon followed the victor's chariot in Caesar's triumphal procession at Rome. Nehru refers to Caesar's classic *"De Bello Gallico"*, penned during the course of his arduous campaigns, which established his reputation as a writer and thinker of the highest order. A man of action, Caesar invaded Britain twice, had a son (Caesarion) by **Queen Cleopatra Ptolemy** of Egypt and after defeating arch-rival **Pompey**, established a dictatorship in Rome. This provoked his untimely murder by a cabal of Senators led by **Brutus** and **Cassius**, an event graphically described by Shakespeare.*" Oh what a fall there was, my countrymen!"* Caesar left a massive footprint on history and future rulers were honoured to take the title of Caesar, Tsar and Kaiser.

His grand-nephew and heir, **Octavian,** took over the Roman Empire, with the titles **Augustus Caesar,** *Imperator* and *Pontifex Maximus,* after a desperate struggle in the East against erstwhile ally **Mark Antony** and his consort **Queen Cleopatra,** culminating in the decisive naval battle of **Actium**. An outstanding builder, during his reign from 23 BC to 14 AD, **Augustus** turned the brick city of Rome into a marble metropolis with the magnificent Roman Forum at its centre! In the lucid language of Gibbon's magnum opus *"Decline and Fall of the Roman Empire, "Augustus wisely rejected military rule and his policy was to reign under the venerable names of ancient magistracy and to collect in his own person, all the scattered rays of civil jurisdiction".*

Despite hiccups like the annihilation of **Quintilius Varus'** three legions, ambushed by **Arminius** at Teutoburger Wald in Germania (9 AD), Rome continued to expand geographically for the next three centuries under capable emperors—**Tiberius, Vespasian, Titus, Trajan, Hadrian, Antoninus Pius, Marcus Aurelius**—albeit interspersed with disastrous rulers like **Caligula, Nero** and **Commodus**. Vespasian and his able son Titus, subdued the turbulent *Jews of Palestine*, destroyed their Temple at Jerusalem in 70 AD and stormed their desert stronghold, Masada. Trajan penetrated deep into Mesopotamia (modern Iraq), while Hadrian's Wall was built by his successor to keep out the wild tribes of Scotland. The virtuous and austere Marcus Aurelius (shown in the movie *Gladiator*), was a Stoic philosopher who detested war, but when the need arose, he spent 8 winters successfully *"campaigning on the frozen banks of the Danube",* according to Gibbon. The best of the emperors lived simple lives, disdaining any pomp which could offend their countrymen, and these good emperors were invariably deified posthumously by the Senate. Many of the later emperors were, unfortunately, weak creatures controlled by the powerful Praetorian Palace Guard, and led dissolute and hedonistic lives.

Though most of the common folk became followers of *Christianity* or *Mithraism,* both monotheistic faiths, the ancient pantheon of Jupiter, Saturn, Mars, Apollo and Venus continued to be worshipped officially by the emperor (as *Pontifex Maximus,* Chief Priest) and sponsored by "the Senate and People of Rome" (SPQR).

In 306, **Constantine** opportunistically seized control of Britain with the help of the veteran legions under his command and declared himself emperor at Eboracum (York). He advanced across Gaul and into northern Italy in 311, to confront **Emperor Maxentius**, his brother-in-law. Defeating the generals sent against him, at Turin and Verona, he marched south along the Flaminian Way, reaching the outskirts of Rome on the 27th of October, 312 AD. That night he had a vision which led him "to fight under the protection of the Christian God" and mark his soldiers' shields with a symbol—a Latin cross with its upper end rounded into a "P". Maxentius, unaccountably, left the protection of the strong walls of Rome, emerging through the *Milvian Bridge* on 28th October and opted to fight with the River Tiber to his rear! His army, despite stubborn resistance, was pushed back and he was drowned in his heavy armour. A panoramic painting in the Vatican, by the great Renaissance artist **Raphael,** depicts the details of this epoch-making battle.

Gibbon praises **Constantine** for his virtue and intelligence and adds, *"His stature was lofty, his countenance majestic, his deportment graceful; his strength and activity were displayed in every manly exercise."* And further that *"he strictly adhered to the domestic virtues of chastity and temperance."* Though a pagan, **Constantine** had a Christian mother (**St. Helena**, discoverer of the "true cross") and gave official support to Christianity by the *Edict of Milan.* An able administrator, he systemetised the Christian Faith, after holding the momentous *Council of Nicea* (325 AD), in which 1000 bishops and religious leaders from all over his empire, participated. The Nicene (Apostles') Creed became the orthodox doctrine of the Church and 4 Gospels were selected from a plethora of such books. Considering the empire too unwieldy to be managed by one individual, he left his heirs as Emperors/Caesars of two separate entities, with capitals at **Rome** (Western Empire) and the newly-founded city of **Constantinople** (Eastern Empire).

The Western Empire quickly contracted as the Roman armies were withdrawn to handle threats nearer home, in Italy itself. The last legions withdrew from Britain in 410, leaving the Britons to fend for themselves. Under Pendragon Arthur (buried at Glastonbury), the Christian Britons managed to hold the pagan Saxon raiders at bay, but only for a while. The now effete Romans, succumbed to barbarian pressure, the city of Rome itself being threatened by **Attila,** King of the **Huns** and sacked successively by the **Visigoths** and **Vandals**. In 476, the last Western emperor, **Romulus Augustulus** was deposed by the barbarian, **Odoacer,** bringing to an end 500 years of imperial rule in Rome.

Constantinople, built by **Constantine** on the site of the ancient Greek city of Byzantium, was triangular in shape, (map Ch.11) and surrounded by water except to the west. It produced a succession of capable rulers who beat back challenges from Persians, Scythians, Dacians, Parthians and Nabateans (of Petra) and preserved the core of the vast Eastern Roman Empire.

Gibbon's magnum opus *"The Decline and Fall of the Roman Empire"*, narrates the sequel in wonderful detail.

Theodosius strengthened the city with additional fortifications (@400AD) and further reformed the Church. The magnificent **Emperor Justinian** (supported by his brilliant general **Belisarius** and the strong-willed **Empress Theodora**) triumphed not only over the Sassanid Persian **King Chosroes** in 532 but also butchered 30,000 rioters belonging to the schismatic Green faction, assembled in the Hippodrome. Belisarius' string of victories in 3 continents, with vastly inferior forces—in Dalmatia (Goths), North Africa (Vandals), Armenia (Persians) and Italy (Ostrogoths) displayed the most varied, creative and unorthodox tactics seen in military history. Second only to Belisaurius in military ability was the eunuch Narses who crafted his own series of triumphs. **Justinian's** judicial *"Code"*, based on humanity and commonsense, greatly influenced all subsequent legal systems. Under him, the city became the centre of Greek and Latin scholarship and his superbly domed *Hagia Sophia* (Divine Wisdom) represents the apogee of Byzantine architecture. Besides its 15 wonderful basilicas, the impregnable megapolis contained a magnificent hippodrome for chariot-racing, 2 grand theatres, over 160 baths, 8 underground cisterns, aqueducts for bringing water from afar, 14 palaces and 5 huge granaries! Its defences included the original Byzantine walls, Constantine's walls and the impregnable triple layered Theodosian walls of the expanded city. Serious schisms developed between the Roman and Greek Churches, based on largely on irreconcilable differences in language and culture. Despite consequent lack of western support, Constantinople continued to serve as a bulwark against invasions from the East. In the evening of his life, the able **Emperor Heraclius**, who had conclusively defeated the powerful Persian Sassanid rulers and consolidated the empire's eastern frontier, was unlucky to come up against the rising tide of Islam in the 7th century. Despite losing to the highly motivated followers of the new faith superbly led by Khalid ibn Walid, Heraclius still managed to save much of his empire. Suffering continuous buffeting from all sides, the city itself survived as the eastern outpost of Christendom with capable rulers like **Leo III** (the Isaurian) managing to repel successive invasions. In 1453, the Ottoman Turks under **Sultan Mehmet II,** finally stormed the megacity, **as** detailed in Chapter 11.

6

BATTLE OF TOURS (732 AD)—
CHARLES MARTEL, THE HAMMER

The decisive victory of **Charles Martel**, *de facto* ruler of the Franks, saved Christian France and Europe, from the rampaging armies of the Caliphate which overran Palestine, Asia Minor and the whole of North Africa in the century following the death of the Prophet Mohamed (632).

Khalid Ibn al Walid who had led the **Koreish** of Mecca to victory over the Prophet's Medinan **Ansar** supporters at **Uhud** in 625, joined the latter soon after. One of the most successful generals in history, he conquered Arabia for Islam and his light horsemen then swept into Palestine. Leading **Caliph Abu Bakr's** armies after the Prophet's death, he thrashed Sassanian **King Yazdigerd's** highly-rated Persians in a series of mobile battles in 633. From his capital Ctesiphon, Yazdigerd sent a strong army under the Khorasan governor Andargazar to intercept Khalid. Since another Persian army under Bahman was following in support, Khalid had to strike quickly and annihilate Andargazar's army which outnumbered his own. The two forces clashed at **Walaja,** east of the Euphrates**,** 30 miles southeast of Najaf in Iraq. After Khalid's frontal attack was repulsed, the Persians counterattacked and the Arab centre caved in. As the Persians were pulled in by the vacuum created, Khalid's cavalry rapidly swept up the flanks and another cavalry force which he had hidden behind a ridge took the Persians in the rear. It was Hannibal's **Cannae** replayed—a classic example of "*double envelopment*", with the enemy decimated.

The story of the Islamic expansion is retold brilliantly by Philip Hitti. The Arabs swept through the Persian Empire and **Caliph Umar** entered the holy city of Jerusalem on foot, a gesture of respect which was replicated by the conquering British general Lord Allenby 1300 years later, in December 1917, after his victory over the Turks in the battle of Beersheba. Defeating Eastern Roman **Emperor Heraclius** in the Yarmuk Valley, **Khalid** occupied most of his empire before he was disgraced and removed by the Caliph on specious charges of corruption. But the great warrior had already laid the solid foundations of Islamic hegemony in the Middle East, which survived despite the assassination of the 2nd, 3rd, and 4th Caliphs (Omar, Osman, Ali)

The **Merovingian** kings of the **Franks** have lately acquired fame, thanks to the books *"Holy Blood, Holy Grail"* (Michael Baigent et al) and *"Da Vinci Code" (*Dan Brown*)* and the popular movie of the latter name which claim that they were blood descendants of **Jesus Christ**! But by the year 700, effective rule of the Franks was firmly in the hands of their *Mayor of the Palace*, **Pepin of Heristal**. After his death (714), his natural son **Charles Martel** succeeded him after a bitter fratricidal struggle, where he displayed his genius for war. He unified the Frankish clans of Austrasia, Neustria, Burgundy and Aquitaine. The "long haired" **Merovingian** monarchs were completely marginalized and the new Caroline dynasty effectively controlled all Frankish territory, albeit as *Mayors*. Charles was now ready to face the ominous Islamic storm from the South.

In 698, **Tariq** who led the Umayad Caliph's armies west-ward in North Africa, crossed the straits of **Gibralter** (Jabar al-Tariq) and invaded Spain, which was ruled by the Visigoths. The Christian **Visigoths** were pushed north and north-west into the Pyrenees and the Asturias. Occupying Southern and Central Spain, the Muslims built the grand Alcazar complex at Seville in 712. The **Emir of Cordoba** crossed the Pyrenees and debouched into **Aquitaine** (Southern France), but was repulsed in 721 near Toulouse, by **Duke Eudo**.

The next **Emir**, **Abdel Rahiman**, brought up a powerful force of 60,000 Berber horsemen, along the west coast of France into Gascony, sacking Bordeaux and ravaging north-wards towards Poitiers, which he besieged, after defeating **Duke Eudo**. His next objective was Tours, 60 miles further north, which reputedly contained immense treasure. In desperation, Duke Eudo turned for help to **Charles Martel** who hurriedly came south, crossing the river **Loire** at **Orleans**. Meanwhile, he advised Eudo *"Do not interrupt their march; they are like a torrent which it is dangerous to stem. Wait till they have loaded themselves with plunder,"*

Most historians, including **Edward Gibbon** and **Sir Edward Creasy**, agree that the Saracens would certainly have overrun France and most of Europe but for the defensive shield-wall of the 30,000 Franks led by Charles Martel (the Hammer) who repulsed the Moslem horsemen, at a site midway between Poitiers and Tours.

Abdel Rehiman's army consisted entirely of *cavalry,* using sword and lance, but seldom the bow. Lightly armed and unarmoured, they were highly mobile but were by now encumbered with a huge mule train of plunder. Their usual tactics consisted of a series of head-long charges which broke up opposing infantry and no contemporary cavalry could match their thrust, ferocity and flexibility. Most of them were North African **Moors**, descendents of Hannibal's Numidian horsemen. **Charles** lured them away from the plains where their cavalry charges were most effective, up into the hills. He dismounted his men and arranged them in a defensive square in a high, wooded area, forcing the Moorish horsemen to charge uphill. While the latter were a totally *offensive force*, with no defensive power, Charles' huge Franks formed a shield wall in *static defense,* with his own private host firmly holding the centre. According to a chronicler, *"The men of the north stood as motionless as a wall—they were like a belt of ice frozen together."*

Tours was a straightforward battle with the **Frankish** *phalanx*, armed with spear, sword, javelin, shield and axe, wearing down the enemy horsemen who continued to charge fearlessly, despite being repeatedly repulsed. It was a rare case where unsupported medieval infantry were able to beat back strong and sustained cavalry attacks. Meanwhile, Frankish scouts and **Eudo's Aquitanians** entered the unguarded Moorish camp, seeing which the Moors rushed back to save their accumulated plunder. In the confusion, the **Emir Abdel Rehiman** was killed. Left leaderless in a strange, cold land, the Arabs retreated headlong back to Spain. Charles could not pursue the fully mounted enemy and was content with securing the huge treasure from the Moorish camp. Stolid Frankish courage, Charles's tactics of inducing the enemy horsemen to charge repeatedly uphill plus the fortuitous death of the Emir won the day for the Europeans.

Though direct Muslim advance into Europe due westward from Asia was firmly blocked by the impregnable megapolis **Constantinople,** Abdel Rehiman's thrust into the soft underbelly of the Continent could well have penetrated deep into Christendom. To quote **Edward Gibbon,** who called him the "hero of the age", *"perhaps the interpretation of the Koran would now be taught in the schools of Oxford, and her pupils might demonstrate to a circumcised people the sanctity and truth of the revelations of Mohamed!"*

In 741, Charles' son and successor, **Pepin the Short**, officially set aside the effete Merovingians and was crowned king of the Franks.

Pepin was succeeded (768) by his son **Charles the Great**, better known to history as **Charlemagne**, who was crowned emperor by Pope Leo III in 800. Charlemagne established the *Pax Dei* over Western Europe, except southern Spain where the Moslem Moors held on grimly till 1492. Unlike his grand-father, Charlemagne used his mounted soldiers as offensive *heavy cavalry* to overwhelm his enemies, eschewing the traditional defensive *shield wall*. Though a fervent Christian, he maintained a warm relationship with his great contemporary, **Harun Al-Rashid, Abbasid Caliph** at Baghdad (of *"Arabian Nights"* fame). **Al Rashid** considered the **Umayad-led Moors** in Spain, rebels against his rule, and hence encouraged Charlemagne to attack them.

But his repeated invasions of Spain failed spectacularly, most notably during the disastrous retreat of **Roncesvalles** (778) which is immortalized in the *"Song of Roland"*. Charlemagne's campaigns north-eastwards against the Saxons were more successful and he forcibly converted and integrated them into his new Western Roman Empire, which included Italy. He could well be considered the founder of the French and German monarchies, ruling his empire from Aachen (Aix-la-Chapelle) in the heart of Western Europe and drawing the disparate peoples of Europe towards a common secular authority. In time, this facilitated Christendom's reaction to Islam when Pope Urban II called for the **First Crusade** (1095) resulting in the establishment of a **Latin kingdom of Jerusalem.** The chivalrous Saladin and Richard the Lionheart light up the bloody Crusades. Belvoir, Montfort and Krak de Chevaliers represent the pinnacle of castlebuilding. The orders of St John/Templars were founded to protect pilgrims. The survival of this Christian/European outpost in the Islamic east for over two centuries led to a massive East-West interaction with important long-term implications—cultural, economic, social, religious,.

7

HASTINGS (1066)—
WILLIAM THE CONQUEROR

Western Europe in the 11th century was in a state of flux but crystallized steadily from itinerant tribes into settled nations, over the next 3 centuries. After the departure of the Romans in the 4th century, Britain was conquered (despite resistance by the legendary King Arthur) by the Angles and Saxons from Germany. The Anglo-Saxons established their kingdoms of Kent, Wessex, Mercia & Northumbria which were unified later by Alfred the Great. Though his successors fought off Viking invasions from Scandinavia the Danish king, Canute and his kin, briefly ruled England before the old Anglo-Saxon dynasty was restored. Pious **Edward**, called the **Confessor**, was crowned king in 1042, but the real power was in the hands of **Earl Godwin** of Wessex and his sons, who led the Saxon nobility. King Edward considered his maternal cousin, **Duke William of Normandy**, his heir.

On Edward's death on 5th Jan 1066, three powerful warriors laid claim to the English throne. Godwin's son the popular **Harold** was approved by the *Witan* and crowned at **Westminster Abbey**, recently built by King Edward, on 7th January. He was immediately challenged by Viking **Harold Hardrada** who revived the **Danish claim.** He invaded northern England in September with a fleet of 300 longships (each 75 ft vessel was rowed by 30 Vikings), accompanied by Harold's estranged brother, **Earl Tostig**. Routing the northern levies of earls Edwin and Morcar at **Fulford** outside **York**, the Vikings threatened the great northern city. The earls should have waited for the king and his host, instead of taking on the 9000 Viking marauders, unsupported.

Meanwhile, the main English army under King Harold himself, was concentrated in the **southeast (Sussex),** anticipating an invasion from **Normandy**. The Normans were descendants of Vikings who had conquered a considerable portion of France. William was the natural son of Duke Robert of Normandy and cousin of the late English king

Edward. Born in 1027, he was orphaned at the age of eight when his father died on a pilgrimage to the Holy Land. Constantly surrounded by danger and rebellion, he was steeled in the arts of war, diplomacy and intrigue. Now at the height of his powers he was an able administrator who kept his turbulent barons and knights under strict control, using the feudal system very effectively. He assembled an **8,000** strong force at the mouth of the little river **Dive** which lies between the Seine and Orme, ready to cross the English Channel.

The elite Norman cavalry was heavily armoured and fought with lance, sword and mace, while the infantry consisted of men-at-arms and archers (using the *short bow* and the *cross-bow*). The invasion was an international enterprise and contained an array of **knights** in search of plunder and fiefdoms. Considering that his army included over 2500 horsemen, transportation across the **Channel** and *logistics* and supply, must have been a major problem for William. Since the Duke's Viking-style longships had a capacity of only 50 passengers or 10 horses, at least 500 ships would have been mobilized—a great logistical feat for the times. Though ready io sail, the fleet was held up at anchor till the end of September, because of adverse weather conditions, a delay which turned out to be most fortunate for William.

When favorable winds finally blew, the flotilla set out, led by the duke's own ship *"Mora"*. William landed at **Pevensey** (in Sussex), on the morning of **28**[th] **September 1066** and immediately marched to Hastings, where the great Roman road to London begins. Here he set up a typical Norman-style wooden castle, as his base of operations.

Harold meanwhile, had led the Saxon army in a rapid march north from London up the great Roman road to confront Hardrada's Vikings at *Stamford Bridge*, 10 miles east of York on the 25th of September. Caught by surprise by the English king's speed of movement, which had won him many a battle in Wales, the Norse host had left their armour on board their ships (12 miles away). The host was divided in two by the river **Derwent when the English army surprised them**. Harold's army, mainly foot soldiers, had covered an astonishing *180 miles in 4 days*, one of the greatest marching feats in history. The huge **Vikings** were the deadliest warriors in the world and their veteran leader, **Harold Hardrada,** was a towering figure, measuring nearly 7 feet in height, but their hurriedly formed line was pierced by the professional English *housecarles* and *fyrd* (militia). The Viking retreat across the lone bridge over the **Derwent,** was covered for some time by a gigantic berserker, wielding a huge battle axe. This warrior, after slaying over 40 Saxons, was finally ingloriously skewered with a spear by a *housecarle* who crept under the bridge.

On the other side of the river, the Norsemen quickly reorganized their array into a ***triangular shield wall,*** being reinforced by warriors led by the young Norse hero **Eiystein Orri**, from the long ships beached at Riccal. Now it was a savage infantry clash between the Vikings and the elite English *housecarles*. But the sudden death of their iconic king, struck by a missile, demoralized the northerners. The fall of **Earl Tostig** and **Orri** (who was betrothed to Hardrada's daughter) left them totally leaderless, though they continued fighting to the last beneath their proud raven banner "*Landwaster*". The remnants of the host under Hardrada's son **Olaf,** were magnanimously allowed to return to the Orkney Isles and Norway in just 24 ships, out of the 300 vessels they had come in! Hardrada's disastrous venture was the last serious Viking invasion that England faced.

Harold was recovering from his hard-fought victory at York on 1st October, when he received tidings of William's landing in Sussex in the southeast. He rushed back to London with his depleted army, mainly mounted *housecarles,* raising such levies as he could, en route. Northern earls Edwin and Morcar were ordered to follow him, with the remnants of their beaten force. Harold had in all, only about **7,000 men**, but could have doubled his army had he waited a few days in London. However, news of the pillaging of his native Sussex countryside by the Normans aroused Harold's impetuous temperament and he moved quickly to take up a strong defensive position which could not be turned, near the modern town of **Battle,** 60 miles south of London on 13th October. A purely defensive battle did not suit his aggressive nature and his previous campaigns in Wales had always been the embodiment of the offensive spirit. But William's knights were the first large-scale cavalry force to ever operate in Britain and Harold probably intended to induce them to attack his strong position and counter-attack when the Normans were tired and worn out from repeated charges.

The 2500 housecarles formed the core of Harold's army but for weight of numbers, he relied on the fyrd, a levy of free men duty bound to serve for 2 months annually. The unarmoured Saxon levy, led by thanes, could number up to 12000 but no more than 4000 could be at Senlac. The English army had no archers or cavalry to speak of.

The east-west **Senlac** ridge which sloped southwards to marshy land was occupied by the Saxons, effectively blocking William's road approach to London in a breadth of around 600 yards. Harold commanded from right of the centre of this line, close to Battle Abbey (later built by William), with his hardy dismounted *horsecarles* ranged around him, 10 ranks deep. This was the spot where the gradient uphill from the marsh was least steep (1:33) and most vulnerable to attack, whereas the slope was steeper towards the east. The **Kentish** men guarded the slope and the faithful **Londoners** were around the king.

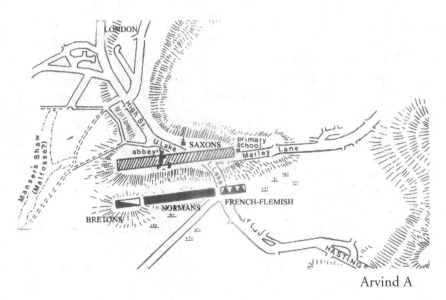

Arvind A

Hastings (Battle Plan)—1066
5

At 6'2" in height, with sandy hair and mustache to match, **Harold** at 43 years, was a truly magnificent figure. The royal *"Dragon of Wessex"* banner and his personal standard, the gem-studded *"Fighting Man"* were planted by his side near a "hoar apple tree". He was accompanied by his doughty brothers, **Earls Gurth** and **Leofwine** who had wisely advised him to leave the battle to them and to wait in London to collect the levies which were arriving daily from all over the country. But this sensible but cautious advice went against King Harold's grain—Contemporary chroniclers, **William of Jumieges** and **William of Poitiers** (the duke's chaplain), have reported the battle in great detail. The *Bayeaux tapestry* (commissioned by the duke's half-brother Bishop Odo) also depicts the entire campaign pictorially. The professional Saxon *thanes* and *housecarles,* armoured and with round shields, battle axes and spears, were flanked by the *fyrd* (militia) on both wings. The *housecarles* were of Danish origin and were arguably the best foot-soldiers in Europe, especially after thrashing Hardrada's Vikings at Stamford Bridge. The best view of the battlefield is from the grounds of Battle Abbey, from the very spot where King Harold fell. The ground slopes downfrom here to the valley in the south, which has fields and several ponds today. The Normans would have to charge up the slope from the valley, which was dotted with water-holes and was quite marshy in 1066.

The duke was relieved to have an opportunity to strike before expected Saxon reinforcements reached Harold. Starting from Hastings very early on the morning of 14th October 1066, the Normans covered 6 miles, came down Telham Hill and reached the marshy plain at around 9.00 am to find the Saxon host looming ahead on the *Senlac* ridge. The two armies were roughly equal In numbers. Going around the Saxon position through the marshy ground was difficult and would have exposed the Normans to a very dangerous attack on their flanks.

They therefore quickly formed line, with **William** (on horseback, armed with a ribbed mace) and his own **Normans**, directly facing **Harold** and his housecarles. He was accompanied by his half-brothers **Robert of Mortain** and **Odo, Bishop of Bayeaux.** The **French** and **Flemish** mercenaries, under **Eustace of Boulogne** and **Roger of Montgomery**, were on the right. The **Bretons** on the left were led by Count **Alan of Brittany**. All three divisions were in 3 orderly echelons of archers, infantry and cavalry, similar to the ancient Roman formation, except that in place of the 3rd line triari, now there were the mounted knights.

The battle lasted nearly 9 hours split in several phases. It opened with volleys by **Norman** *archers* who (who shooting uphill) could not make any impression on the *shield wall* of the Saxon phalanx, further protected by a trench and hurriedly devised earthworks. The whole line of **Norman** *infantry*, armed with spears, swords and kite-shaped shields then charged uphill to be met by a storm of missiles—sling-stones, axes, javelins— flung by fyrdmen placed in front of the Saxon army. There was then a prolonged hand-to-hand struggle, with the Saxon battle cries "Out, out" and "Holy Cross", ringing out aloud. As his infantry withdrew in good order, William's elite knights charged in, led by the minstrel **Taillefer** singing *the Song of Roland,* but they floundered in the boggy ground. The duke himself was unhorsed and the battle was at a critical stage. William removed his helmet so that his men could see that he was alive. On the left, Alan's Bretons were rolled back downhill, hotly chased by the shire levies, who were however cut down by the Bretons who turned when they reached level ground. Despite clear instructions from Harold to maintain position, the indisciplined levies could not be controlled and this feigned retreat was repeated by the Bretons to good effect. It is also probable that the Saxons charged downhill to replenish their depleted stock of missiles. The French on the right also made a feigned retreat, with the same result. **Fuller** opines that Harold could have ordered a general advance at this juncture, instead of trying to maintain the shield wall. The forward momentum would have overcome the archers and infantry. True the knights would have escaped, but they would be useless without archers and infantry, In hindsight, this appears as a good option. Despite the slaughter, the Saxon line was still intact (with reinforcements coming in) at 4 pm when the final bloody phase began, with just 2 hours of day light left.

 William now combined his *3 striking arms* to good effect. The *archers* raised the trajectory of their volleys and the *infantry* and *cavalry* charged in as the Saxon *shield wall* was raised to meet this new angle of fire. This was much like Napoleon's tactics integrating artillery, infantry and cavalry holistically, described in Ch.17. The Saxon *phalanx* began to buckle as the Normans gained a firm foothold on the level ground at the top of the ridge. **Harold's siblings** were both killed, Gyrth's bronze helmet smashed in by William himself. A little after sunset, with the battle still in suspense, Harold staggered as an *arrow hit him in the eye*. As he leaned on his shield in agony, a group of 4 Norman knights rode in and cut him down. A fierce melee raged around his body until his faithful housecarles were slaughtered to the last man, below the banners of the legendary "*White Dragon*" and the bejeweled "*Fighting Man*". Around **4000 Saxons** and **3000 Normans** were killed, many in the pursuit in the late evening and night of the battle. A large group of pursuing Normans rode into a deep ravine (later named **Malfosse**), where most were killed by the Saxons who turned and rallied for one last time.

 Most of the surviving *housecarles* fled the country opting to serve as mercenaries abroad, with many joining the elite **Varangian** guard at **Constantinople**. The northern Earls, **Edwin and Morcar**, quickly made peace with William, leaving no other serious claimants to the throne. Some Saxon chiefs, like **Hereward the Wake** (immortalised by **Charles**

Kingsley) from the fens of Ely, conducted guerilla operations for some time against the occupying Normans. **Sir Walter Scott's** *"Ivanhoe"*, provides a vivid picture of continuing antipathy between the Saxons and their Norman overlords, a century after the Conquest.

Harold's mangled body was identified by his mistress, Edith Swan-neck, and buried by the Normans on the beach near Hastings. The last English King was later reinterred in Waltham Holy Cross Abbey, London, which he had founded in 1060. On Christmas day 1066, **William the Conqueror** was crowned king of England by the archbishop of York at **Westminster Abbey**. It was the last time that a wholly foreign army and leader would win the throne of England through battle. To ensure better control and administration, William compiled the *Domesday Book* (1086), listing the details of all land holdings in England. He assigned large swathes of real estate to his knights, establishing the new *feudal system*. For instance, Roger de Beaumont and William de Warenne became Earls of Leicester and Surrey, respectively, holding lands bestowed by the king, with subordinate barons and knights owing allegiance, in turn, to them. But he ensured that his vassals' estates were scattered over different parts of his kingdom, to prevent rebellion. The **Norman Conquest** drew England away from its wild Scandinavian/ Viking connection and united it to the more sophisticated world of western Europe founded by Charlemagne. Heraldry and the institution of knighthood and chivalry were developed. **French** *language, law* and *culture* entered insular England, since the English monarchs simultaneously continued to hold large parts of France down to the mid 16th century.

The dynasties that followed William the Conqueror,—Plantagenets, Tudors, Stuarts, Hanoverians, Saxe-Coburg-Gotha (Windsor)—have all been of William's bloodline for 1000 years. The transplantation of the **Norman** *feudal system* and its mingling with the traditions and institutions of **Saxon democracy** (like the *Witan*) ultimately led to the creation and development of the English constitutional monarchy and bicameral parliamentary system as we see it today.

8

INDUS (1221)—GENGHIS KHAN, THE SCOURGE OF GOD

No compilation of effective war leaders would be complete without the inclusion of the *master of mobile warfare*, the embodiment of insatiable ambition for conquest and the incarnation of pitiless cruelty—**Genghis Khan**. Scion of a ruling Mongol family, **Temujin** as he was named, lost his father Yesugai, to poisoning by the Tartars, and struggled for survival in the inhospitable Mongolian terrain. Forming a useful alliance with the Maronite Christian Khan **Toghrul**, head of the powerful **Kerait** tribe, Temujin defeated the **Tartars** (1202) and built up a devoted following of nomadic archers who were attracted by his commanding personality and great leadership qualities. He had a striking appearance—tall, green eyed, with red hair and long beard. A great organizer and brilliant strategist, he taught himself the fundamentals of *siege-craft* and soon mastered this art in order to successfully wage war against the Chinese who were adept at fortification. By 1207, after a series of battles and skirmishes, he brought the Keraits, Naimen, Merkits and other tribes under his sway, taking the title "*Khan of Khans of the nine white yak-tails.*" In 1211, he crossed the Great Wall and attacked the Chin empire with 180,000 soldiers, defeating the Chinese decisively at **Wei chuan** in 1213, sacking their capital **Peking** (1215).

Using the excuse of an attack on a Mongol caravan in 1219, he next attacked the powerful **Khwarazm empire**, around the Oxus-Jaxartes Rivers, south east of the Caspian and Aral seas. Attempting to defend his entire border, **Sultan Mohammed Shah** spread his forces (3,00,000 strong) along the Jaxartes but several 10,000-strong Mongol "*tumens*" pierced the defences at various weak points and the Sultan fled westward to an island in the Caspian sea. The Mongol cavalry could travel faster than any other troops, penetrating passes and crossing rivers with ease. They stormed **Bokara** and **Samarkand** in Trans Oxiana (between the

Jaxartes and Oxus rivers.). The Sultan's son **Jallaludin Shah** repulsed the invaders under the *Orlock* **Juchi**, at Parwan near **Ghazni**, far to the south east. But **Genghis** himself moved swiftly across the Hindu Kush mountains and caught up with Jallaludin as he tried to cross the Indus River to the safety of India.

The opposing forces were roughly equal in numbers—around 60,000 each. **Jalaludin, facing north** occupied a strong defensive position, with his right flank on the Indus and his left protected by a mountain ridge. Genghis' army of 6 *tumens* advanced at dawn on 24th November 1221 with their leader stationed in the centre, identified by his standard of 9 white yak-tails. The Mongols were armed with the short composite bow of 300 yards range, sword, 2 javelins, dagger and a wicker shield. Each horseman was self-sustaining with water-proof hide for river-crossing, fish-hooks, iron pot, rations of millet, yoghurt and smoked meat. Stirrups and saddles gave the rider stability when shooting arrows or combat in a confused melee. They were organized into *"tumens"* (of 10,000) and *"hordes"* of 3 tumens under *orlocks*. Jalaludin's army was equally mobile and was a heterogeneous mix of Central Asian Turkomans, Tajiks, Uzbeks and Kanghis—all fierce horsemen.

Opening the battle aggressively, north-facing **Jalaluddin** ordered **Emir Malik** on his right to attack along the western bank of the Indus. As the Mongol left was driven back, Jalaluddin reinforced Malik by depleting his own left wing. Obviously, he hoped to accomplish an envelopment of the Mongol left by using overwhelming force here. He then led a massive charge in the centre to pin down Genghis and prevent him from strengthening his beleaguered left. It was an excellent tactical move but the wily Genghis saw through his intentions and took a calculated risk. Leaving his centre to fend for itself, he himself led his elite black-clad imperial Guard (10,000) on to the exposed left flank of Emir Malik's attacking force. Simultaneously, he also detached a *tumen* from his right wing to ride around the protective western ridge and fall unexpectedly on the weakened Khwarazmian left. Both moves succeeded completely and the Khwarazmian army was totally annihilated in this classic maneuver of double envelopment—a perfect riposte to Jalaludin's attempt to turn the Mongol left! Only 700 of the vanquished foe escaped, with **Jalaludin** himself cutting his way to the Indus and leaping in, standard in hand, from atop a 50-foot cliff. Genghis was moved to exclaim *"Fortunate is the father of such a son!"* But his admiration did not lead him to be merciful to the valiant man's young children—all were cast into the Indus to drown. Jalaludin fled to the court of **Sultan Iltutmish** in Delhi, where he lived for 3 years. Returning to resist the Mongols, he was murdered in Azerbaijan in 1231.

Genghis then suppressed several rebellions ruthlessly and in 1226 decisively defeated the **Tanguts** and razed their city of Erikaya. Soon after, he was badly injured in a boar-hunting accident near **Tashkent**. This affected his health adversely, turning his thoughts towards religion. Though an ardent follower of **Shamanism**, he was all along surprisingly tolerant of other religions. His massacres and extravagant displays of cruelty were essentially *only an extension of policy*.

Victorious to the last, Genghis died in 1227, at the age of 60, leaving his vast empire intact to his sons, who divided it into 4 *Khanates*— Iran, Turkestan, the Golden Horde in Russia and the Great Khanate of China, under **Oghotai.** Invasions of Europe continued under the brilliant *orlock* **Sabutai**. Genghis chose to be an enigma even in death, being buried in an unknown place near the River Onon in his native Mongolia and modern archeologists are still painstakingly seeking clues to ascertain the exact site of his grave, which reputedly contains a huge treasure trove. Apart from his massive footprint on *mobile warfare*, his fecund direct descendents (today numbering nearly around 18 million!) included the ferocious destroyer **Timur, Babur** and the **Moguls** who ruled Delhi (1526 to 1857). Many ruling families, stretching all the way into Russia and Eastern Europe are descended from Genghis. But his grandson Kublai Khan, founder of the Yuan dynasty of China was the most memorable thanks to the annals of Venetian traveler Marco Polo who served him from 1271 to 1294. Arguably, the loveliest fragment of English poetry ever written was Coleridge's opium induced *Kubla Khan* beginning.

> *"In Xanadu did Kubla Khan a stately pleasure dome decree,*
> *Where Alph the sacred river ran, through caverns measureless to man,*
> *Down to a sunless sea . . . ."*

About Genghis, Jawaharlal **Nehru** observes—*"Strange that this fierce, cruel and violent feudal chief of a nomadic tribe should fascinate a peaceful, non-violent and mild person like me, who am a dweller of cities and a hater of everything feudal!"*

9

BANNOCKBURN (1314)— ROBERT BRUCE, SCOTLAND RESURGENT

The great clash of arms at Bannockburn in 1314 was the successful culmination of 20 years of bitter conflict for Scottish independence. It began when England's **Edward I,** as arbitrator, upheld the claim of **John Balliol**, to the Scottish throne, over his rival **Robert Bruce**, in 1292. King Edward had recently subjugated **Wales,** building a ring of impregnable castles (Harlech, Caernarvon, Flint, Conway, Beaumaris) designed by the peerless James of St. George, around the rugged mountain region of Snowdonia, to hem in the turbulent Welsh. A consummate commander and administrator, Edward had earlier put down the rebellion of the English barons led by Simon de Montfort (1265) and established a rudimentary parliamentary system. He entertained grand ideas of establishing English hegemony over the entire British isles. He soon proclaimed himself suzerain of Scotland, which atrocious claim was resisted by all patriotic Scots. Symbolically, Edward I carried away the Scottish coronation **Stone of Scone** (Jacob's pillow, according to myth) to Westminster Abbey. It was only returned to Scotland in 1996, exactly 700 years later. **King John Balliol**, who fell out with the English King, was exiled. The leadership of the freedom movement devolved surprisingly on **William Wallace**, an ordinary knight from Paisley (Glasgow) who defeated the English at **Stirling Bridge** (11th September,1297). As a 15000 strong English army under John de Warenne (Earl of Surrey) and Hugh de Cressingham advanced, the Scots positioned themselves half a mile to the north of the bridge over the Forth and attacked after 6000 of the enemy had crossed, annihilating them and killing Cressingham. Scottish co-commander Andrew Murray, was mortally wounded and Wallace became, despite his humble origins, Guardian of Scotland.

The story of his unequal struggle against the powerful armies of **Edward I**, is recounted in heroic detail in Jane Porter's historical novel "*The Scottish Chiefs*".

Sir William Wallace did not belong to any of the leading Scottish baronial families but his intrepid spirit, which earned him the title "**Braveheart**", kept the freedom struggle alive for **Robert**, grandson of the original claimant **Robert Bruce**. Edward hurriedly returned from campaigning in France, moved his government north to York, assembled an army of over 20,000 at Roxburgh and invaded Scotland. Wallace was defeated by Edward at **Falkirk** (1298). The English and Welsh archers (using *longbows* made of yew) decimated the 4 stubborn Scottish *schiltron* hedgehogs of spearmen with sustained volleys, followed by a charge of the heavily-armoured English knights. Undeterred, Wallace continued his guerilla war and kept the torch of Scottish freedom burning till 1305, when he was betrayed to the English and tried for treason (though he had never been a subject of Edward). He was hanged, drawn and quartered at Smithfield in London as graphically depicted in the film "**Braveheart**", starring **Mel Gibson**. Celebrated in legend and song, **Wallace** was the noblest of heroes and his martyrdom united the Scots as never before. A competent general with a penchant for guerilla tactics, Wallace was unlucky to come up against a truly great commander, Edward I, with half-a-century of varied military experience in England, Wales, France and Palestine. Though most of Wallace's leading captains—**Andrew Murray**, **John Grahame**, **Macduff**—were dead by 1305, his spirit lived on till the independence movement was revived by **Robert Bruce**, earl of Carrick and Annandale, grandson of the original contender to the throne. The **Bruces,** owning extensive estates on both sides of the border, initially swore fealty to Edward I of England, but young Robert later joined the Scottish patriots. Undisputed leader of the freedom movement after Wallace's death, he was excommunicated by the Pope in February 1306 for the murder of rival claimant **John Comyn** in Dumfries monastery, but received strong support from **Bishop Robert Wishart** of Glasgow and the nationalist clergy of Scotland. **Robert Bruce** was crowned king at **Scone** in **March 1306** following established custom, with several leading Scottish bishops and earls present. King Edward's extreme reaction to the coronation was predictable and Bruce suffered a series of terrible defeats, Undeterred, he soldiered on, giving rise to the legend of "Robert Bruce and the Spider". Mighty warrior that he was, Edward I soon had Scotland back in his vice-like grip, taking castle after castle using an assortment of formidable siege engines including his giant *trebuchet* "**Warwolf**". His stream of victories earned him the sobriquet, "*Hammer of the Scots*". **Robert Bruce** fled to **Ireland** with his brothers and close followers, but his mother, wife and daughter were captured and barbarically treated by the English, being hung up in open cages outside the walls of Berwick Castle.

Fortunately for the Scots, the aged Edward I died in 1307 and Bruce returned to Scotland. Bruce's valiant band carried on guerilla warfare in South-West Scotland, where he was a major feudal landowner, but two of his brothers were captured and suffered Wallace's cruel fate. The new king, **Edward II** (first English *Prince of Wales*), lacked his father's perseverance and genius for war, though he was physically strong and brave enough.

The Scots won a series of small victories, captured one castle after another (Perth, Linlithgow, Dumbarton, Roxburgh, Edinburgh). They even began provocative cross-border raids into Yorkshire and Lancashire, led by the meteoric **Sir James 'Black' Douglas**. By 1314, strategic **Stirling,** a spur castle, remained the main English stronghold in Scotland. **Edward II** personally moved north with a large army since the English Governor, **Sir Philip Mowbray,** had agreed to surrender it, if not relieved before 24th June. The castle was a *force multiplier* and a small garrison could tie down a besieging army several times its size. The fall of Stirling would have been catastrophic for the English because of its strategic location on the main road to northern Scotland.

It is not surprising that all the 3 decisive battles of the Scottish war of Independence—**Stirling Bridge** (1296), **Falkirk** (1298) and **Bannockburn** (1314)—were fought within a few miles of each other. The first, won by Wallace, created the spark of freedom; the second won by Edward I, almost put out the ensuing fire; the third, won by Bruce, re-established Scotland as an independent country. This area, near the mouth of the **Firth of Forth**, is critical for any invasion into the Scottish heartland from Edinburgh and the south. **Falkirk** was fought in a wooded region just south of the boggy marshland where **Stirling** and **Bannockburn** are located, and all 3 battles were fought by English armies on their way north from lowland **Lothian**, along the east coast. This is also the strategic east-west line along which the Romans had built their **Antonine Wall**, to keep out the wild Picts of the north. Stirling was called the "*gateway to the Highlands*" since it was wellnigh impossible to cross the Forth at any place downstream (east) where it was too broad, or upstream since the castle was located on a spur of the Ochil hills, where the Highlands begin. It is much like the strategic **Kurukshetra-Panipat**

area, which any army invading India from the north-west has to pass through, to reach Delhi and the Gangetic heartland. **Stirling castle** is the HQ of the Argyll and Sutherland Highlanders and the visitor from India can view many items in the regimental museum, which were originally spoils taken from **Tippu's Srirangapatnam**, after its fall in 1799.

Edward II's army was nearly 20,000 strong and was confident of outright victory in a pitched battle, thus putting an end to the war. There were 2500 heavy cavalry (knights) and 2000 Welsh long-bowmen, along with highly trained infantry, plus state-of-the-art equipment, including siege engines (*battering rams, catapults, trebuchets, siege towers* etc.) With resplendent banners and burnished armour, the English army was a magnificent sight as it mustered at **Berwick-on-Tweed** and moved north, just 2 weeks before the deadline of 24th June, agreed on between Edward Bruce and **Philip de Mowbray**, governor of Stirling. On mid-summer's eve, the English arrived before the ford across the Bannockburn (stream). To oppose them, the Scottish force consisted of 8,000 regular soldiers, mainly battle-hardened *pikemen* trained to form *schiltrons* (large circles, with 15 foot spears forming a protective hedge). There were also 500 horsemen and about 3000 militia. Utilising the terrain to good effect, **Bruce** placed his soldiers in 4 divisions across the **Stirling road,** which he dug up, leaving only a narrow gap between the wooded hills in the west and the marshy bog in the east. The divisions were led from south (right) to north respectively by the **king**, brother **Edward Bruce**, **James Douglas** and the king's nephew **Thomas Randolph, earl of Moray.** Governor Mowbray rode down from Stirling to meet his monarch on the 23rd and persuaded King Edward to send 600 cavalrymen under **Lord Clifford** through the eastern gorge, where they would not be seen by the Scots, straight to the castle, less than two miles away and thus "technically" relieve it. But they were spotted by Scottish skirmishers and **Randolph** moved to intercept them. The English knights repeatedly charged Randolph's 2 infantry *schiltrons* spiritedly, but to no avail. The cavalry charges gradually weakened and the horsemen retreated. As they gathered to reorganize, the Scot foot-soldiers did the unthinkable—they charged straight at the English cavalry! Outnumbered 3 to 1, it was a morale-booster for the Scots to see the heavily armoured English knights flee precipitately before them, losing nearly 100 of their number in this unusual mini-battle.

Simultaneously, the recklessness of **the Bruce** led to an unforgettable incident on the southern part of the field. A young English knight, **Henry de Bohun** from Gloucester's division, noticed a lone figure riding back and forth in front of the Ist division. Observing the crown on his helmet, de Bohun identified the horseman as the Scottish king himself and charged directly at him with pointed lance. Bruce was mounted on a small grey palfrey and carried no lance but he skillfully dodged de Bohun and pole-axed him with his battle-axe, splitting his skull. Had de Bohun succeeded in killing the Bruce, the Scots would have been left leaderless and kingless on the eve of the main battle; but it was typical of Bruce to wantonly expose himself to danger and accept any challenge. Today, there is a magnificent statue of King Robert Bruce to mark the spot, which is the best vantage point from which to view the battle field.

After overnight skirmishes, the armies were ready to face each other on the morning of **24**[th] **June**. From the marsh where they were, the English struggled to cross the gorge and enter the field to the west where the 4 Scottish divisions were waiting in *schiltrons*. The English command was disunited and confused, unlike Bruce who personally oversaw every stratagem, delegating the finer details of the tactics to the 3 divisional commanders, who were his brother, nephew and James Douglas (his closest friend and *alter ego*). The battle was a magnified replica of what had happened on the previous day. **Edward II** had learnt the wrong lessons from the Englih victory at Falkirk. He did not realize that *cavalry* could destroy *schiltrons,* but only after they were broken up by archers' fire. As the charge of the English knights was beaten back by the 6 unbroken *schiltrons* of Edward Bruce, James Douglas and Randolph, the English archers in the rear hit their own knightly comrades with "*friendly fire*". At this point, some Scottish militia and camp-followers were sighted atop Gillies Hill in the background. Mistaking them for Scottish reinforcements or reserves, the English mass panicked. As Bruce ordered the Scottish *schiltrons* to push forward, the disorganized English knights were pushed back into the gorge and even into the marshy carse beyond, where horse and man floundered in their heavy armour. Sensing the opportunity, Bruce now threw in his reserve of 500 cavalry and the division of Highlanders and Isle-men with broad *claymores* (under Angus Og McDonald), which he had hitherto held in reserve. The slaughter of the English began, with the gallant young Earl of Gloucester, Sir Robert Clifford, Sir John Comyn (son of the murdered Sir John), Sir Giles Argentine and many other noble knights being butchered. Their very numbers and heavy equipment now proved a bane, but some did manage to get to the Forth and swim across. King Edward himself rode through to Stirling castle but Mowbray, bound by his agreement with Edward

Bruce, honorably refused to let him in. With just a few knights, the king made a wide detour to the west and dashed back south to Dunbar, with stragglers being picked off by the rampaging Scots. The **Earl of Hereford** cut his way west with a few horsemen to Bothwell Castle on the Clyde, but was taken prisoner there. Bruce was able to exchange for this very important captive, his queen, his daughter Marjorie, his sister Mary and old Bishop Robert Wishart of Glasgow!

Bannockburn, the greatest moment in Scottish history, was won by Robert Bruce after 18 years of unrelenting struggle and proved that superior enemy numbers and weapons were ultimately no match for the indomitable national spirit and patriotism of the Scots, who now considered themselves truly a nation.

The 15 years of Bruce's reign after Bannockburn were generally successful, though far from peaceful. Using his family ties with the great Irish feudal house of Ulster, he put up his brother **Edward** as **High King of Ireland** (1316) and even went personally, to assist him. This pan-Gaelic alliance was a far-sighted idea but failed because the Irish could not see any difference between English occupation and Scottish rule by **King Edward Bruce**. The latter was defeated and killed (1318), putting an end to Scottish involvement in Ireland.

Meanwhile, Scottish borderers like Douglas and Randolph kept the English in the northern counties on tenterhooks with sporadic raids, until Bruce and Edward III sensibly signed the Treaty of Edinburgh-Northampton (1328) to end hostilities. Even more importantly, Bruce made his peace with the Church of Rome and Pope John XXII lifted his excommunication in 1328. Robert Bruce died in 1329, of leprosy, and was succeeded by his infant son **David II**. **Robert Bruce** was buried at Dumferline abbey. His friend **Sir James Douglas** carried his heart (in a silver casket) on a pilgrimage to the **Holy Land**—a journey which ended en route, in a desperate battle against the Moors of Granada in Spain. On David II's death, he was succeeded by **Robert II**, son of the Bruce's daughter Marjorie, who had married **Walter Stewart**. Nearly 300 years later (1603), Robert Bruce's Stuart (Stewart) descendant, James VI of Scotland, succeeded Elizabeth I to the English throne as James I. This established the rule of the Stuart dynasty over the whole island (England, Wales, Scotland) with the **Union of the Crowns. The Union of Parliaments** followed in **1707**. It is ironic that the Union may be undone by the rise of the Scottish National Party at a time when David Cameron, a Scot, is the British Prime Minister!

10

RELIEF OF ORLEANS (1429)— JOAN OF ARC

The legacy of William the Conqueror as Duke of Normandy, ensured that the kings of England continued to hold vast territories in France. These holdings were enhanced by advantageous marriages contracted with French heiresses so that by the 14th century, English monarchs held huge chunks of France, albeit as nominal vassals of the king of France. The claim of the English king **Edward III** to the French throne itself, led to the **Hundred Years War** (1338-1453), which commenced with thumping English victories at **Crecy** and **Poitiers** (1350), where English long-bowmen and knights under the king and his son **Edward (the Black Prince)** laid low the flower of French chivalry, even taking the French king **John II** prisoner. The effigy of the Black Prince, the greatest warrior of the age, at Canterbury Cathedral, displays a powerful physique and determined features. The 6 ft English longbow, made of yew, ash or elm, and a range of over 350 yards, was the gamechanger in the conflict. In expert hands, it shot 3ft long arrows at 10 times the rate of the crossbow.

Nevertheless, the war dragged on desultorily, with the Peasants Revolts and the Black Death taking their toll in both countries. The population of England was now less than 5 million, against France's 12 million. However, the enthronement of the dynamic young English **King Henry V** in 1413, changed the tenor of the war. In 1415, Henry V won the decisive battle of **Agincourt** and was accepted as heir by the demented French **King Charles VI,** by the Treaty of Troyes. His own son, the **Dauphin Charles**, was disinherited. Henry's claim to the French throne was bolstered by his marriage to Princess Catharine, daughter of Charles VI in 1420. Fortunately for France, the brilliant Henry V died soon after, leaving an infant (Henry VI) as successor. William Shakespeare wrote about Henry V.

"Too famous to live long,
England never lost a king of so much worth"

But the English and their Burgundian allies controlled much of France, including Paris, and the Dauphin was yet to be formally crowned as **Charles VII** at Rheims, where French kings were traditionally anointed. In 1428, Orleans on the River Loire, was significant as the main stronghold of the **Orleanists** (Dauphin Charles' faction). The **Duc d' Orleans,** leader of the Orleanists and nephew of the late king was still kept as a captive in England after being taken prisoner at Agincourt, 13 years previously. The other powerful feudal magnate, the **Duke of Burgundy**, openly sided with the English. Regular skirmishes took place around Orleans and the fall of the city seemed imminent, despite the courage and activity of **Count Dunois**, natural son of the late duke of Orleans.

The political and military situation changed dramatically with the arrival on the scene, of **Joan of Arc**, *la Pucelle* (the Maid). Joan was a 17 year-old from the village of Domremy in northern France, who claimed to have seen divine visions and heard angelic voices urging her to lead the French armies to victory. Motivated by intense patriotism, she travelled south and met the Dauphin at Chinon Castle, near Tours. When she convinced him of her destiny, he gave her an army to relieve Orleans, the only French-held stronghold north of the Loire River. This was definitely the turning point of the 100 Years War.

Lying on the north bank of the wide and shallow Loire, **Orleans** was a quadrilateral defended by strong walls and 34 towers. On the southern side of the town, a bridge led to an island protected by 2 towers called "**Tourelles**", from where there was a drawbridge to the southern bank, which was itself guarded by guns behind formidable earth-works. 70 new-fangled **cannon** (bombards) were on the city walls—probably the earliest such use in European history.

The **English Regent, the Duke of Bedford** realized the strategic significance of Orleans. **Thomas Montague, Lord Salisbury**, who led the 12,000 strong Anglo-Burgundian army, perceived that the **Tourelles** towers were the key to the defense of Orleans since most of the supplies reached the city from the South through this ingress. After heavy bombardment by the English, the French abandoned the southern bank, the island fort (Isle St. Antoine) and the Tourelles and withdrew into the city (23rd October 1428). The English promptly occupied these strong points, repaired them and commenced bombardment of the city from this close vantage position. However, a French cannon accidentally discharged by a boy, killed the able Salisbury and command passed to **John, Lord Talbot**.

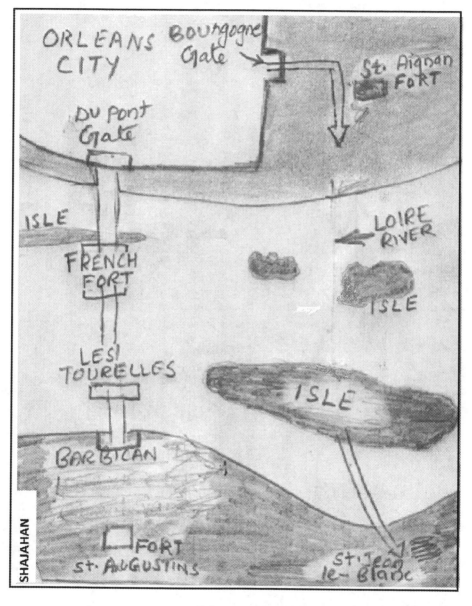

Orleans—1429

6

In November the English withdrew into winter quarters, leaving only a token force before the city. This respite enabled Dunois to enter the city with reinforcements, raising the garrison's strength to **12,000**. In December, 1428 the new English commander **John Talbot**, intensified the siege by commencing to build a semi-circle of forts on its northern side. **Talbot** was an experienced commander and built 2 forts (St.Laurel to the west and St.Loup to the east), north of the Loire to prevent the entry of supplies from that direction, but he did not have enough soldiers to either cover the entire perimeter or to take the city by assault. Since the town's land-ward perimeter was 2000 yards long, any besieging line of fortification would need to be about 4000 yards long!

An attempt by a French-Scottish force, under Count Dunois, to cut off 300 wagon-loads of food supplies from Paris to the English army, led to the victory of the latter, at Janville, in what was called the "**Battle of the Herrings**". The innovative **Sir John Fastolf** successfully made a hedgehog of wagons for his archers to defend. After this setback, the besieged were disheartened and there were now plots within Orleans to hand over the city to the English or the Burgundians. Orleans being the only town north of the Loire in French hands, its fall would have been disastrous for the patriots since it was midway between English-held Paris and the Dauphin's ad-hoc capital, Bourges in the south.

Clad in white armour, carrying a consecrated banner emblazoned "*Jhesus Maria*" and riding a black charger, **Joan** reached Orleans on 29th April 1429. She wore the consecrated sword taken from the shrine of St.Catherine and first went to church where the '*Te Deum*' was chanted. The effect of her enthusiasm on French morale was unbelievable. As for the English, they were paralyzed at her boldness and kept within their forts. Joan wrote to Talbot "*The King of Heaven demands your surrender.*" But the English insultingly shouted back, "*Vacher-cowgirl!*"

On 4th May, the newly aggressive French soldiers attacked and captured the outlying fortress of St. Loup, after a fierce assault. The English then abandoned Fort St. Jean le Blanc on the south bank. They however, continued to hold onto the bridgehead (**barbican**) fort on the south bank and the **Tourelles** which were occupied by 500 men-at-arms under **Sir William Glasdale.** Joan called out to him "*Glasdale, you have called me a harlot, but I have pity on your soul.*" Joan's fierce attack on the bridge-head was repulsed and she was severely wounded under the collarbone by an English arrow which found a chink in her armour. The English jeered as the Maid withdrew, but to their horror, Joan reappeared like a ghost on the field, urging on her soldiers and leading them with her banner held high. At this critical juncture, acting without orders, the Orleans city militia boldly improvised a bridge of planks (bailey-bridge) from Isle St. Antoine and attacked the **Tourelles**, taking the defenders in the rear. **Glasdale** had too few men to hold both strong points and decided to abandon the bridgehead on the south bank and pull back to the Tourelles. As he withdrew across the draw-bridge, it was hit by a cannon shot and he fell into the Loire and drowned in his heavy armour.

By the 15th century, **knights** were clad in multiple layers of protective materials—padded clothes below a hauberk of flexible chain mail, over which there was plate armour and an embroidered surcoat. Breastplates, gauntlets, greaves and elaborate helmets kept improving and the best armour was manufactured in Milan, Nuremburg, Augsburg and Toledo. Knights carried a long, heavy sword (suitable for thrusting and slashing) in its scabbard plus a heavy mace or battle-axe for smashing in helmets, apart from the mandatory shield with its distinctive heraldic device to identify the owner. These 2-handed swords had long hilts and large pommels for better balance. Horses too, were heavily armoured. Knights would carry a lance when charging in echelon, using the momentum of man and beast (both armoured) to full effect. They had to be well-trained and went through a long apprenticeship as pages and squires, before knighthood was conferred. **Chivalric orders** like those of the Garter, St. George and the Golden Fleece were honours instituted by monarchs to motivate their martial followers.

Even after the invention of gun-powder, mounted knights continued to be the critical strike force on any medieval battle-field, countered only by similar cavalry or a hedgehog formation of spearmen or sustained flights of arrows from longbows or cross-bows. Lesser folk would be on foot, wielding spears, swords and bows and would have inferior protection against missile and weapon attack. Large companies of mercenaries were employed during the 100 Years War. Sir Arthur Conan Doyle relates the story of Sir Nigel Loring in *"the White Company"*. Many such freebooting companies roamed Europe, ready to fight for any paymaster. The Duomo in Florence boasts a magnificent fresco by Ucello of the *condottieri* leader, "Giovanni Acuto", who is interred there. He is actually the English knight **"Sir John Hawkwood",** who after his French adventures, fought bravely for the Italian city-state. Italy continued to be the playground of the *condottieri* who were employed by war-lords like **Cesare Borgia** (protagonist of **Machiavelli's** *"The Prince)*. Siege engines too had developed over the years and the late 14th century also saw the introduction of cannon, mainly in the attack on and defense of forts, citadels castles and cities.

Matchlock muskets were followed by the more reliable *wheel-locks* which were further improved by adding a thrusting **bayonet** in the early 17th century, to replicate the spear. By then, the heavily armoured knight was extinct and heavy cavalry swords replaced the lance in the charge, followed by the addition of pistols. The stage was set for Europe's bitter wars of religion and the advent of the great pioneer of modern warfare— **Gustavus Adolphus, King of Sweden.**

But to return to the plight of the Anglo-Burgundian army besieging Orleans. After the death of **Glasdale,** they were now leaderless, demotivated and without ammunition and provisions.

The English on the Tourelles **islet** were forced to surrender and Joan led her victorious army into Orleans. The Anglo-Burgundians blew up their siege-works surrounding the city and withdrew unhindered, since **Joan** refused to fight them on a Sunday. The siege was effectively over!

Joan's army quickly recaptured several strategic bridges and towns on the River Loire. An English army under **Sir John Fastolf** (caricatured by Shakespeare in his plays "Henry IV" and "Henry V" as Sir John Falstaff) was defeated at **Patay**, the first English defeat in 80 years of incessant warfare. Other French victories followed, and after the recovery of Rheims, Charles VII was crowned there on 17th July 1529, sealing his legitimacy as monarch. **Prof. Edouard Perroy** says, *"Now Charles, whom Joan had hitherto called 'Dauphin' was indeed King!"*

Joan continued to lead the French to successive triumphs. Hence the question arises—"Was Joan a great general?" Not technically, since she was not trained in military strategy or tactics. But she relied on the advice of experienced military men like Count Dunois, Xaintrailles and La Hire and her own sound commonsense. And with her divine sense of mission, she was indeed an *inspirational leader* who overnight transformed her demoralized men into a victorious national army.

On 23rd May 1530, she was captured by the **Burgundians**, while leading a reckless sally outside the walls of **Compiegne**, which she had recently captured. Nobody came forward to ransom her and she was sold to the hated English who put her on trial at **Rouen** for heresy, by an ecclesiastic court headed by the vicious **Bishop Couchon**. The main charge against her was for cross-dressing-attire as a page, male armour etc.

Receiving no legal help, she was condemned as a heretic, burnt at stake and her remains cast into the River Seine.

Though the 100 Years War meandered on for another 22 years, the French people were now entirely with King Charles VII and the momentum was so strongly with him, that the English cause became hopeless. Charles occupied Paris and held a Parliament there. Joan's heresy trial was set aside by Pope Callixtus III, after a thorough study, in 1456 and Joan was canonised and made a patron saint of France. Over the years, St. Joan became an international cult figure, a subject for Voltaire, Schiller, Verdi, Tchaikovsky, Mark Twain, Jean Anouilh, Brecht, Bernard Shaw and various films (Ingrid Bergman starred in the 1948 version) and operas. And it all originated with her successfully raising the siege of Orleans!

The return of the defeated armies to England precpitated the Wars of the Roses with the dynastic houses of Lancaster (White) and York (Red Rose) fighting each other to the point of mutual annihilation. R L Stevenson's novel *"The Black Arrow"* gives a thrilling account of this struggle which culminated at Bosworth, with Lancastrian Henry Tudor ascending the throne in 1485. Lord Lytton's *"The Last of the Barons"* depicts the extinction of the feudal nobility in this bloody civil war. Good leadership was displayed by Richard Neville (Earl of Warwick) and Yorkist brothers Edward IV and much maligned Richard. Shakespeare, who lived under the Tudor Queen, Elizabeth I, portrayed a veritable monster in his *"Richard III"*, an image reinforced by Lawrence Olivier's brilliant depiction on stage and screen. Extensive reading and research at Leeds University's Brotherton Library radically modified my impression about "Crouchback" Richard and his 3 year reign.

With the expulsion of the English, unified France rose from the ashes to gradually become the leading power in Europe (despite destructive civil wars between the Catholics and Huguenots) under **Louis XIV, the Sun King.** The emergence of Great Captains like **Turenne** and **Conde**, apart from excellence in all the arts of peace—architecture, literature, music, philosophy and painting—ensured her place as the leading nation in Europe by the 1650s.

11

FALL OF CONSTANTINOPLE (1453)— MEHAMET II

On 6th July 1449, the last emperor of the Eastern Roman Empire was enthroned as **Constantine XI,**. Unlike his great 4th century predecessor, the first **Constantine** who founded Constantinople, made Christianity the official religion of the empire and presided over the historic Council of **Nicea** (325), this last Emperor had no achievements of note, or resources to fall back on. But he soon proved that he was definitely not lacking in courage and resourcefulness. Succeeding his childless brother, John VIII Paleologus, he set about restoring **Greek Orthodox** ties with the long-estranged **Roman Catholic Church** and organizing the administrative and military systems to face the grave threat menacing the city, the last remnant of the great Eastern Roman Empire.

By the mid-15th century, **Constantinople**, the epitome of culture and civilization, was a ripe fruit ready to be plucked. The flood of **Ottoman Turks** from the east led by Sultan **Bayazid** had totally encircled it by 1395. Fortunately, he was defeated in the east by Timur and taken prisoner as recounted in Christopher Marlowe's blank-verse epic *"Tamerlane"*. **Sultan Murad's** siege of the city was foiled in 1422, but he penetrated deep into Europe, invading Transylvania where he was stopped by **Hunyadi (John Corvinus)**. But in 1448, Hunyadi's army of 24,000 Hungarians, Poles and Germans was slaughtered at **Kosovo**, a replica of an earlier battle there (in 1389) when the Christian pan-Serbians were similarly decimated. The memories of both doleful Kosovo events still reverberate in the Balkans. **Radovan Karadzic**, during his trial at the Hague for the alleged genocide of Muslims, even cited the ancient tribulations of **"Holy Serbia"** to justify his actions! The recent capture and ongoing trial of Serbian **Gen.Ratko Mladic** has again reopened ancient wounds and memories.

Murad's son, **Mehamet II** (1451-1481), inherited at 20, his father's dream of conquering the great city. He was brilliant, persevering and resourceful and had inherited the astonishing good looks of his Albanian Christian mother. Totally ruthless, his first act as Sultan, was to drown his infant brother, and he was soon known among his subjects as "*Hunkar*" or "the drinker of blood." He greatly admired his adversary **Vlad Drakul, Prince of Wallachia**, for his ingenious torture methods like nailing the turbans of Turkish envoys to their heads for refusing to uncover before him. Or impaling 18,000 Turkish prisoners in serried ranks, after a battle. In **Bram Stoker's** creative fiction, Drakul has been transformed into **Count Dracula**, the Prince of Vampires!

Mehamet was a master of deception. **Edward Gibbon** says *"peace was on his lips, while war was in his heart."* He quickly made peace with John Hunyadi, the Venetians, Bosnia, Wallachia and Serbia and built the stronghold of **Roumelia-Hisar** in 4 months, just north of Constantinople. Along with a smaller fort on the Asian shore, it controlled the Bosphorus where it was at its narrowest and cut off the city from its corn supply sources in the Ukraine. Every action of the Sultan was like a chess move and he unerringly anticipated all possible contingencies. He was undoubtedly the first great gunner in history, using artillery, made by the Hungarian gun-founder Orban and manned by Christians, to great effect in all his engagements. Consequently, 12 great bombards and 14 batteries of lesser guns constituted the back-bone of his war strategy against the beleagured city.

The **Turkish army** included **15,000 *Janissaries*** (the most formidable soldiers in the world), trained ***Bashi-bazouks*** and massed provincial levies (*Azab*)—a total of 200,000 soldiers. The elite *Janissaries* were recruited as boys from the Sultan's Christian provinces, forcibly converted to Islam and were like military monks, forbidden to marry and totally disciplined. Armed with bow, sword and mace, the *janissaries* (new soldiers) wore knee length coats of mail and white peaked caps reinforced with iron plates. The Ottoman fleet, though not very efficient, numbered over 200 warships of various kinds, including sailing ships and oared galleys.

"To meet this formidable array outside the walls of Constantinople, Constantine had nothing!" observes **Gen. J F C Fuller** in his *"Decisive Battles of the Western World"*. And within the city itself, he had just a few hundred mercenaries plus two dozen moth-eaten galleys in the harbour. His fervent appeal to the 80,000 citizens yielded just **5000 volunteers** to join the inevitable life and death struggle. Nevertheless, the last Emperor proved as much a man of action as the first Constantine had been, 1100

years earlier. His reply to a peace overture from the Sultan speaks for itself, *"To surrender the city is beyond my authority!"*

His first action was to repair the 13 miles of ancient, dilapidated walls which surrounded the city. The outer fortifications of the triangle-shaped city, the perimeter of which the author traversed on foot, consisted of

1. The **sea wall in the north**, along the Golden Horn (the main harbour) from Xylo Porta, east to the Acropolis, was 3 ½ miles long.

2. The **5 ½ mile wall** along the sea of Marmara **in the east** ran from the Acropolis, south-west to the Golden gate, where it joined the land wall.

3. On the **landward west**, the 4 mile long wall built in the 5th century by **Theodosius II** was still a formidable obstacle against attack. It was a triple barrier consisting of a 12m. high inner wall with 112 massive towers; a 9m high outer wall; plus a breastwork and a 20m wide water ditch as the first line of defense. The Lycus stream which ran through this wall between the Gate of San Romano (7th hill) and the Adrianople Gate (6th hill) created a weak point at the 5th Military Gate. The extreme northern part of this western fortification (between the Circus gate and the Xylo Porta) was protected only by a single layer of wall, without even a defensive moat.

The only occasion when the city was taken by storm was in 1204, helped by a naval attack through the Golden Horn. A crusading Catholic army, led by Venetian *Doge* Henricus Dandolo, ostensibly on its way to liberate Jerusalem from Sultan Saladin forced its way in, ravaging and looting the city! Coincidentally, St. Mark was the patron saint of both Constantinople and Venice and the famous bronze horses now embellishing the façade of the Cathedral of St. Mark in Venice were carried away from the Byzantine Hippodrome! In his historic meeting in 2004 with Greek Patriarch Bartholomew on the occasion of the 8th centenary of the vile deed, Pope John Paul II said *"How can we, even at a distance of 8 centuries, not feel the pain and disgust?"* The Patriarch accepted this apology in a true spirit of reconciliation and co-operation.

The ancient Greek wall of Byzantium protected just the palace area while Constantine the Great's 4th century city wall had practically disappeared. However, the 1500 year old Theodosian triple wall is in fair condition even today and must have been considered formidable in 1453. But it could not bear the weight and recoil of the heavy cannons which were becoming an essential part of siege and defensive equipment.

Galata (Pera), north of the Golden Horn, was a neutral enclave held by the **Genoese.** Its Taksim Square is famous today as the gathering point of protesters and demonstrators. A massive chain boom from here to the Acropolis of Byzantium, supported by floating barrels, restricted entry by ships into the Golden Horn itself. Ancient **Byzantium** (founded by Greeks in 667 BC) in the north-east corner of the city, around which new Constantinople had been built in the 4th century, was protected by another line of even older walls. It contained Justinian's wonderful domed **Cathedral of Hagia Sophia** (Divine Wisdom), the **Hippodrome** (for chariot-racing) with its great **obelisk of Thotmes** transported from Luxor, vast imperial palaces, impressive basilicas, huge underground water cisterns and other important structures.

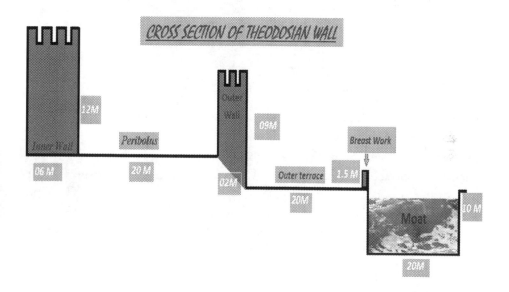

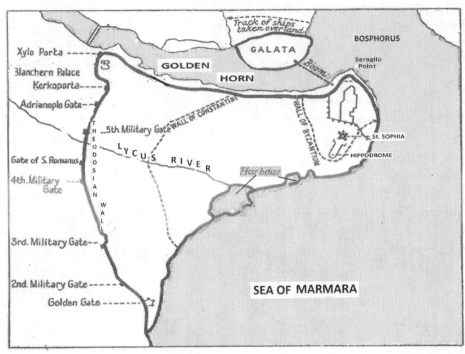

Shajahan

Constantinople, Section of Theodosian Wall

7

Because of the longstanding theological schism between the **Roman Catholic Church** and the **Greek Orthodox Church**, Constantinople had hitherto received no help from the west. Constantine XI acted speedily. The doctrinal question (*filioque* dogma) of whether the Holy Spirit proceeds from "both the Father and the Son" was quickly resolved. Papal supremacy was also accepted in a service held in the Hagia Sophia in December 1452. But the Papacy itself was under severe strain and the Pope's appeal to the monarchs of Europe to save the eastern megapolis, evoked no response. The Christians of northern Spain (Navarre, Castile and Aragon) were in the process of finally terminating Moorish rule in southern Spain (Granada). The Hundred Years War (1338-1453) had totally exhausted England and France. As for the Germanic Holy Roman Empire, it was famously described as *"not Holy, Roman or an Empire"*! Aeneas Piccolomini (later **Pope Pius II**) wrote in anguish," *Look at*

Christianity! It no longer has a head. Neither Pope nor Emperor is esteemed. Each ruler seeks nothing beyond his own kingdom."

Constantine XI received effective help only from Italian **condottieri** (mercenaries) numbering around **2000** and **Cardinal Isidore** from Ukraine, who bravely sailed into the Golden Horn with a couple of ships and 400 soldiers. Militarily much more valuable was the arrival later, of the experienced Genoese soldier **John Giustiniani**, along with 700 men in 2 large ships, accompanied by **Johann Grant**, expert German engineer and artillerist. The emperor immediately appointed **Giustiniani, commander-in-chief** of the city forces, a position which he fully justified with his outstanding energy, organizational skills, creative tactics, audacity and unwavering courage. **Sultan Mohamet** meanwhile, reduced several small island forts on Prince's Islands in the Sea of Marmara, cruelly impaling the defenders in his customary way. He appeared before the western land wall of Constantinople on 5th April 1453, with his army in **4 corps**, each under a **pasha**. He massed his best troops in the low-lying **Lycus valley**, where he perceived a weakness in the fortifications, under his **Grand Vizier, Halil Pasha.**

Constantine, consequently moved his headquarters to this point, enjoining **Gustiniani** to be there in person. But the overall length of the walls was just too much for his **9000 soldiers** who were now thinly spread out along the 13 miles of land and sea defences. Bombardment by the Turkish artillery commenced on **12th April**, at the 5th Military Gate in the low-lying **Lycus valley**. Fortunately for the besieged, these giant cannons could fire only 7 or 8 times per day due to overheating problems and the defenders quickly repaired the damage caused. The defenders, however, found that the recoil impact of their return fire, caused considerable damage to their own 1000 year old walls! After a week of desultory cannonade, **Mohamet** suddenly ordered a general assault on the western land wall and the harbour boom simultaneously. With yells of *"Yagma! Yagma!"* the Turks rushed the outer ditch. But the defenders were well-placed and ready, opening a withering fire from handguns, cannon, crossbows and catapults, to sweep the attackers back. **Grand Duke Loukas Notaras**, Constantine's Chief Minister, also beat back the **naval assault** on the boom, to the great chagrin of the Sultan.

Two days later, 3 large Genoese warships and a grain ship came within sight of the city. 145 Turkish galleys under **Admiral Sulaiman Baltoglu Pasha** rowed out to attack them, but the huge sailing ships effortlessly crashed through the Turkish fleet to reach the vicinity of

Seraglio point unharmed. They were stranded here, as the wind dropped, and the Turks rowed out to surround them. A desperate action ensued, with the Genoese repelling the boarding parties and destroying several galleys with rocks and pots of combustible *Greek fire*, holding off the attackers for over 2 hours! A sudden puff of wind enabled the Christian ships to move again. The boom was lowered and the ships safely entered the Golden Horn. The furious Sultan thrashed his admiral with a stick, in frustration! **Sultan Mohamet** was checked but certainly not check-mated and he now realized the importance of controlling the Golden Horn, to force Constantine to further disperse his little army. Seventy Turkish ships were transported over rollers along the ground, north of the Genoese-held enclave of Galata for about a mile, into a stream which flowed into the Golden Horn. **Mohamet** thus had his own fleet in the Golden Horn, circumventing the boom chain protecting it from naval attack from the Bosphorus in the east. Consequently, Constantine's position was rendered practically untenable. The disheartened defenders besought the Emperor to escape while there was still time, but he gallantly turned down the base suggestion. *"How could I leave the churches of our Lord, the clergy and my own people in such a plight?",* he replied.

The heavy bombardment continued into May, along with intermittent assaults by 50,000 Turks around the **San Romanus Gate**, just south of the Lycus stream. On May 18th, the Turks brought up a huge wooden assault tower, a *"helepolis"* or city taker, but the innovative Giustiniani blew it up with gunpowder barrels rolled down the escarpment slope. Next, *mining* was attempted on the walls near the Adrianople Gate in the northern segment of the western wall, but engineer **Johann Grant** frustrated this underground operation by drowning the miners with water from the Golden Horn or cutting them down in desperate hand to hand subterranean clashes. There were now strong rumours of the impending arrival of a Papal fleet and also of a Hungarian army, to relieve the besieged Christians.

A lesser leader than Sultan Mohamet would have given up the siege, as advised by several of his commanders, including Hallil Pasha. Instead, the Sultan commenced a continuous attack on the entire 13-mile perimeter of the land and sea walls, putting unbearable stress on the dwindling garrison. Focus was on **3 sections** of the western wall— the Adrianople Gate, the Lycus valley and the 3rd Military Gate—with particular emphasis on the second. Simultaneously, the fleet kept up a cannonade on the sea wall in the east. On **27th** and **28th May**, the Turkish camp was buzzing with unusual activity and the defenders feared the worst.

For us in the 21st century, it is impossible to understand the all-pervasive influence of religion on the Byzantines or the complex and intricate nature of the relationship between **Patriarch** and **Emperor**. Byzantines did not conceive of the divine as something remote. The reality of God, Christ, the Virgin Mary, the Archangels and the Saints was accepted by the entire populace and religious devotion here possessed an oriental mystic quality, quite different from that of western Christianity. (Attending the Greek Orthodox mass celebrated by Patriarch Bartolomew was an unforgetable experience for the author) On the night of **28**th **May**, the defenders—Genoese, Venetians and Greeks—led by the Emperor and the Patriarch, joined in prayer in the great church of Holy Wisdom (**Hagia Sophia**), to cries of **kyrie elieson**, an event described by **Brice**—"*The last Christian service in St. Sophia is surely among the most tragic and moving events in history*". The symbiotic relation between the Byzantine Church and State conceived by Constantine the Great and developed over eleven tumultuous centuries, had entered its final tragic act!

The Emperor sensibly decided to man only the outer walls, locking the gates in the inner wall, since the garrison was now down to **4000 men**. At **2.00 am on 29**th **May 1453**, the Turks launched a ferocious all-round attack. In the breached Lycus sector, the bashibazuks, the Anatolians and janissaries were in separate echelons, all equipped with scaling ladders and iron hooks. When the first two groups failed in their assault, **Mohamet** launched his **12,000 *elite janissaries*** but still could not break through the ingenious defensive arrangements contrived by the innovative Giustiniani. A freak incident led to the city's fall. Half of a mile to the north of the Lycus, there was a small postern called **Kerkoporta (Circus Gate)** which had been bricked up many centuries ago. This had recently been opened up but forgotten. Some 50 Turks unexpectedly entered through this, taking the defenders in the flank. They moved south to the Adrianople Gate and hoisted the red Turkish crescent flag, after pulling down that of St. Mark. They were however quickly checked here, and the frontal attack in the Lycus area was also severely repulsed, by the **Emperor** and **Guistiniani**.

Unfortunately, at this critical stage, a stray projectile struck the latter and he was carried away from the fray, grievously wounded. In the ensuing panic, a group of janissaries forced their way into the city, through the gate in the inner wall opened for Guistiniani. **Constantine** called out *"the city is taken but I am still alive!"* and gallantly galloped into the midst of the enemy with his personal bodyguards in a desperate attempt to stem the tide but was surrounded and cut down. His badly mangled body was later identified by his boots of imperial purple adorned with the distinctive gold buckles featuring the unique Imperial double-eagle. Guistiniani was carried on board a Genoese ship anchored in the Golden Horn and evacuated to the island of Chios in the Aegean Sea where he died in terrible pain, a few days later.

The fall of the city was sudden, as the Turks penetrated the defences simultaneously at several points and streamed in, isolating those defenders who bravely continued to fight on around the massive Golden Gate bastion and the southern part of the Theodosian Wall. At 4 pm, Mohamet made his triumphal entry through the Edirne (Adrianople) Gate, riding directly to the inner city area of **Byzantium** where the citizens had taken refuge in and around the Hagia Sophia, the ultimate sanctuary of the God-fearing. Dismounting in front of the great church, he symbolically placed a handful of earth on his turban, taking full control of the city. The Sultan then ordered the execution of all the prominent Greek nobles, including Grand Duke Loukas Notaras and his son and permitted his rampaging soldiers to plunder and ravage the city for 3 days.

An Imam dedicated the **Hagia Sophia** as a mosque (Aya Sofiya) to Allah, which it continued to be till 1934, when the great patriot and secularist, **Mustafa Kemal Ataturk**, removed the whitewash on the walls, exposing the beautiful Christian mosaics and paintings underneath. The Ataturk pointedly rededicated it as a national museum. The altered Turkish name of the city, **Istanbul,** however continues to this day. Sultan Mohamet allowed the anti-Rome monk George Scholaris to ascend the Patriarchal throne as **Patriarch Genadius** and did not interfere unduly in the internal administration of the Greek Orthodox Church. Though most of the places of worship like the great Chora Church and the Cathedral of St. Irene were also converted into mosques, the Patriarchate in the Fener district still caters to the spiritual needs of the Orthodox faithful. Nobel Laureate, Orhan Pamuk refers to the *husn* or spirit of melancholy pervading the megapolis. Despite the liveliness and revelry in Taksin Square and modern Galata area, one can sense a feeling of cloying sadness underlying the thickly populated poor quarters in the shadow of the old walls.

Pope Nicholas vainly ordered a counter-attack to recapture the city, but no European monarch responded to his passionate call. A succession of energetic Sultans followed Mohamet, the greatest being his grandson, **Sulaiman the Magnificent**, a contemporary of Queen Elizabeth and Akbar. He employed the great Christian architect **Mimar Sinan** for putting up exquisite edifices like the **Salmaniye** and **Shahzade Mosques**. The **Sultanahmet (Blue) Mosque** and the **Topkapi Palace** put up by his successors also evoke admiration. The early Ottoman Sultans were also competent soldiers. For the next two centuries, Europe was continuously threatened by the Turks, until the pressure was relieved by the naval triumph of Don John of Austria at Lepanto (1571) and John Sobieski's massive victory at Vienna (1683). But even in the 21st century, the fear of the 'ferocious Turk' is not confined to the Balkans and has even estopped Turkey's admission into the European Union.

However, the Greek *diaspora* just before and after the cataclysmic fall of 1453 brought beneficial results for the West, through the dissemination across Europe of Byzantine scholarship, philosophy, literature and art, bringing a new secular element into the traditional milieu. This led to the blooming of the **Renaissance,** as the Greek light spread in Italy and the rest of Europe. In the field of painting alone, the works of **El Greco** (who settled in Spain) inspired the schools of Zurbaran, Velasquez and even Goya. As for Italy, Venice itself produced the remarkable Giorgione, Tintoretto, Veronese and Titian. The astounding flowering of the high Renaissance witnessed the contemporaneous careers of the incomparable Florentine trio— **Michelangelo**, **Leonardo Da Vinci** and **Raphael**!

Cut off from the spices, gems, silks and exotic products of India and China, Europe hastened to discover a western route, with Columbus undertaking his voyage (funded by Queen Isabella of Spain), less than 40 years after the fall of the megacity. Portuguese sailors under the patronage of Prince Henry the Navigator criss-crossed the globe. Vasco da Gama also quickly discovered an alternative oriental route, going around the Cape of Good Hope in 1498 to avoid the victorious Ottoman Turks who controlled the eastern Mediterranean and the Spice and Silk Routes.

12

TALIKOTA 1565
& THE DESTRUCTION OF VIJAYNAGAR

No medieval Indian characters are probably as widely remembered to-day as the clown-jester-poet-minister **Tenali Raman** and his imperial patron, **Krishnadeva Raya**, who reigned from 1509 to 1529. Thanks to the plethora of anecdotes, comic books, films, TV serials, cartoons and folklore in which they figure, they have come alive in the public imagination, along with the city in which they lived—**Vijayanagar**. However, a modern visitor to the ruins of this megapolis will find fewer Indian sightseers than foreign tourists, and the extensive archeological digs are also mainly foreign funded. Led by Prof. Nobura Karashima, Japanese historians, in particular, have shown extraordinary interest in **Hampi** and its past. Karnataka celebrated 2009 as the 500th anniversary of the coronation of **Krishnadeva Raya**, but the other South Indian states over which he ruled, have been rather tardy, despite the outstanding contribution he had made to their economic, cultural, artistic and literary development.

During its heyday in the early 16th century, **Vijayanagar** was indeed a wonder for travelers like the Italian Nicolo Di Conti, the Persian Abdur Razzaq, the Russian Anastasio Nikitin and the Portuguese adventurer Barbosa, with its 7 concentric lines of fortifications and its hundred temples. In fact, Domingo Paes described it as *"large as Rome."* However after the cataclysm in **1565**, Caesar Frederici wrote *"The city of Beznagar is not altogether destroyed but is empty; dwelling therein are only tygres and wild beasts."*

Situated a few miles from the railway station at **Hospet** (near Bellary), Vijayanagar, according to tradition, was founded in 1342 by the Telugu-speaking brothers, Harihara and Bukka, on the mythical site of **Kishkinda** (the monkey kingdom of Bali, Sugreeva and Hanuman.). With the blessings of the Sage Madhavacharya of Sringeri, it grew into a strong bulwark against the marauders from the north. Even after the ascent of the powerful **Deccani kingdoms—Ahmednagar, Bijapur, Berar, Bidar** and **Golconda**—the Vijaynagar empire continued to prosper, mainly due to **foreign trade** with the Portuguese and Arabs through the ports of Goa and Bhatkal.

This great granite city on the **Tungabhadra River**, was the capital of a powerful empire encompassing practically the whole of **South India**. It prospered even as it carried on its incessant wars with the 5 Muslim Sultans to the north for control of the fertile Raichur *doab*. **Robert Sewell's** seminal work 19th century work, **"A Forgotten Empire"** reproduces the chronicles of the foreign travelers and presents an inspiring story of the recovery of South India under the Vijaynagar rulers after the destructive forays of northern invaders, Malik Kafur and Mohamed Bin Tughlak.

The empire reached its zenith under **Krishnadeva Raya (1509-29)**, who annihilated the Deccani armies at the **battle of Raichur (1520)**. Under him, the empire covered *5 language zones*—Telugu, Kannada, Tamil, Malayalam and Marathi—and his revenue came from 60 seaports, with vast territories giving him tribute—Rajamundri, Vellore, Tanjore, Mylapore, Kollam, Kondavid, Madurai, Tinnevelly, Malabar. A visionary builder, he constructed huge irrigation tanks, temples and towns and the massive statue of Vishnu in his '*avatar*' as the man-lion **Narasimha.** A connoisseur of music and dance, he built the great '*gopuras*' and dance halls in the temples of Kanchipuram, Chidambaram, Kalahasti (the *gopura* collapsed recently) and Hampi's own sacred Virupaksha shrine on the banks of the Tungabadra.

The narrative of **Domingo Paes** (1520), details the grand celebrations for the 9-day Navaratri festival and also gives a graphic account of the great monarch's daily routine. "*The king is accustomed to drink a quartilho of gingely oil before daylight and anoints himself with this. He covers his loins with a small cloth and takes in his arms great weights; then he exercises with a sword and wrestles with a wrestler. After this labour, he mounts a horse and gallops around till dawn.*" All this, before his daily temple visits and regular work! Prof.**Nilakanta Sastri** says of him "*Pre-eminent as a warrior, Krishnadeva Raya was equally great as a statesman, administrator and patron of the arts.*" But the hubris of his successors soon led to the fall of the realm when it seemed to be at the zenith of its glory.

Aliya Rama Raya of the Aruvida family was the son in law of the great Krishna Deva Raya. After ruling as regent from 1542-50, he imprisoned the rightful heir, nephew Sadasiva Raya, and continued to rule the empire along with his brothers **Tirumala and Venkatadri**. A consummate intriguer, he played clever politics with the Deccani kingdoms, often acting as a mediator. First joining Ahmednagar, Bidar and Golconda to attack Bijapur, he switched sides in 1558. Rama Raya's efforts to maintain the *Balance of Power* in the Deccan was successful for more than 20 years, as he adroitly joined the weaker side against the stronger alliance. As the sole Hindu ruler in the region, his survival strategy was impeccable (and necessary). But his egregious deceitfulness and insufferable arrogance finally provoked the young sultans of **Ahmednagar, Bidar, Bijapur and Golconda** to form an offensive alliance against him, since they were co-religionists and also closely related to each other by marriage. Only the distant kingdom of **Berar** refrained from joining in. Vijayanagar was geographically vulnerable since the capital was located too close to the disputed Raichur *Doab* and the northern boundary of the Empire. Any major defeat in the *Doab* would result in a mobile enemy arriving at its gates in a matter of hours, before the city could ready itself for defence. The hubris of the Rayas resulted in a total state of unpreparedness for such an eventuality in 1565.

The four allied armies converged on the plains just south of Bijapur and marched further towards the south-east. **Rama Raya** sent **Tirumalai** with a strong force to stop the coalition armies at the **Krishna River.** **Tirumalai** put up earth works and cannon at the only ford, but the Sultans managed to evade him through a ruse and continued their southward march through the fertile countryside in the pleasant January weather. Though **Ferishta** gives a figure of 900,000 and 400,000 respectively, for the Vijaynagar and allied armies, this is certainly an exaggeration. The over confident Rama Raya, with his subsidiaries and feudatories, marched north with probably around 150,000 foot soldiers, 15,000 horsemen, 100 elephants and 30 cannons (with Portuguese gunners). His Muslim adversaries had 80,000 infantry, 30,000 cavalry (on Persian horses), 35 elephants, 40 cannons (manned by Turkish gunners) and 2000 foreign archers.

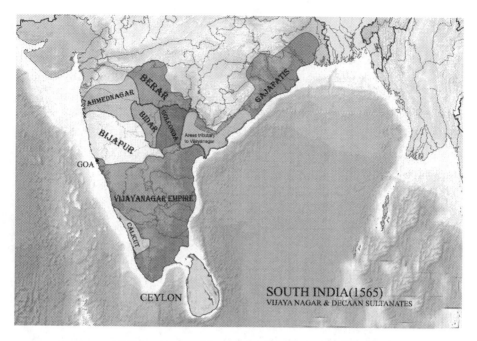

Vijaynagar and Bahmani Kingdoms—1560
8

Though much stronger on paper, the Vijaynagar forces were led by 3 aged brothers, whereas the 4 Deccani Sultans were in the prime of their manhood. The former, carried on litters, or riding elephants, were far less mobile and active than the Sultans, who were mounted on fleet Arab horses. The ace Turkish gunners gave the Sultans a distinct edge, as also the metal cross-bows of their archers against the bamboo bows of the Hindus. Further, the Rayas were unsure about the loyalty of their Muslim mercenaries, led by the **Gilani** brothers who had only recently defected from the army of the Bijapur Sultan.

The two huge armies met near **Tengadi (Talikota),** 50 miles south east of Bijapur on **26th January 1565.** Ninety year-old year old **Rama Raya,** at the centre of the Vijayanagar array, directly faced Hus**sein Nizamshah of Ahmadnagar; Venkatadri on the right** opposed the **Golkonda** and **Bidar** forces under **Ibrahim Qutb Shah** and **Ali Baridshah**; while **Tirumalai on the left** faced **Ali Adilshah** of **Bijapur** and some **Marathas** led by **Ghorpade.** There were also **mercenary** contingents, mainly Turks, Iranians, Deccanis and Sidis, in both armies.

After a massive cannonade from both sides, Venkatadri on the right wing ploughed through Barid Shah's divisions and Qutb Shah was also forced to retreat. But a contingent from **Nizamshah's** central force shored them up. Rama Raya was therefore able to penetrate the weakened Ahmednagar army, while Tirumalai on the left also pressed the Bijapur forces hard. While matters seemed to be going well for the Vijaynagar forces in all three sectors, **Rama Raya's** litter was knocked over by a charging elephant and he was taken prisoner and brought before the Nizam Shah. The latter, activated by a visceral hatred for the Raya, had him beheaded immediately. The display of the Raya's head held aloft on a spear, caused panic in the Hindu ranks, where there were already rumours of treachery by their Muslim mercenaries, led by the **Gilani brothers**. All of a sudden, they fled pell-mell, pursued by the victorious allied army. What a contrast to the aggressive reaction of the Swedes on losing their charismatic king, Gustavus, at Lutzen.

There was no attempt to defend the city, which was well protected by the **Tungabadra River** in the north and by massive *multiple lines* of fortifications on all other sides. With both his brothers dead, **Tirumalai** recovered some treasure from the city and escaped south to **Penukonda**.

The now defenseless the city of **Vijayanagar** was looted and pillaged continuously for 6 months. "*Never before in the history of the world has such havoc been wrought so suddenly on so splendid a city*"-says **Sewell**. Fire and gunpowder were used to augment the destruction, but even what remains today is truly magnificent. The temples—Virupaksha, Vithalasamy, Hazara Rama and the pagodas on Matanga hill—still inspire awe—along with the famous Hampi bazaar, Lotus Mahal, the elephant stables and palace complex. But most awesome is the ferocious 20-foot high monolithic granite statue of **Ugra Narasimha** (with lion's mane and bulging eyes), which survived all efforts to destroy it. The fall of Vijayanagar had its particular impact on the fortunes of Portuguese **Goa**. According to **Robert Sewell** "*Goa rose and fell with Vijayanagar, as the latter was the market for the former.*"

Tirumalai's Aruvid dynasty of Rayas retained some prestige, though no real power, in their new location (**Penukonda**), but the great empire broke up, with each local Nayak setting up his own independent kingdom. The **Deccan Sultans** continued their internecine bickering and were soon swallowed up by the expanding **Moghul Empire** under **Akbar.** Vijayanagar's attempt at establishing Hindu hegemony in the Deccan was replicated by **Shivaji** in the 17th century, but the Marathas also came up short against **Abdali's** Afghan raiders in 1761 at Panipat (Ch.16).

13

SEKIGAHARA (1600)— IEYESU TOKUGAWA, SHOGUN

Barring the repulse of the Mongol invasions at Hakata Bay (in 1274 & 1281), with the assistance of timely *kamikazes* (divine winds), **Sekigahara** (1600) was arguably the most important battle ever fought in Japan. It established the **Tokugawa Shogunate** which ruled the country for over 250 years. The Tokugawas were finally overthrown only because of foreign intervention, subsequent to the aggressive visit of a US squadron under Commodore Perry in 1853.

Though occupied by a homogeneous people who came from Korea (except for a small group of indigenous Ainu), the islands of Hokaido, Shikoku, Honshu and Kyushu had been in constant feudal flux for centuries. The '*Samurai*' warriors of the two swords, followed the rigid *Bushido* code and served their '*daimyos*' (barons) loyally in their incessant civil wars. **Samurai Strategy** can best be understood through studying "*The Book of the 5 Rings*", written by the 17th century duelist **Miyamoto Musashi**. On the other hand, the black-clad *ninja* assassins, used a variety of poisoned weapons (swords, *suruken* disks, knives, arrows) to bring silent death to whomsoever they targeted. '*Ronin*' (masterless *samurai*) were mercenaries, outside the *Bushido* system. Traders, farmers and other non-combatents were generally left undisturbed by the warring factions, as long as they paid protection money.

The **Emperor**, residing in **Nara** (and later, **Kyoto**) on the main **Honshu Island**, was considered divine (descended from goddess Amateresu). But power was effectively with a member of the **Minamoto, Tairo** or **Fujiwara** family, ruling as military dictator or "*Shogun*". Continuous civil war between these powerful clans was a feature for centuries, with the **Ashikaga** family retaining the Shogunate for a long period till 1568 when **Odo Nobunaga**, scion of a minor noble house, marched into **Kyoto**, the imperial city. When he was murdered in 1582, **Toyatomi Hideyoshi**, a commoner, succeeded him. An able ruler, he banned Christianity, organized the administration and invaded Korea. Ruling from his great castle at **Osaka**, this de facto ruler of Japan, never took the title of *Shogun,* but he made all the other daimyos swear that they would support his son, after his death. However, soon after his demise, the greatest of the war-lords, **Ieyesu Tokugawa**, predictably set himself up in his own fief **Edo (Tokyo),** far to the East, quietly building diplomatic bridges with various clans—Date, Maeda, Mogami. Hideyoshi's young heir, **Hideyori**, continued to live in **Osaka Castle**, which even today overwhelms the visitor with its wide moat, massive walls and a six-storey pagoda keep, ensconced in the midst of beautiful gardens and orchards. The **divine emperor** (revered but powerless) resided at **Kyoto**, a few miles to the north in the extensive imperial palace. The unfolding story is related in **James Clavell's** well-researched novel **'Shogun'** and the magnificent film of the same name.

Ieyesu Tokugawa soon faced stiff opposition from the other barons, particularly the *daimyos* of **Satsuma** and **Choshu** who held great estates on the south-western island of **Kyushu**, where Portuguese missionaries (pioneered by St. Francis Xavier) and traders had established themselves. Fire-arms had recently been introduced by the Europeans into this medieval milieu and it was a period of change and transition for Japan in all spheres—social, political, economical, religious and military.

Theoretically, the realm was now ruled by 5 regents from the leading families (Maeda, Mori, Ukita, Kagekatsu, **Tokugawa**). Power had historically been focused in the central **Osaka-Kyoto** region, but this time the main contenders were from the **East (Tokugawa)** and the **West** (alliance led by **Ishido Mitsunari**). Totally ruthless and a master of strategy, Ieyesu **Tokugawa** played a waiting game. When his eldest son and heir was accused of treason by Nobunaga, he had induced the boy to commit "*Seppuku*" (ritual suicide), in order to save the Tokugawa clan from annihilation. Patience was his forte, but he could be bold at the right time, having fought 90 battles!

In 1600, from his **Tokyo** Headquarters, **Tokugawa** unexpectedly moved South-west at lightning speed, capturing Gifu castle on the Tokyo-Kyoto road and threatening the national power centre of Kyoto-Osaka, which was under Ishido Mitsunari's control. **Ishido** was caught by surprise by the large number of allies which the geographically isolated Tokugawa picked up.

The westerners lacked unity of command and purpose, with some daimyos wanting to invade and plunder Tokugawa's home province. They also wasted 10 days on a fruitless siege of **Fushimi** Castle, near Kyoto. **Ishido** then decided to move with his allied army eastwards through the narrow **Sekigahara Pass** to block Tokugawa's route to the west, leaving 1,500 men to garrison **Ogaki Castle**. In the foul and rainy weather, **Ishido Mitsunari's** men erected palisades to protect themselves from Tokugawa's powerful cavalry and positioned themselves in a **North-south** alignment. **Ishido** himself was on a mountain spur on the **extreme left** (North) with a good view of the battle field. In the centre were 10,000 men under **Ukita Hideie**, while the right wing of 8000 was led by **Kobayakawa Hideaki**. Overall it was a very strong defensive situation for the westerners.

Skirmishing took place throughout the night and there was heavy exchange of fire between *match-lock arquebusiers* on the two sides, this fire arm having been introduced recently in Japan by the **Portuguese**. But the longbow (*yumi*), heavy club (*kanabo*), the shafted spear (*naginata*) and the samurai sword (*katana*) were still the most popular weapons in both armies. The charge of the elite *samurai* horsemen generally decided the outcome, though the footsoldiers did also play a significant role in the fighting.

At 8 am on 21st October, 1600, **Tokugawa's** centre attacked **Ukita** fiercely amid the frantic throbbing of the giant *Taiko Drums* and attacks then took place all along the line. The western allied army was numerically superior and initially appeared to beholding their own. After several hours of fighting, **Ishida** sensed the crucial moment and signaled to his ally **Kobayakawa**, positioned on a hill on the right, to launch his planned attack. To his dismay, the latter failed to respond as he had been induced by **Ieyesu Tokugawa** to change sides. Instead, **Kobayakawa's** forces crashed into ally **Ukita** from the flank and a rout of the westerners quickly followed. Only a few of the **Satsumo** *cavalry* cut their way through and escaped west, to distant Kyushu island. **Ishido Mitsunari** was captured on the battlefield and executed at **Kyoto**, after 3 days of torture. **Kobayakawa** later committed suicide, probably out of shame at betraying his allies and breaking the rigid **Bushido code**. The battle-field betrayal by Kobayakawa replicated the action of **Lord Stanley** at **Bosworth (1485)** in the climactic battle that ended the English Wars of the Roses, another bitterly fought civil war. **Stanley**, ostensibly allied with **Richard III**, abandoned him on the field of battle and suddenly joined rebel **Henry Tudor**. This led to the latter's victory and enthronement of the Tudor dynasty. Similarly at **Talikota** (1565), the defection of the Gilani brothers caused the defeat of the Vijaynagar army. At **Plassey (1757), Clive** bribed **Mir Jaffar** to betray **Nawab Siraj-ud-daula of Bengal** and thereby won the decisive battle.

Soldiers understand defeat and are often prepared to fight to the last in a lost cause. But betrayal utterly saps morale.

The battle of **Sekigahara** decided the course of Japanese history for the next 250 years. **Ieyesu Tokugawa** became **Shogun** and after a long siege of Osaka Castle, Hideyoshi's heir, **Toyotomi Hidaeyori**, committed suicide. The **balance of power** shifted to **Tokyo (Edo),** in the east of Honshu Island, though the divine Emperor continued to live in Kyoto. **Ieyesu** built a great fortress in **Tokyo**, on the site of what is now the Imperial Palace. The **Tokugawa Shoguns,** who were ardent Budhists**,** banned Christianity and all relations with foreigners on pain of death. The uniquely insular Japanese culture (with stylized *No* drama, *Kabuki* plays, elegant paintings and *haiku* poetry) flourished under the xenophobic Tokugawas. When the Shogunate was finally overthrown in 1868 by the restoration to power of the **Emperor Meiji,** their longtime enemies from western Kyushu island (daimyos of Satsumo and Chosu) played a leading role in the **Tokugawa** downfall—sweet revenge after 268 years of suppression**.** The **Emperor** recruited the peasants and equipped them with Enfield rifles and Gatling machine-guns. He abolished the anachronistic samurai system and the die-hard samurai who resisted were massacred near Kagoshima, in Kyushu Island, in 1877. This dramatic story is depicted in *"the Last Samurai"*, starring Tom Cruise.

Despite this brutal suppression, the aggressive *samurai spirit* lived on, fuelled by successful wars against Korea, Russia and China. They boldly took on even the British and Americans, finally leading to the cataclysmic defeat of Japan in the 2nd World War with A-bombs dropped at Hiroshima and Nagasaki (August 1945). The samurai spirit still survives, albeit in altered form, judging from the annual rituals (honoring the ashes of the war dead) at the **Yasukuni Shrine**, in which the Prime Minister personally participates. The ashes of Netaji Subhash Chandra Bose are reputedly enshrined here (or at the Renkoji Shrine?), along with the Japanese war heroes. The *Bushido* Code underlies the do-or-die *business strategies* of Japanese companies—Sony, Mitsubishi, Honda, Toyota—in the World market. These are are widely admired, but cannot be easily replicated by others, without the deeply embedded Japanese *samurai* spirit. The remarkable discipline, stoicism and fortitude of the Japanese people emerge every time a major catastrophe occurs—nuclear disaster, earthquake or tsunami—even all together as at **Fukushima!**

14

LUTZEN (1632)—GUSTAVUS ADOLPHUS, LION OF THE NORTH

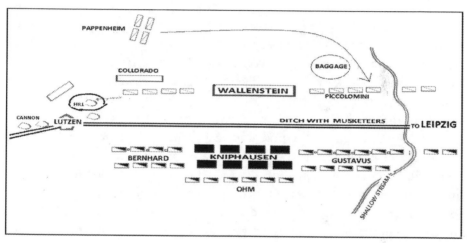

By Arvind A

Lutzen (Battle Plan)—1632

9

The Thirty Years War (1618-48) was one of the most bitterly contested and destructive conflicts ever fought, and it utterly ruined and ravaged Germany, as vividly depicted in Berthold Brecht's influential play, *'Mother Courage'*. Though commonly considered a religious conflict between **Protestants** and **Catholics,** the war was essentially a struggle between the 2 great European dynasties—the **Bourbons** of France and the **Habsburgs** of Austria and Spain. The so-called "Protestants" were marshaled by his grey eminence **Cardinal Richelieu** (of *Three Musketeers* fame), first minister of France, to break the Imperial **Habsburg** ring around his country. He managed to get the support of the Protestant rulers of Sweden, Denmark, the Dutch

Republic, England, Scotland and several German princelings, while the Emperor of Austria was supported by the Catholic rulers of Spain and Bavaria. This was the beginning of the great secular tradition of France, with its First Minister, a Cardinal, leading an all-Protestant alliance against three Catholic powers. Dynasty and nationality were becoming more important factors factors than religion in the Balance of Power game. After 12 years of desultory fighting, the war suddenly came alive with the arrival in Germany in 1630 of the dashing Swedish king, **Gustavus Adolphus**, who has been called the "Father of Modern War".

Battles of the Middle Ages had been mainly won by cavalry, since individual foot soldiers could not withstand the shock of heavily armoured horse men. Then, massed pike men (Swiss) and long-bowmen (English), were found as answers to the cavalry conundrum. These new tactics were further improved by the Spanish by using musketeers on the flanks, to support the Pikemen. This relegated the cavalry to a skirmishing role or of firing pistols at the enemy, instead of charging headlong and using the natural momentum of their mass and speed.

Highly educated and a polyglot, Gustavus had come to the throne at the age of 17 in 1611 and straight-away plunged into a pre-emptive war with aggressive neighbor Russia. He was a brilliant organizer and introduced innovative all-arms integration to maximum effect— logistics, cavalry, infantry, mobile artillery. He modified infantry tactics by changing the pike to musket ratio to (1:2), increasing the latter to enhance fire power, while retaining just sufficient pike men to keep out cavalry charges. He switched over from *match-lock* to the more reliable *wheel-lock* musket. Cross-training was also undertaken to develop a multi-skilled army, capable of inter-changing roles.

Lately, cavalry had been trained to ride up and shoot with pistols but Gustavus went back to the traditional cavalry charge, using impact and weight to full effect. Gustavus' cavalry consisted of heavy horse and dragoons (mounted infantry). The former carried a long sword and two pistols and charged 3 deep, straight at the enemy. Royalist Prince Rupert and Parliamentary general Oliver Cromwell successfully copied Gustavus' cavalry tactics during the English Civil War (1642-49). Gustavus' cavalry and infantry units were smaller (600 to 1000) and more mobile than the opposing Imperialists (@2000). The Swedish army was also intermixed, with cavalry not just on the wings of the formation. Ten mobile 4-pounder guns were assigned to every regiment.

Gustavus' focus was on mobility, discipline, administration and leadership and he trained and nurtured a core group of competent generals, including his chancellor **Axel Oxenstiern**. He took excellent care of his soldiers—Swedes, Irish, Germans and Scots—and was adored by them for his austerity, piety, charismatic personality and thick red-gold hair for which he was nicknamed *"the Lion of the North"*. Gustavus understood the threat to the Baltic Sea and the Protestant North from the advancing power of the Catholic Hapsburg Emperors of Austria led in the field by the brilliant but unscrupulous Czech mercenary, **Count Albrecht von Wallenstein**. In a strategically astute move, Wallenstein had already fused the different European war-theatres into one mighty conflict in the heart of Germany, a conflict which he could easily control from his own power-base. **Gustavus** headed a tiny kingdom (Sweden) with few resources and was funded by his wealthy allies—England, Holland and France. Landing in **Pomerania** in July 1630, he soon gathered an army of 30,000 and decided to invade the hereditary Hapsburg possessions (Austria, Bohemia, Silesia) instead of joining the on-going conflict in Germany which was then the main theatre of the war. **Wallenstein** was in disgrace at that time and the Austrians and Bavarians under **Count Tilly** and **Pappenheim** besieged the Protestant city of Magdeburg and sacked it, putting the inhabitants to the sword. This induced all the threatened German Protestant princes, including the Elector of Saxony, to join Gustavus, who soon commanded an army of 50,000 soldiers. He moved on Liepzig and confronted **Tilly** at *Breitenfield*, 5 miles north of the town.

The 74-year old **Tilly**, a master of traditional Spanish tactics, formed 2 lines in 17 squares of 2000 each. The 6000 cavalry were on the flanks, commanded by the dashing **Pappenheim** (right wing) and **Isolani** (left). Though 40,000 strong and competently led, the Catholic army had only 26 guns. Moving rapidly south, Gustavus camped 1 mile away, on 16th September,1631 and spent the night discussing plans with his captains— the canny Scot **Sir John Hepburn** and Swedish **Field Marshals Horn** and **Baner**. The next morning, the 2 armies met, and the mobility of Gustavus' army, particularly the artillery, won the day, helped by a wild, uncontrolled and wasted cavalry charge by Pappenheim at the pike men and musketeers on the Swedish right. Deprived of cavalry support, Tilly's infantry veterans (who lovingly called him "father") nevertheless fought to the very end against the main Swedish force and were practically decimated where they stood. General Monro, who led the Scottish contingent, described it as a victory of *"mobility over weight"*. To make matters worse for the Catholics, **Tilly** was mortally wounded in a battle at the River Lech in April 1632, while defending the Bavarian heartland.

But like **Hannibal** (after *Cannae,* hesitating to attack Rome), **Gustavus** failed to move decisively on **Vienna**, the Imperial capital. Instead, he penetrated deep to the south-west capturing **Erfurt, Coburg,** and **Nuremburg** (in **Bavaria**) and besieged **Ingolstadt,** but ran short of funds and men. On **Tilly's** death, the Austrian Emperor had been forced to reinstate **Wallenstein** in a desperate move to contain the rampaging Swedes. The wealthy Wallenstein, now Duke of Freidland, raised his own mercenary army to counter the Swedes. **Gustavus** hoped to draw **Wallenstein** behind him by attacking the **Bavarian** heartland, but the wily Imperial commander saw through the ploy and instead attacked **Saxony** in the north, to cut off the Swedish line of communication. It was now a gripping chess game between the 2 grandmasters—**Gustavus** and **Wallenstein**—with each trying to out-think the other. Several such fascinating military duels—**Hannibal** vs. Scipio, **Napoleon** vs. **Wellington**; **Rommel** vs. **Montgomery**; come to mind!

Failing to lure Wallenstein south, Gustavus was himself compelled to turn north in October to re-establish his line of supply with Sweden. The first round had clearly gone to the Imperialists. But advancing rapidly, the Swede caught up with Wallenstein near Leipzig. Since cold weather was setting in, **Wallenstein** had just sent off **Pappenheim's** cavalry. Left with just 25,000 men he was withdrawing towards Lutzen to set up winter camp when **Gustavus** (who had 12000 foot and 7000 horse), suddenly decided to attack. Unfortunately for **Gustavus**, a cavalry unit from the imperial rearguard stumbled on his advance guard and fought a delaying action, giving Wallenstein time to set up his defences and summon back Pappenheim's 8000 strong cavalry detachment.

Wallenstein had his right on a mound with 3 wind mills, and the town of *Lutzen*. On his left was a little stream and in front (to the south) was the *Lutzen-Liepzig* road, a causeway lined with ditches, which he deepened for defence against the advancing Swedes. He posted his infantry in the centre, with cavalry along the flanks and most of his 30 cannon on the mound. His disposition of resources was flawless and he could afford to wait on the defensive till **Count Pappenheim** reinforced him. But he had not reckoned reckon with the audacity and innovative genius of Gustavus.

Knowing that **Pappenheim** (8000 horse) was on his way to support **Wallenstein**, **Gustavus** advanced at first light on 16ᵗʰ November, but heavy fog forced him to halt. His army was in 2 lines, with the infantry in the centre. Like Napoleon against Wellington at Waterloo, he had to dislodge Wallenstein from his strong defensive position, before Pappenheim arrived. He therefore personally led the strong right wing (Finnish and Swedish horse), sweeping aside the Spanish musketeers lining the road/causeway and endeavored to envelope the enemy's left wing, but heavy mist intervened. **Gustavus** was unable to wear armour because of an old wound and was also conspicuous with his customary red sash. He was wounded in the arm, but advanced again when the fog lifted, driving back **Piccolomini's** heavy cavalry. **Pappenheim's** timely arrival steadied the imperialist left, but he fell mortally wounded and panic seized the Catholics again. Meanwhile the Swedish left and centre also made headway and victory was in sight. The fog again descended suddenly and **Gustavus,** with just 3 companions accidentally rode into an enemy unit and was shot repeatedly. His blood-stained horse reached his army, signaling his death.

This great loss only spurred his men to a superhuman effort and they made a supreme push to win the day. **Prince Bernhard of Saxe-Weimar,** on whom command devolved, captured the windmills and the battery on the imperial right, in a violent attack. Wallenstein wisely made a strategic retreat, losing 10,000 soldiers, while the Swedes lost around 5,000 men in what was a conclusive victory for them. But Gustavus' death deprived them of his charismatic leadership, though their generals were competent enough. The war dragged on for another 16 years, mainly because of the initiative of France, its able first ministers **Cardinals Richelieu** and **Mazarin** and its great captains, **Conde** and **Turenne**, but it was Gustavus who had reshaped the future of war itself! **Napoleon** admiringly said, 150 years later, *"Gustavus Adolph etait anime des principes d' Alexandre, d' Annibal et de Cesar"*.

The peace of Westphalia (1648) brought to an end 30 years of incessant warfare, with the Hapsburgs cut to size. The ascendance of France, its Sun King **Louis XIV** and its *generation next* of great generals— **Turenne** and **Conde**—was established. **Gen. JFC Fuller** observed sagely, *"The Thirty Years War was both the deathbed of German medieval civilization and the cradle of Franco-Prussian rivalry. When the war finally ended in 1648, France was powerful and centralized, while Germany was totally disrupted. **Marshal Turenne's** soldiers little knew the hatred which* *they engendered in the Germans by their destructive incursions across the Rhine, indulging in rapine, plunder and looting. This pent-up feeling led to the creation of a martial Prussia (and later, a unified Germany) as a challenge to French hegemony, under the leadership of* **Frederick the Great** *and* **Count Bismarck***, in the 18*th *and 19*th *centuries."*

Two years after Lutzen, **Count Wallenstein** was murdered by his ungrateful and suspicious Emperor. A sad fate indeed, for the man who had saved the Austrian Empire and could truly be ranked right next to the Great Captains of War in ability. **Gustavus** was succeeded by his infant daughter **Christina,** who later abdicated the Swedish throne, became a Catholic, settled in Rome and was eventually buried with great fanfare in St. Peters Basilica—one of only three women buried in the grotto. A strange destiny indeed for the sole heir of Gustavus Adolphus, the champion of the Protestant faith!

15

BLENHEIM (1704)—MARLBOROUGH, THE FIRST CHURCHILL

By the advent of 18th century, the art of war had reached a stage of stagnation. *Logistics* became all-important, as strategy became circumscribed by requirements of transport, provisions, grass, water and munitions. The pre-eminence of siege warfare established the reputation of the rival engineering masters of fortification—Marshals **Sebastian Vauban** of France and **Baron von Cohorn** of the Dutch Republic. In fact, Vauban's '*Lines of Brabant*'-a cocktail of canals, rivers and star-shaped forts (like Lille)—was virtually impenetrable. Stretching from Antwerp to Louvain to Namur, all in modern Belgium, this curtain effectively protected the northern border of France. Therefore, the defensive invariably triumphed over offense, and avoidance of battle through "*Strategies of Evasion*", was the order of the times. Even the great French marshal **Turenne**, became a past master in this negative science, out of sheer necessity.

It is only with the rise of **John Churchill, Duke of Marlborough**, that there was a shift away from this type of inconclusive warfare and a return to the offensive as pioneered by **Gustavus Adolphus** and perfected by **Cromwell** and **Conde**. The invention of the *Socket Bayonet* fixed on the *Flintlock Musket*, eliminated Pikemen and simplified battlefield tactics. The number of firing lines was reduced to 3 or 4 and battalions shrank to just 800 men. After firing at close range (@ 50 feet), the infantry made a bayonet charge, under cover of the smoke. The cavalry also came very close to the enemy, before charging in at full gallop, sword in hand.

John Churchill, son of Sir Winston Churchill, an impoverished English country gentleman, was born on 6th June 1650 and served with distinction in various units of the army between 1667 and 1701. He was close to **Catholic James II**, having been the king's gentleman of the bedchamber. His sister Arabella was the monarch's mistress even bearing him a son, James Fitzjames, Duke of **Berwick**! In 1709, the latter was to lead a Franco-Spanish army to victory over an Dutch-English force at Almanza. But Churchill opted for the **Protestant** cause of **Mary** (elder daughter of the king) and her husband **William**, the Dutch Stadtholder, during the Bloodless Revolution (1688), which ousted James II. He had already seen service at land and sea in the English, and even the French, forces! But in 1676, when recommended for a high appointment in the French army, the French ambassador wrote disparagingly to Louis XIV *"M de Churchile is too occupied with pleasures"*. When not engaged with affairs of State, he had indeed led a hectic hedonistic life during the dissolute Restoration period (1660-85) indulging in many simultaneous liaisons. He had dangerously shared a mistress, (Barbara Castlemaine, Duchess of Cleveland), with James' predecessor, the rakish Charles II, once even having to jump out out of the lady's window to save his life (and her honour!)

Despite these peccadillos, before his premature death, William III, aware of Churchill's considerable martial and diplomatic talents, appointed him **Captain-General** of the Anglo-Dutch armies in 1701. Calmness of temperament, high intelligence and a rare ability to tolerate fools, coupled with his varied experience of war and diplomacy, soon catapulted him to the position of (arguably) the greatest English general ever. To maintain the Balance of Power in Europe, Churchill had to oppose rampant France and its **Sun King, Louis XIV,** militarily, diplomatically, economically and politically. His multifaceted career is brilliantly depicted in the biography '*Marlborough*' by his descendant, Nobel Literature Prize winner, Prime Minister and 20th century war leader—**Sir Winston Churchill.**

Unlike in the 30 Years War (1618-48), when hostilities commenced on 17th May 1702, England, now allied with the United Provinces (Holland) and Austria, faced France and Spain, both ruled by Bourbons. The Bourbon duo, constituting a solid geographical block, had the advantage of operating on interior lines, whereas the 3 partners in the Grand Alliance were geographically apart and were in danger of being defeated piecemeal. France and Spain, also enlisted the support of Portugal, thus sealing off the Mediterranean and almost all European ports, to English and Dutch trade. Landlocked ally Austria, was surrounded on all sides by enemies— indeed a difficult situation overall, for Churchill, recently created 1st Duke of Marlborough by **Queen Anne,** James' younger daughter, who had succeeded her brother-in-law, William.

Marlborough's initial task was to prevent his allies, **Holland** and **Austria,** being over-run by enemies. He personally led the 90,000 strong Anglo-Dutch forces against France in the United Provinces (Holland), while the distinguished **Prince Eugene of Savoy** led the Austrian army in **Italy** against the numerically superior Franco-Spanish combine under Marshal Vendome. After expelling the French from the Maas and lower Rhine Valley, Marlborough next prepared for an invasion of Germany.

In a cleverly devised geopolitical strategem, Cadiz in Spain was threatened by an English fleet carrying 14,000 troops under the Duke of Ormonde. The positive effect of this was unfortunately offset by the powerful Catholic **Elector of Bavaria** joining France, permitting **Louis XIV** to order a move against the Austrian capital, Vienna. After French **Marshal Villars** linked up with John George, the Elector of Bavaria, the French army under **Marshal Vendome** in Italy, was instructed to move north to join the French-Bavarian forces and *"finish the war by annihilating the Austrians"* according to Louis XIV's explicit instructions. With 60,000 French and Bavarian soldiers threatening Vienna, the Austrian situation was desperate and Emperor Leopold recalled his best general, **Prince Eugene,** from Italy (like Carthage had recalled Hannibal in 202 BC), to save his capital.

Portugal was wooed back by Marlborough, by sending an Anglo-Dutch army to Lisbon and substituting French Claret with Portuguese Port, in imports to England! But Marlborough still had to save the Austrian emperor at any cost, since the ambitious French plan was to place the **Elector of Bavaria** on the Imperial Throne and completely dominate Europe. A quick military decision was not possible in the Netherlands because of the formidable French fortifications (including the Vaubon's Lines of Brabant). Marlborough and his close ally in English politics, Chief Minister **Sidney Godolphin,** nevertheless, needed a spectacular victory to reinforce their position in Parliament, as well as to reassure Queen Anne about the viability of the Grand Alliance.

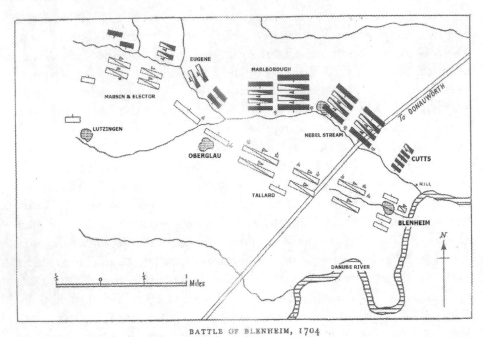

BATTLE OF BLENHEIM, 1704

By Shajahan

Blenheim (Battle Plan)—1704
10

So far, the main war in Europe was fought separately in 2 theatres—the **Netherlands** and **south Germany.** This suited France, with its central position. The Duke therefore took the bold step of suddenly transferring the English army far to the east to support Prince Eugene and save Vienna by threatening Bavaria. Though the strategic concept was clear, execution of the plan was a formidable logistic task—crossing great rivers and roadless terrain. The Quartermaster-General, **Lord Cadogan**, had to plot the line of march, locate places to camp, arrange depots for food, shoes, ammunition, 2000 wagons, 100 tons of oats daily for 15000 horses etc.

As usual, English naval dominance created a welcome diversion. **Austrian Arch-duke Charles**, supported by English troops, landed in Lisbon claiming the Portuguese throne, while the **Rock of Gibraltar** in Spain was taken by assault—it is in British hands even today! Handing over the defense of the Netherlands to the Dutch general **Overkirk**, with 60,000 Dutch troops, Marlborough dashed east from Liege to Cologne (16th May1704) and Bonn, surprising the French and even his Dutch allies, who were not privy to his high-risk 'Danube plan'. As he moved further east to Coblenz and Mainz, the Dutch were unnerved at the prospect of facing the formidable French forces alone. However, Marlborough enjoyed the complete support of **Queen Anne,** whose closest confidant was his wife **Duchess Sarah.** He personally had a close relationship with **Anthony Heinsius, Grand Pensionary of the Dutch Republic** and hence could afford to take such great political risks. At 53, he still had to make a reputation as a Great Captain and was lucky to partner **Prince Eugene,** 13 years younger, but rated the ablest general living. To make a comparison, both Napoleon and Wellington completed their illustrious careers by the age of 45! According to a contemporary report "*He looked remarkably young with a complexion that would put the fair sex to shame. With the features of a classical hero, his charm was irresistible to men and women alike*".

After covering 250 miles, Marlborough reached the vicinity of Ulm, on the Danube, where he was joined by forces under the **Margrave of Baden,** while Eugene with his small army kept **Marshals Tallard** and **Villeroi** at bay, near Strasbourg close to the Rhine, in the west. To supplement his hazardous 250-mile supply route from the Netherlands, the Duke needed access to friendly German states lying to the north-east. He therefore captured the town of **Donauworth,** which commanded a bridge across the Danube, after fiercely storming the fort of Schellenberg, since he lacked engines to besiege it.

Surprisingly, instead of immediately attacking the Bavarian capital, **Munich,** and taking the Elector out of the war, he wasted the whole of July burning Bavarian villages, hoping perhaps that this would induce the Elector to sue for peace. Tallard, meanwhile, slipped away from Eugene, marching rapidly east through the Black Forest to join Marsin and the Elector south of Ulm on 5th August. Bluffing Villeroi to remain in place by leaving part of his small army near the Rhine, Eugene in turn, took a short-cut through Wurtemberg to link up with Marlborough, on 6th August. Despite this confluence of forces, they were outnumbered by the Franco-Bavarian army (60,000 vs 70,000) which took up a strong defensive position south of the *Nebel brook,* just where it meets the **Danube River.**

Marshal Tallard commanded the French right and centre, with its right flank protected by the great river. He had the villages of *Blenheim* and *Oberglau* (3miles apart) on the right and left respectively, of his sector. **Marshal Marsin** and the **Elector** commanded the left wing, with the village of *Lutzingen* protecting their left flank. They arrayed their forces right up against the 15 foot wide Nebel stream, using it as a defensive moat, whereas Tallard kept his soldiers within Blenheim (9 battalions) and

Oberglau (12 battalions), to fully utilize the defensive potential of these fortified villages. The French in these villages could sweep the British with crossfire as they re-formed after crossing the Nebel. Tallard also stationed 7,000 soldiers between the 2 villages. Marsin had 51 squadrons of cavalry and 12 infantry battalions and held Lutzingen strongly, the entire Franco-Bavarian line stretching 5 miles from east to west.

The 60,000-strong forces led by Eugene and the Duke, were thoroughly heterogeneous—Austrians, Hessians, Hanoverians, Prussians, Dutch and 10,000 English/Scots, but the two leaders thought (and fought) as one—a rare case of 2 great equals co-operating perfectly in jointly leading an army. Reconnoitering forward, Marlborough ascertained the preponderance of forces on the enemy's right (Tallard) and decided to surprise him by directing the main attack there, while Eugene kept Marsin busy with a small force. The keys to the French defense were Blenheim and Oberglau villages, from which positions Tallard could launch flank attacks on any troops moving between them. The Duke's plan was to focus initial attacks on the villages and tie down their sizeable garrisons, allowing his other forces to slip through in between—a very risky venture, conceivable only by the boldest. He could not even be sure, initially, whether Tallard would try to oppose the Nebel crossing or fall back and use the villages themselves as the main defence.

The duke commenced his move at 3 a m, but Tallard, (holding a strong position) could not believe that he would attack such a strong position without at least a (3 to 1) superiority and assumed that the enemy was in retreat! The advantage in the initial cannonade went to the French, but at 7 am, the duke sent in **Lord Cutts** with a mix of 14,000 infantry and 5,000 cavalry across the brook, using bailey bridges. After crossing the stream, Cutts was to halt in a shallow dip in the meadow and attack Blenheim village only on further orders. The duke was awaiting word from Eugene who was toiling through difficult terrain away to the west.

At 12 noon, Prince Eugene's ADC came riding in and Marlborough turned to his generals calling out, *"Gentlemen, to your posts!"*. Cutts' allout attack caused the excitable **Marquis de Cleambault** (commanding the Blenheim garrison) to panic and he called in all available French reserves to support him. Soon, 12,000 men (12 battalions) were needlessly packed into the little village, leaving Tallard with just 9 battalions to challenge the British forces pouring in between Blenheim and Oberglau! But the first English attack failed, as did the second. The superb French *gendarmerie* cavalry then made a counter charge which was barely beaten back by the English cavalry.

Marlborough made preparations for a third attack, but he called it off when he saw that his purpose had been served—over 12,000 French soldiers were now holed up in Blenheim. But things were not going well for him around Oberglau to the west, where 10 of his battalions (under the Prince of Holstein-Beck) were repulsed by 9 French battalions, including the famous Irish refugee brigade—'the *Wild Geese*'. A gap opened up in the English line through which Marsin boldly propelled a cavalry charge. The duke galloped to the scene and plugged the gap with a cavalry brigade borrowed from Prince Eugene, who was himself fighting a critical battle against the Elector in the far west. The French attack was contained and they were soon bottled up in Oberglau, like their compatriots in Blenheim to the east. It all depended now on Eugene holding on in the west with his weakened forces, since the English were rampaging freely in the east.

At 4:30 p m the duke set his centre in motion. Guessing his intention, Tallard brought in his last 9 reserve battalions, south of Oberglau, to try and save the day. The French pushed back the advancing Hanoverian infantry and the issue was in balance till English cannon shattered them with a whiff of grapeshot. Mounted on a white charger and wearing the Star of the Garter, the handsome duke, riding well forward, was indeed a magnificent figure. Intuitively sensing the critical moment, at 6 pm., Marlborough ordered a general advance. With trumpets blaring, kettle drums beating and flags flying, the cavalry swung into a trot as they closed with the still resilient French cavalry who had the reputation of being the finest of the time. But the latter had had enough. They fired just one volley from their pistols and suddenly turned and fled, including Lous XIV's elite household cavalry *(the Maison de Roi)*. With Marshal Tallard's forces broken in the east, Marsin and the Elector in the west, sensibly ordered a general withdrawal to prevent an envelopment of their flanks by the triumphant English and Austrians.

After 17 hours in the saddle, the duke hastily scribbled a note to his wife which was delivered 10 days later at Windsor, *"I have not time to say any more, but to beg you to give my duty to the Queen and let her knew her army has had a glorious victory. Mons. Tallard and 2 other generals are in my coach."* None of the 3 defeated commanders (Tallard, Marsin and the Elector) had made a serious tactical mistake, but Eugene's stubborn holding action and Malborough's sheer audacity of conception and execution won the day against superior forces positioned behind strong defences! As Robert Southey wrote in his poem *"After Blenheim"*, it was indeed *"a famous victory"*, the greatest in Europe since Gustavus' triumph at Lutzen in 1632. The French soldiers isolated at Blenheim and Oberglau villages were captured en masse, encumbering Marlborough with over 15,000 prisoners. The 40 year European primacy of France (and Louis XIV) was broken, Vienna (and the emperor) were saved, the Catholic Stuarts' chances of regaining the English throne were blown away and English Naval Supremacy was established for 200 years.

Arvind A
Marlborough/Eugene Routes

Europe—1700
11

The grateful nation (and Queen Anne) gifted John Churchill, the magnificent 16,000-acre Royal Estate of Woodstock, near Oxford. The grand ducal palace, appropriately named **"Blenheim"** was designed by Hawksmoor and Vanbrugh, and surrounded by an exquisite garden by Capability Brown. Marlborough's great descendant, Sir Winston Churchill, born here, went on to provide leadership in an even greater crisis for England and against an even more dangerous enemy—Adolph Hitler! Marlborough's string of three further victories—**Ramillies** (1706), **Oudenarde** (1708) and **Malplaquet** (1709)—led to the peace of Utrecht. Out of the Queen's favour and no longer indispensable, he was dismissed in 1712, ostensibly for corruption. But the duke was reinstated by **Hanoverian George I**, who succeeded his cousin, Queen Anne on the English throne in 1714. Though France was apparently the loser in the war, its significant gain was in breaking the Hapsburg Ring (Spain, Austria) around it. Meanwhile unnoticed by all the belligerents, the barbarian Russian bear (under the visionary Tsar **Peter the Great**) established itself as a major player on the European stage, with a thumping victory over the erratic military genius, **Charles XII** (of Sweden) at Poltava in 1709.

As an ominous portent of future German hegemony, **Frederick II, the Great** (Elector of Brandenburg and King of Prussia) in a magnificent display of pyrotechnics, fought off successive enemies several times his size. At one stage, he (with only distant Britain as an ally) confronted the combined forces of Austria, France, Russia, Saxony and Sweden! He was indeed greatest in times of crisis. Napoleon said admiringly of him, *"What distinguishes Frederick is not his maneuvering skill but his audacity. He abandoned his line of communication and often acted as if he had no knowledge of the art of war!"* Thomas Carlyle called him *"the last of the Kings"* since he was a throwback to the medieval period, when Kings personally led armies in the field. Over decades of war, he managed to consolidate his scattered territories—Prussia, Brandenburg, Cleves, Pomerania, Mark—into a single solid mass by annexing various segments, including Silesia and parts of Poland.

Though his father had left him a well-trained army, Prussia was strategically weak, being surrounded on all sides by aggressive neighbours and possessed no natural boundaries in the form of formidable rivers or insurmountable mountain ranges. The European situation was fragile after the Empire was inherited by Maria Theresa in 1740. Utilising the confused conflict situation of the War of the Austrian succession (1740-48) and the Seven Years War (1756-63), Frederick managed to aggrandize himself, winning great battles over the Austrians at Rossbach and **Leuthen** in 1757, and adding Silesia to his realm. He was history's outstanding exponent of ceaseless attack even with inferior forces, which he massed to gain superiority at the point where he attacked. **Leuthen** was a spectacular example of *flanking attack in oblique order*, modeled on the Theban tactics at **Leuctra** (371BC) against the Spartans and a fore-runner of **Assaye,** where **Arthur Wellesley** decimated the Marathas. Napoleon called Leuthen, *"a masterpiece of movements, maneuvers and resolution, all in perfect conformity with the principles of war."*

With Frederick fighting against tremendous odds, surrounded by enemies on all sides, Rossbach and Leuthen were must-win battles that literally saved Prussia from extinction. Memories of Rossbach, At one stage he had only distant England as an ally with all the nations of Europe arrayed against him. Consequently, Leuthen, Zorndorf, Torgau and other high-risk victories dominated German history and the German psyche. Out of this arose a sense of superiority which ultimately led (under **Bismarck** in the latter half of the 19th century) to a united and aggressive **Germany** replacing **France** as the Continental superpower. It also ended 600 years of almost continuous Anglo-French rivalry. But before that came the epoch of the great wars of the French Revolution and the Napoleonic era.

16

ABDALI 3RD BATTLE OF PANIPAT (1761)— MARATHA ECLIPSE

14th January 2011 was the 250th anniversary of the cataclysmic defeat of the **Maratha empire** which then dominated much of the Indian sub-continent. Out of the maelstrom of the forces competing in the Deccan after the fall of Vijaynagar (1565)—the Mughals and the kingdoms of Ahmednagar, Bijapur, Berar, Bidar and Golconda—had risen the new power of the Marathas. Their charismatic leader, **Shivaji Raje Bhonsle** was greatly influenced by his mother Jijabai and his guru and advisor, Dadoji Kondev. Later, his preceptor, Swami Ramdas enjoined him to revive the glory of Vijaynagar and its great Emperor Krishna Deva Raya. With his power centered around Poona, Shivaji, the master of guerilla warfare and siege-craft, captured dozens of Western Ghat hill forts and kept at bay huge armies led by Afzal Khan, Shaista Khan and other leading Mughal and Bijapur generals, who referred to him derisively as "the mountain rat", but could never get the better of him. He was crowned *Chatrapati* in 1674 and was even able to fight off Mughal armies personally led by **Aurangzeb** himself, until his death in 1680.

Despite a prolonged war of succession, the Maratha territories kept expanding in all directions. The Brahmin *Peshwas* (prime ministers) Balaji Viswanath (1713-20) and Bajirao (1720-40) then became de facto rulers, holding court from the grand Shanwar Wada palace in Poona, while Shivaji's descendents were pensioned off as *Maharajas of Satara* and *Kolhapur*. Thereafter, the Maratha generals became semi-independent and held sway over their respective domains—**Bhonsle** (Nagpur), **Gaikwad** (Baroda), **Holkar** (Indore), **Scindia** (Gwalior), **Patwardhan** (Sangli) and seafaring **Kanhoji Angre,** based on the Konkan coast. On the occasions when they came together, the *Maratha Confederacy* was indeed a formidable force.

By 1760, the British East India Co. had established itself in India mainly due to the military genius and guile of **Robert Clive** who successfully overcame the French (under Dupleix) and their Indian proxies in the south, and Nawab Siraj-ud-daula of Bengal at Plassey in 1757. The only power in the sub-continent, capable of challenging them now, was the Maratha confederacy.

The Marathas' strident war-cries *"Har, Har Mahadev"* and *"Jai Bhavani"* spread terror as the mobile raiders over-ran central India They soon controlled Delhi, the seat of the Great Moghul, under the illustrious **Peshwa Baji Rao** and his sibling (and alter ego) **Chimaji Appa**. Though both died a few days apart in 1740, the Maratha momentum was carried forward by their sons, **Peshwa Balaji Baji Rao (Nana Sahe**b) and **Sadasiv Rao "Bhau** who were themselves destined to die a few days apart in 1761!

Meanwhile, following in the footsteps of Persian ruler **Nadir Shah** (who sacked Delhi in 1739 and carried away the Kohinoor diamond and the Peacock Throne), his protégé, the Afghan **Ahmed Shah Abdali,** raided India 5 times, from 1742 onwards. In his horrendous campaign of 1756, Abdali was particularly severe on the pilgrim city of **Mathura** and much innocent blood flowed into the sacred Yamuna. In late 1757 led by Malhar Rao Holkar and Raghunath Rao, brother of the Peshwa Balaji Baji Rao (Nanasaheb**),** a powerful Maratha army marched north-west, seeing that Abdali had retired to Afghanistan to avoid the inclement summer of the Indo-Gangetic plains. The Marathas easily took Lahore, Multan and Peshawar from their Afghan governors, advancing without much opposition since Abdali was caught up in a civil war at home. But Abdali was not a man to meekly accept Maratha hegemony in North India.

For his fifth and final invasion of Hindustan, the Afghan ruler gathered together a host of Uzbeks, Hazaras, Afghans, Pashtuns, Tajiks, Turkomans and Kazaks in the customary manner of all northern raiders. Invitations to invade Hindustan and promises of support came from Rohilla chief **Najib Khan** (who ruled over the upper reaches of the Ganga-Hardwar, Saharanpur) and the radical cleric **Shah Waliulah** who wrote *"The plight of the Muslims is pitiable. All control of government is in the hands of the Hindus"*.

Unfortunately, the Maratha forces were widely dispersed. The Peshwa and his valiant cousin **Sadashiv Rao "Bhau"** were engaged in the south in the Nizam's territories where they won a major victory at **Udgir,** using artillery effectively, thanks to **Ibrahim Khan Gardi,** who had been trained by Frenchman Charles de Bussy at Hyderabad, Meanwhile, **Dattaji Scindia** and his nephew **Jankoji** were trying to extract *chauth* tribute from the Rajput rulers of Jaipur, Jodhpur and Udaipur. **Raghoji Bhonsle** was attempting to push east into Bundelkhand in a move to reach the holy cities of Allahabad and Benares and **Damaji Gaekwad's** cohorts were busy in Gujarat. Nanasaheb Peshwa's grand design to conquer Hindustan therefore led to a wide dispersal of the Maratha forces at a time when the Afghan wolf was at the gates. The Maratha campaigns won territory and tribute but made too many enemies at this critical time. Peshwa Nanasaheb was a competent diplomat and administrator, but no great shakes as a war leader, unlike his illustrious father Baji Rao, who invariably led his armies from the front. To make matters worse, the Peshwa was terminally ill. The political situation in 1759 was unsettled as the Scindias moved into the Ganga-Yamuna *doab* to attack Najib, against the wishes of senior commander **Malhar rao Holkar.**

The latter's *bête noir* was Maratha ally **Suraj Mal**, the Jat ruler of Bharatpur, who had killed his only son Khande Rao (whose widow **Ahalyabai** later ruled Indore). New Emperor **Shah Alam** and his Wazir Imad-ud-daulah were at loggerheads, with both secretly soliciting aid from both Abdali and the Marathas! The Mughal empire was a pale shadow, but imperial *firmans* were useful to legitimse conquests all over India, although the emperor's writ scarcely extended beyond the city walls. As the popular doggerel went, *"From Delhi to Palam, is the realm of Shah Alam"*. Abdali set out from Kandahar in September 1759 with his heterogenous army of 60,000 freebooters who poured in through the Khyber and Bolen Passes, pushing back **Sabaji Scindia** from Peshawar and overcoming stubborn Sikh resistance at Lahore. Dattaji and Jankoji Scindia, who were now besieging Najib Khan at Shukratal, near Hardwar, moved west to the Punjab to link up with Sabaji's defeated forces on 8th December 1759. Abdali and Najib moved on the Scindias before Holkar could join them from Rajasthan. In a skirmish on 10th January at **Barari Ghat,** resisting the Afghan crossing of the Yamuna, Dattaji Scindia was killed and Jankoji and Sabaji were wounded and the ragged remnant of the Scindia forces fled south to join the army headed by Malhar rao Holkar.

Urgent appeals were sent to Peshwa Nanasaheb at Poona who decided to send the bulk of his Deccan forces, under the victor of Udgir, 30 year old **Sadashivrao "Bhau".** Nominally though, the Peshwa's 17-year old son and heir **Viswas Rao** would be in command of the 50,000 strong army, which included 15,000 highly mobile Pindari horsemen, besides 10,000 *Gardi* musketeers, 11,000 elite *Huzurat* household cavalry and contingents led by various *sirdars*—Shamser Bahadur (natural son of the late Peshwa Baji Rao and the beautiful **"Mastani"**), Yeshwant Rao Pawar, Damaji Gaekwad, Balwant Rao Mehendele, Manaji Paygude. No longer the swift and mobile guerillas of Shivaji and Baji Rao, Bhau's army was burdened with luxurious tents, accoutrements, cooks, barbers, harriers and about 20,000 pilgrims intending to visit holy places in North India! Since Bhau was given only Rs.6 lakhs cash plus *hundis* for Rs 3 lakhs encashable at Indore, it was presumed that the force would have to live off the land. Starting on 15th March 1760 from Sindkhed, near Aurangabad, they moved slowly but directly north, reaching Gwalior on 1st June and the Chambal area therafter, suffering from an early monsoon and having difficulty moving the heavy artillery across rivers and through the ravines. Holkar and **Surajmal** (the Jat raja of **Bharatpur**) who joined Bhau, suggested following the time tested guerilla methods of Maratha warfare, after leaving the heavy Gardi cannons and the host of noncombatants at Gwalior.

Bhau, after his success at Udgir, relied greatly on his powerful artillery but he would have done well to at least get rid of the noncombatants. It is said that an angry Holkar commented, *"The proud Brahmin deserves the fall he is heading for."* Reaching Agra on 14th July, Bhau sent Holkar and Surajmal ahead to take Delhi. The journey of 900 miles had taken 120 days, because of the large number of campfollowers and the ineptitude of the Marathas in handling the numerous river-crossings.

Negotiations were now opened with Abdali, who insisted on having Sirhind as the border whereas the Marathas wanted the Indus as a barrier. Their only ally Surajmal of Bharatpur, left in a huff, when he was denied custody of Delhi. The Marathas were thus left friendless in a strange land, led by a commander who had never campaigned beyond the Narmada River and was quite unfamiliar with the topography, peoples, languages and culture of north India. Beset with money and supply problems, Bhau shifted his camp to the Shalimar Gardens outside Delhi, while Abdali was at Shahdara, east of Delhi, the armies being separated by the Yamuna in flood. Both sides were playing a waiting game. Besides collecting supplies and money, Bhau had to arrange boats and was also trying to wean away Shuja, Nawab of Oudh who was a Shia, unlike Abdali and his friends, who were Sunnis. Confident that Abdali could not intervene across the Yamuna, Bhau attacked and took Afghan-held **Kunjpura**, 120 miles north of Delhi, using his Gardi artillery to deadly effect, on 19th October, 1760—*Dussera* day.

The Marathas strictly observed auspicious days for important events. With the Yamuna still in flood, the Marathas then left on a pilgrimage to Kurukshetra, on 25th October. Abdali used the opportunity to cross the Yamuna unchallenged near Baghpat, helped by local Gujars, with the Maratha patrols caught napping. But he still hesitated to attack this powerful southern army. Bhau established his entrenched camp just south of the town and fort of Panipat, 9 miles west of the Yamuna and 50 miles north of Delhi. Nearby was the legendary Kurukshetra field where the Kauravas and Pandavas had their final death-struggle, while Panipat itself was the site of 2 great battles in the 16 th century.

In 1526, the Sultan of Delhi, **Ibrahim Lodi**, had been slain here by the Timurid invader **Babur,** ruler of Fergana and Samarkand, who then laid the foundations of the Moghul Empire in India. In 1556, the army of Babur's teenaged grandson Mohamed Jalaludin 'Akbar', led by Bairam Khan, defeated **Raja Hemu's** indigenous coalition to firmly establish Moghul hegemony in north India. Hence the battle that took place there in 1761 is referred to as the 3rd Battle of Panipat. All the three battles at Panipat resulted in overwhelming victories for the invaders from the northwest!

A consummate diplomat, Abdali had enlisted the aid of the Rohilla chiefs **Najib Khan** (of Saharanpur) and **Dunde Khan** (of Bareilly) and the Shia Nawab of Oudh, **Shuja Ud-Doulah**. He also cemented alliances with several Hindu rulers. The Maratha Confederacy, on the other hand, had alienated even the Sikh Jats (including Alai Singh of Patiala) and the powerful Rajput rajas of Jaipur, Udaipur and Jodhpur.

On 29th October, on the advice of the astute Ibrahim Khan Gardi, the Marathas set up camp around Panipat Fort, at the intersection of the present National Highway with the Sanauli Road and entrenched themselves for a long stay, even as Abdali set up his camp 6 miles to the south-east. Short of money and supplies, the Marathas soon had to depend on their Delhi agent for the former and scoured the countryside for the latter. They lost many warriors in skirmishes, including the aged but active **Govind Pant Bundela**, who was surprised near Ghaziabad on 20th December, while foraging across the Yamuna. They were now virtually under siege, being without winter clothing and short of food and ammunition. Being strict vegetarians they could not even slaughter and eat their bullocks! While starvation and insanitary conditions prevailed in the static Maratha entrenchments, Abdali moved his camp thrice to avoid living in such vile surroundings. Bhau's desperate attempts to negotiate through Nawab Shuja of Oudh were blocked by Najib Khan who exhorted Abdali to permanently get rid of the *kafirs* who were *"a thorn in the garden of Hindustan"*.

On his part, the ailing Peshwa from his luxurious Shanwarwada Palace, instructed Bhau to exterminate the *gilcha* Afghans. But he delayed his own promised move north with a supporting army, dawdling near

Paithan to contract a marriage with a 9 year old girl! Nanasaheb appeared totally distracted and unable to come to terms with reality, beginning his slow movement north only on 31st December 1760. The only feasible course of action for Bhau was to fight his way out, since Abdali refused to attack his impregnable position, while Najib Khan's Rohillas tormented the southerners with wildcat attacks on foraging parties.

On the night of 13th January, 1761 (Winter solstice, *Makar Sankrant*), there was a meeting of the top Maratha leaders. Ibrahim Khan mooted the desperate idea of forming a huge defensive hollow infantry square with the powerful cannons in front blasting their way south-east in oblique order to the north-facing Afghans. Led by the French-trained Gardi musketeers and followed by the main host, after reaching the Yamuna, the Marathas could move south along its western bank to Delhi, which they still held.

Both were tactics prevalent in European warfare. Wellington at Waterloo (1815) successfully formed infantry squares to repel Napoleon's cavalry charges and Frederick the Great had a penchant for *flanking attack in oblique order*. But as soon as the lateral movement began led by the 10,000 strong *Gardi* musketeers, Dunde Khan led his 14000 Rohillas and 3000 Persian cavalry to block their way, forcing the Maratha line to turn right. This converted the battle into a traditional face to face confrontation, with Abdali's line outflanking the smaller Maratha army in the west. Thus, Bhau in the centre with the 11,000 elite *Huzurat* (Peshwa's household cavalry), now had artillery expert Ibrahim Khan Gardi commanding to his left and *sirdars* Dattaji Scindia and Madhavrao Holkar to his right. Numbering over 45,000, but half-starved and demoralised, the Marathas faced south, into the winter sun, stretching along the Sanauli road.

The 60,000 Afghans, facing north, were aligned south of the Sanauli road, their left formed by **Shah Pasand Khan's** 3000 horsemen and 15000 Rohillas (under **Najib Khan).** On their right were Persian cavalry **(Barkudar Khan)** and **Dunde Khan's** 14,000 Rohillas. Their centre was led by Nawab Shuja of Oudh with 60 artillery pieces and Abdalli's **Wazir Shah Wali Khan** with 20,000 Afghan horsemen and the remaining 15,000 Rohilla Pathan cavalry. When the Maratha left wing (*Gardi* infantry) met Abdali's right at around 10 am, the other extremities of the opposing armies (Holkar and Najib) were still 4 miles apart, in the west. **Abdali,** who never led from the front, directed the battle (on an elephant?) from the rear centre, escorted by his Slave battalion, as his army advanced in a northerly direction before dawn on 14thJanuary1761. Though his position in the rear was considered cowardly by Marathi historians, this enabled him to overview the battlefield and exercise good control over his forces, unlike Bhau who was soon totally embroiled in the confusion.

The initial artillery barrage went in favor of the Marathas. Their left wing of 10,000 French-trained Hyderabadi Gardi musketeers, under Ibrahim Khan, routed Dunde Khan's Rohilla cavalry on Abdali's right. Meanwhile Sadasivrao Bhau, mounted on an elephant, led the *huzurat* cavalry in a furious charge against the Wazir's Afghan cavalry in the centre. The Wazir appealed to Nawab Shuja for help, but in vain and the Afghan army was soon split down the centre. Though Najib Khan on the Afghan left fought off Jankoji Scindia, it looked as if Bhau in the centre could clinch the battle, but his horses were half starved and badly winded after their fierce up-hill charge of over 2 miles. Intuitively sensing the decisive moment, Abdalli sent forward his reserve of 3000 musketeers (Qizilbash) and 500 swivel-mounted cannons on camels, which fired over his own troops right into the midst of the exhausted *huzurat* cavalry positioned in the Maratha centre.

By 4 pm, **Sadasivrao Bhau's** centre had no reserves to supplement his dwindling horsemen and he watched helplessly as nephew **Viswas Rao** was shot and mortally wounded as he fought from his elephant *howdah*. Dismounting from his own elephant, Bhau mounted his horse and led 3 desperate charges at the head of his personal guard. Unfortunately, seeing the 2 empty *howdahs*, the Maratha rank and file assumed that both their leaders were dead and lost heart. At this juncture, 2000 renegade Afghans who had been fighting on the Maratha side, threw off their distinguishing saffron headgear and joined their brethren. Malhar Rao Holkar, the born survivor, fled westward from the right wing before actually engaging the enemy. Bhau had 3 horses killed under him but continued fighting on foot till he was surrounded and butchered, along with the cream of Maratha manhood including Yashwant Pawar, Shamsher Bahadur and Manaji Paygude. Young Jankoji Scindia was grievously wounded and captured, while Ibrahim Khan and his Gardis on the left fought on unsupported. This group of gallant South Indian Telangis was ultimately surrounded and massacred to the last man.

Of the Maratha host, only 15,000 escaped south to Gwalior, including Bhau's wife **Parvathibhai** who was saved by the loyalty of Janu Bhintada and protected by **Raja Surajmal** of Bharatpur. Over 6000 women and children were taken prisoner and their subsequent fate was truly tragic. Grant Duff writes *"They retained the women as slaves but ranged the men in lines and amused themselves in cutting off their heads."* Many Maratha warriors, who survived, chose not to return home after their defeat. According to the *Sunday Indian* (24th Jan.2011), their descendents (*the Road Marathas*), following ancient customs and celebrating Maratha festivals, still reside in the Panipat region and meet annually at the *Kala Aam (Black Mango)* memorial monument, the site of the disastrous final stand of Sadasiva Rao Bhau.

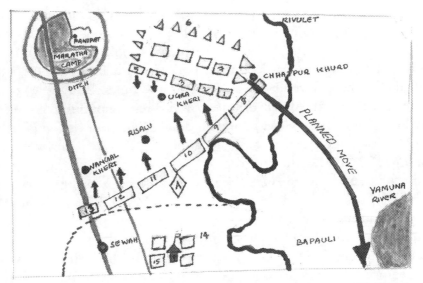

By Shajahan

Panipat (Battle Plan)—1761

12

1) Ibrahim Gardi

2) Damaji Gaekwad

3) Bhau, Viswas rao, Huzurat cavalry

4) Jankoji Scindia

5) Holkar

6) Support troops

7) Noncombatants

8) Barkudar Khan

9) Rohillas (Dunde)

10) Grand Wazir

11) Shuja

12) Najib Khan

13) Pasand Khan

14) Afghan Camp

15) Abdali Slave Troops

A) Abdali position

The Maratha host was essentially 2 separate armies. The *huzurat* cavalry, the *gardi* infantry and artillery were elite forces on whom Bhau relied. The *gardis* were European (Charles de Bussy) trained, and had won battles at Udgir and Kunjpura for him. The traditional Maratha forces (light cavalry) on the right were unable to face the better-mounted Afghans who had bested them at Bararighat and in a series of subsequent skirmishes. Bhau lost the battle tactically because though powerful, his artillery lacked mobility, unlike Abdali's camel-mounted guns.

Maratha failure to enlist allies because of their hegemonistic attitude and the unreasonable levy of "*Chauth*" and "*Sardeshmuki*" tax on neighboring rulers, was also a major cause of the defeat. Abdali on the other hand, had struck diplomatic deals even with Hindu leaders and also appealed directly to Muslims (especially Sunnis), in the name of religion. He also cleverly held back a tactical reserve force which he unleashed at the critical time to annihilate the victorious but exhausted, enemy centre.

Abdali was the very last of a long line of successful raiders from the North-West, but he could not establish his domain in India despite decisively defeating the dominant power, the Marathas. Returning home with immense booty, he left his son **Taimur Shah** at Delhi, but the Afghans were soon pushed out by their implacable enemies, the Sikhs, who retook Amritsar and Lahore and established their own powerful kingdom in the Punjab under **Maharaja Ranjit Singh**. The strong symbolism of the Maratha defeat is signified by naming of the Pakistani "*Abdali*" missile, just as the (Mohamed) *Ghori* was named to counter the Indian *Prithvi* (Prithviraj Chauhan) missile by reviving memories of the 12th century battle of Tarain.

Nanasaheb Peshwa received the dire tidings of the death of his son and cousin and the destruction of his great army while crossing the Narmada with reinforcements. As dramatically narrated in Marathi, *"Two pearls have been dissolved, 27 gold coins have been lost and of silver and copper, the cost cannot be cast up"*. The Peshwa returned to **Poona,** retired to a temple on Parvathy Hill and died soon after, a totally broken man. Young Jankoji Scindia of Gwalior and the valiant Ibrahim Khan **Gardi**, both severely wounded, were captured and executed by the Afghans, despite the intervention of Nawab Shuja of Oudh. But the latter managed to ransom and save 7000 Maratha soldiers.

Though they revived briefly under Peshwa Madhavrao and Jankoji's uncle **Mahadji Scindia** and **Nana Phadnis,** who both survived the Panipat disaster, the Marathas had lost their aura of invincibility. This mortal blow to the Maratha psyche made it possible for the British to conquer India, step by step. The Mughal emperor and Nawab of Oudh were defeated at Buxar (1764), the Rohillas crushed (1777), Tippu was killed at Srirangapatnam (1799), the weakened and disunited Maratha subedars decisively beaten by Arthur Wellesly (1803) and finally subdued (1818), the Sikhs beaten (1849). Finally the suppression of the mass uprising of 1857, led to firmly establishing British rule in India!

17

WATERLOO (1815)—
NAPOLEON, THE FALL OF THE TITAN

The advent of the 19th century saw the '*Man of Destiny*', **Napoleon Bonaparte,** dominating Europe as he strode it like a colossus. But his beginnings as the son of a minor Corsican nobleman gave no indication of the meteor-like career that lay ahead. Born in the Italian-speaking isle of **Corsica** (which had recently become a part of France) in 1769, the main influence on him throughout his life was his mother, Letizia, or Madame Mere, as she was later known. He was sent at the age of ten, to the French Military School at Brienne, where he quickly mastered French. Moving to the elite '*Ecole Militaire*' in Paris, he passed the 2-year course in 1 year and was commissioned into the artillery. At the artillery school at Auxonne (1785-88), he became the star pupil of the Commandant, Marshal du Theil, principal proponent of the new *Blitzkrieg*—swift concentration at a given point, breakthrough and destructive pursuit. Here, the young Napoleon imbibed the fundamental principles of warfare, particularly the effective use of mobile artillery. He learnt that a battle-plan plan should be flexible, with multiple courses of action constantly available to the proponent. Consequently, his fertile mind was always filled with alternatives, enabling him to delay tactical decision-making until the last critical moment, invariably catching his opponents on the wrong foot. Hence, no two Napoleonic battles are exactly alike, though one perceives 2 basic offensive patterns—a *flanking attack* or an *irresistable frontal assault* (as at Waterloo)—with subtle variations of these thrown in unexpectedly, to confuse the enemy. With Alexander and Hannibal, Napoleon completed the triumvirate of all-time super Grand Commanders, winning through all-out attack. The only battle which he fought completely on the defensive, was **Leipzig** in 1813, where he lost against overwhelming odds.

The chaotic conditions prevailing after the French Revolution (1789), provided him with ample opportunities to distinguish himself. Revolutionary France was a *'nation in arms'* boldly asserting its individuality against the monarchs of Europe, starting with the famous *'cannonade at Valmy'*. **Napoleon** was promoted brigadier-general at the age of 24, after he re-took the port-city of **Toulon** from the British. In 1795, he saved the Revolutionary Government by ruthlessly dispersing a rampaging Paris mob with a *'whiff of grapeshot,'* killing over 100 of the rioters and was raised to the command of the Army of the Interior. He married the beautiful and influential **Josephine Beauharnais,** a widow with 2 grown children, and set up residence at La Malmaison on the outskirts of Paris.

Nehru, in his *'Glimpses of World History'*, said—*Napoleon had, like Akbar, an extraordinary memory and a perfectly ordered mind. He said 'I* ***close one drawer and open another. The contents of the drawers never get mixed up.'*** His supreme talents were made even more productive by his enormous energy, capacity for hard work (the busy bee was his chosen symbol), mathematical and logistic skills, geopolitical comprehension and his meticulous attention to detail. In recognition of his obvious leadership potential, Napoleon was next given a truly Herculean task at the age of 27—leading an army across the Alps into Italy in March 1796, to fight the combined armies of Austria and Piedmont. Though lacking in discipline, his young conscripts were bold, self-reliant and intelligent marauders, ideally suited for Napoleon's elastic tactics. Winning a dozen battles, including the classic operations at Lodi Bridge and Rivoli, he knocked the Austrians and Piedmontese, out of the war, by synergistically integrating infantry, artillery and cavalry. He also began building a splendid team of generals, starting with **Murat** (cavalry leader *non pareil*), **Augereau, Soult** and **Berthier.**

His invasion of **Egypt** (1798) was an ambitious geopolitical move, a prelude to military tie-ups with the **Shah of Persia, Tippu Sultan** of Mysore and other anti-British potentates in the East. But he was thwarted by British naval might unleashed by **Admiral Horatio Nelson,** who destroyed the French fleet at the Battle of the Nile, aborting Napoleon's grandiose Oriental plan. Despite these travails, he conjured up a fantastic victory over the Mamelukes, his pre-battle speech inspiring his men, *'Soldiers, from the summit of these Pyramids, 40 centuries look down on you!'* The team of scholars who accompanied him to Egypt, included archeologists who founded the science of 'Egyptology 'and discovered the tri-lingual "**Rosetta stone**", which led to the decipherment of the ancient hieroglyphic script.

Returning to a chaotic situation in France, he led a coup and made himself First Consul with Abbe Sieyes and Roger Ducos as the other Consuls. He now focussed on improving the administrative system, restoring Roman Catholicism and also thoroughly modernizing the legal system by formulating the *'Code Napoleon'* which forms the basis of European jurisprudence, even to-day. While preparations to invade arch-enemy, England, were under way, **Napoleon** crowned himself *Emperor of the French* in the Notre Dame Cathedral, in the presence of the Pope. He organized a new Imperial system of subordinate Kings, Dukes and Princes, creating the Imperial Guard, setting up the elite St. Cyr Military Academy, instituting the prestigious *Legion of Honour* and appointing 18 Marshals of the Empire! But his victories at Ulm, Austerlitz and Jena were counterbalanced by the destruction of the French fleet at Trafalgar (1805) by Lord Nelson, who was however mortally wounded in the battle. This naval defeat effectively broke Napoleon's Continental System and his European embargo on English goods. But in 1807, Napoleon recovered the initiative, defeating Russian Tsar Alexander at Freidland and forcing him to sign the Treaty of Tilsit.

Now at the pinnacle of his career, he got embroiled in Spain, where he installed his elder brother, the incompetent Joseph, as King, leading to a long, debilitating struggle. Goya depicts the gruesome nature of this war. Spanish *guerillas* (the word was coined here) aided **Arthur Wellesley's** English army in inflicting a succession of defeats on the Emperor's best marshals—Soult, Massena, Junot, Marmont, Jourdain. In his effort to create a dynasty, Napoleon divorced **Josephine** (who had not borne him any children) and married **Marie-Louise,** daughter of the Austrian Emperor, after defeating the Austrians at Wagram. Having a son by her, he made his own brothers, Jerome and Louis, kings of Westphalia and Holland respectively, and appointed brother-in-law Joachim Murat (the fiery cavalry commander), king of Naples. He then compounded his troubles in Spain by a disastrous invasion of Russia in 1812.

He had learned nothing from the failure of the attack on **Peter the Great's** Russia by the erratic genius **Charles XII** (of Sweden), in 1707. He should have encamped for the winter in Smolensk but pushed on impetuously. Though Napoleon won Borodino and several other battles, the 67-year old Russian **General Kutusov**, made a deep strategic withdrawal, even burning and abandoning holy **Moscow** to the French invaders, as described in Tolstoy's *War and Peace*. The severe Russian winter decimated the 450,000 strong *Grand Army* and Napoleon returned alone on 19th December 1812 to Paris to face a truly daunting situation, with the armies of all Europe ranged against him. Even his former Marshal, Bernadotte, whom he had nominated Crown Prince of Sweden, was now among his enemies.

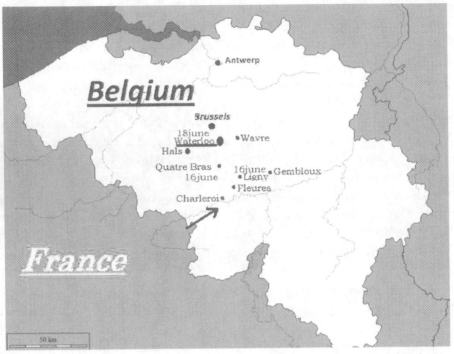

By Shajahan

Battles of Ligny (16th June), Quatre Bras (16th June)—1815
13

Heavily outnumbered on all fronts, 1813 was a disastrous year for Napoleon. He suffered a horrific defeat fighting defensively against heavy odds at **Leipzig** in Germany. By 1814, he was cornered in the vicinity of Paris. Prematurely aged and balding at 44, with his slim figure grown corpulent, he nevertheless fought with his customary panache and aggression, inflicting successive defeats on the contracting ring of enemies—Prussians, Austrians, Dutch, Russians and English—brilliantly utilising his central position, but to no avail. Forced to abdicate, he was exiled to the island of Elba, off the coast of Italy. The Austrian Metternich and his own former Foreign Minister Talleyrand, were the architects of the Pan-European political schemes against him. The **Bourbon Kings** were restored, but while the Allies were still conferring at Vienna how to redraw the map of Europe, Napoleon escaped from Elba, and landed near Cannes on the southern coast of France on 1ˢᵗ March 1815.

In what is called *'The Hundred Days'*, he was greeted with wild enthusiasm in his march north to Paris. He boldly confronted the French army sent against him with, *"Soldiers of the 5ᵗʰ, will you fire on your Emperor?"*, to which they responded, *"Vive l'empereur!"* After just a few months of the misrule of the grossly obese **Louis XVIII** and his Bourbon clique, the nation yearned nostalgically for the return of the heroic days of 'the *little Corporal'*. Below average height (5'4"), Napoleon had a large head with a broad forehead and hair which he wore long till his Egyptian campaign (1798). His persona exuded irresistible charisma, thanks to his regular features, expressive eyes and his brilliant conversation—even the great **Goethe** became his ardent admirer. As he neared Paris, King Louis XVIII fled and the rapidly changing attitude of the French authorities can be summarized thus:

"The Tiger has broken out of his den, The Ogre has been 3 days at sea,
The Wretch has landed at Frejus, The Buzzard has reached Antibes
The Invader has arrived in Grenoble, The General has entered Lyons,
Napoleon slept at Fontainebleu last night, The Emperor will proceed to the
Tulieries today
His Imperial Majesty will address his loyal subjects tomorrow"

Napoleon was at his energetic best as he prepared to face the multinational forces ranged against him by adding 80,000 veterans to the 200,000 strong standing army, plus young conscripts. According to **Caulaincourt**, his Foreign Minister during the **Hundred Days,** *"He seemed to extract men, horses and guns from the very bowels of the earth"*. Against this, 5 powerful allied armies were preparing to invade France— Wellington's 95,000 Anglo-Dutch soldiers, Blucher's 117,000 Prussians, 200,000 Austrians, 150,000 Russians and an Austro-Piedmontese army across the Alps in Italy. Wellington and Blucher were both within striking distance, just across the border in Belgium. Napoleon's strategy was to quickly destroy them before the others could come to their help—a perfect plan, under these must-win circumstances. He could never hope to win against the allies' combined strength and any sort of honorable peace was out of question since all the kings of Europe mortally feared his unsurpassed ability and unbounded ambition, as well as the formidable impact of France's *'levee en masse'*. Moreover, for centuries, the Rhine estuary and little Belgium (the Cockpit of Europe), had possessed a great symbolic value in the eyes of the French people and a victory here over Wellington would boost morale.

Napoleon once said *"When drawing up a plan of action, I magnify every danger, every disadvantage that can be conceived. My nervousness is painful though I conceal it from everyone."* But once the decision was made, his iron resolution and unbounded energy overcame all difficulties.

Unfortunately, apart from his paucity of human and material resources, Napoleon was deprived of the services of his superlative team of generals and marshals. Moreau, Poniatowski, Junot, Bessieres, Lannes, Duroc and Berthier (his reliable chief of staff) were all dead; Bernadotte and Marmont had joined his enemies and brother-in-law Murat (the dashing cavalry general) was embroiled in Naples, vainly trying to win back his kingdom. Leaving the able Marshal Davout in Paris as War Minister and Suchet to guard the Alps, Napoleon took along **Soult,** as chief of staff, and Marshals **Ney** and **Grouchy** to command the left and right wings of his army of 110,000. His strategic plans were brilliantly conceived, but unfortunately, Soult had never before held a staff job at any level. Ney and Grouchy were noted for raw courage but did not possess the creativity and intelligence required to think and act independently, or even to grasp the subtleties of Napoleon's grand scheme and to spontaneously formulate solutions to the problems which came up in the short but complex campaign lying ahead. But the 5 corps of around 15,000-20,000 each were competently led—1st (d'Erlon), 2nd (Reille), 3rd (Vandamme), 4th (Gerard) and 6th (Lobau), with the cavalry under experienced generals Lefebvre, Milhaud and Kellerman.

Prince Gerbhardt von Blucher, the 73-year old Prussian commander, had his 105,000 men stationed on the heights around Ligny, south-east of Brussels. Along with his proven military ability and mental toughness, there was a streak of visceral hatred for the French in general, and Napoleon in particular. He also had absolute control of the Prussian army, drilled and trained in the grand tradition of Frederick the Great and capably officered by the likes of Gneisenau, Scharnhost, Bulow, Pirch, Clausewitz and Ziethen.

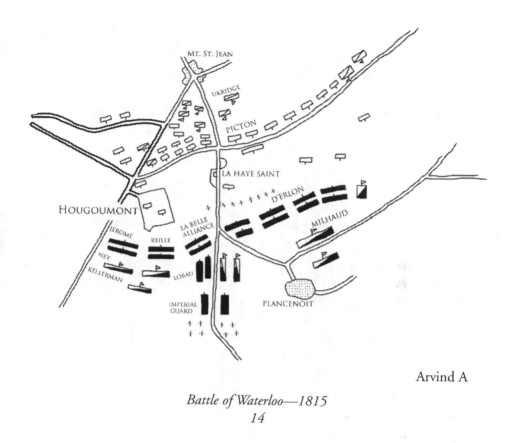

Arvind A

Battle of Waterloo—1815
14

Born in 1769 (like Napoleon), the English commander **Arthur Wellesley** came from noble but impoverished Anglo-Irish stock and had his early education at Eton. Hence the famous quote attributed to him, *"The battle of Waterloo was won on the playing fields of Eton".* After a year at the French Royal Equestrian Academy at Angers (France), where he learned French, good manners and horsemanship, he was commissioned into the British Army in 1793 and saw active service in Flanders. Promoted Colonel in 1796, he was sent to India, his brother, **Richard Lord Wellesley,** being appointed Governor-General in 1797. **Haider Ali** and **Tippu Sultan** of Mysore, had been implacable foes of the British, fighting them in three full-scale wars. On the outbreak of the 4th Anglo-Mysore War (1798), British strategy called for several armies to converge simultaneously on Tippu's capital Srirangapatnam—the Nizam's forces, the Marathas, the Bombay contingent and the Madras contingent. Col. Arthur Wellesley was with the last, which was led by Gen.Harris.

Tippu, no mean general, contested every inch of his territory. Arthur Wellesley distinguished himself in a sharp encounter at Mallavally, east of Srirangapatnam, before the Sultan was finally cornered in his island-city in the Cauvery. After breaching the north-west part of the wall with concentrated cannon-fire, a fierce assault was made, with the Argyll Highlanders wading through the Cauvery River, which was at its pre-monsoon low. Tippu personally led the desperate defense of the breach, but a watergate (½ a kilometer to the east of the breach), was opened by traitors and the defenders of the breach were taken by surprise from the rear. Tippu died fighting as the city fell on 4th May, 1799. War trophies from Tippu's palace are displayed in the museum of the Argyll Highlanders in Stirling Castle, Scotland. Wellesley, wounded in the fighting, was appointed Governor of Mysore for his contribution to the victory. The **Wadiyars** were reinstated as kings of Mysore and Tippu's sons were held in Vellore Fort, where there was later to be an abortive revolt by the sepoys in 1806, in their favour.

As Governor, Col.Wellesley chased and killed the notorious bandit, **Doondiah Wagh** and brought peace to Mysore. Promoted Major-General in 1802, he led a 24,000 strong army in the 2nd Anglo-Maratha war the following year, winning crucial battles at **Assaye** and **Argaon**. The victory at **Assaye** was brilliantly crafted, with a risky oblique order of battle, much like Frederick's at **Leuthen** in 1757, against the Austrians.

Returning to England, he was made Chief Secretary for Ireland. In 1808, he succeeded **Sir John Moore** in the Iberian peninsula after Moore's death at *Corunna*. He set about grooming a team of generals—Beresford, Pakenham, Rowland Hill (later Postmaster-General)—and thrashed the French Marshals **Nicolas Soult** and **Auguste Marmont** at Porto, Talavera and Albuera. With inferior forces, he then held the defensive lines of Torres Vedras in Portugal and captured Ciudad Rodrigo and Badajoz. Entering Spain, he comprehensively defeated the French, under Marmont, at Salamanca, for which he was promoted full General and made Earl of Wellington. In 1813, with Napoleon forced on the defensive after his Russian debacle, Wellington crossed the Pyrenees and invaded France, as part of the overall Allied strategy. On Napoleon's abdication in 1814, he was made Ambassador to France. When the Emperor returned in triumph from Elba in March 1815, he (now Duke of Wellington), assumed command of the combined British, Dutch and Belgian forces (80,000 infantry, 14,000 cavalry, 196 guns), around

Brussels. To his east was Blucher, with 105,000 foot, 12,000 horse and 296 cannon. Both armies were dispersed in loose corps and would take some days to concentrate and hence would be caught napping, if everything went as per Napoleon's plans.

After arrangement of his available forces near the Belgian border, to lull the suspicions of his enemies, Napoleon delayed his own departure from Paris till 12th June. Napoleon's soldiers were the greatest marchers in history—Marshal Bernadotte's men once covered 85 miles in 60 hours— and by the 15[th,] the bulk of Napoleon's army was at Charleroi across the border in Belgium, ready to strike at either Wellington (north-west at Quatre Bras, 25 miles south of Brussels) or Blucher (north-east at Ligny). Ney, with Reille's corps, was to engage the duke. Grouchy (Vandamme's 3rd and Gerard's 4th corps) on the right, supported by Drouet d'Erlon's 1st corps, was to annihilate Blucher's Prussians, and drive their remnants eastwards to **Gembloux**, back along their line of supply.

Both attacks were launched on the 16th, but Ney countermanded Napoleon's written orders and pulled back **D'Erlon's corps** from **Grouchy's** force, depriving the right wing of the crushing victory envisaged by Napoleon. After Vandamme was pushed back, the Imperial Guard made a spectacular bayonet charge to sweep the Prussians out of Ligny. Old Blucher, leading the Prussian cavalry to repel this attack, had his horse shot under him. Bruised from the fall and narrowly escaping capture, the old fieldmarshal was dragged to safety. The shattered Prussians managed a strategic withdrawal, not east towards their base, as per orthodox military theory, but north to **Wavre**, contrary to the advice of Blucher's Chief of Staff, General Gneisenau. Blucher's move (inspired by gin, rhubarb and garlic), enabled him to maintain contact with the Duke, whose forces were pushed north by Ney, from **Quatre Bras,** along the Brussels Road, to Waterloo. Ney was uncharacteristically overcautious and missed his own chance of a decisive win over the British, who thus managed to effect a strategic withdrawal northward to Mont Saint Jean, near Waterloo.

The headstrong French marshal was ideally suited for the intended role of smashing the opposing force, but at **Quatre Bras** he (and Reille) were unduly wary of the Wellington's penchant for setting defensive traps, which had repeatedly foiled French marshals in Spain. They were also slowed down in their pursuit by a heavy thunderstorm. Wellington who was at a ball in Brussels on 15th night when he was informed of the French advance across the border, remarked, "*Napoleon humbugged me,* *by God! He has gained 24 hours on me."* Expecting a flanking attack on Brussels, he had posted a mixed cavalry-infantry force at Nivelles, west of Quatre Bras, the latter being lightly held. Napoleon's failure to win decisively with either the right wing as planned (**Grouchy vs. Blucher** at **Ligny**) or the left (**Ney vs. Wellington** at **Quatre Bras**) was primarily because D'Erlon's corps could not effectively assist either wing. As a result of Ney countermanding Napoleon's original orders, the corps wasted valuable time and effort marching between the two wings. Ney reported to Soult at 10 pm: *"I have attacked the English position with the greatest vigour but an error of Count d'Erlon deprived me of a final victory"*. After Ligny, Blucher's forces regrouped at **Wavre** to the north while his would be pursuer, **Grouchy,** blindly stumbled east, towards **Gembloux!** Actually, it was the obtuseness of Ney and Grouchy that deprived Napoleon of decisive victories over the Allied forces at Ligny and Quatre Bras, followed by a final killer blow at Waterloo. Gen. Fuller remarks—*"For a man of Grouchy's limited intelligence, all that was required was a simple instruction, '**Prevent the Prussians marching to Welligton's assistance**'With such generals as Ney and Grouchy, Michael and all his angels would have definitely lost the campaign!"*.

Blucher contacted the duke (the master of topography), who had now taken up a strong position, further north on the Brussels road near the hamlet of Mont St. Jean, just south of Waterloo. In typical Wellington style, his soldiers were ordered to lie down on the reverse side of a ridge to protect them from the master-gunner Napoleon's expected initial cannonade.

He carefully distributed his experienced English divisions to stiffen the Belgian-Dutch forces. He also sent a 17,000 strong force to Hal, 10 miles west, another typical safety first move to prevent a flanking move by Napoleon on Brussels. But this overcautious positioning condemned the force to remain unused, in the critical battle the next day. On his uncovered eastern flank, he anticipated Prussian support to come up soon. The two armies were roughly equal in numbers (70,000 each) The French were slightly superior in cavalry and artillery, but had to force a quick victory, before the Prussians arrived to support the duke. Wellington's Army was a heterogeneous force, with a core of disciplined British veterans whom he had led in Spain, whereas Napoleon's force was solidly French, inspired by lofty ideals of *le patrie'* and motivated by intense personal loyalty to their beloved Emperor. Though the Duke apparently lacked the common touch, he was a very competent general and a no-nonsense leader, with varied experience and an unbroken string of victories. As at Zama (202 BC), where Scipio outwitted Hannibal to decide the future course of history, at Waterloo also, the lesser genius overcame the greater, fighting the very last of his great battles.

On the morning of 18th June, Napoleon with 72,000 men faced Wellington with 68,000 soldiers. Napoleon's overall plan was straight forward—let loose a massive artillery barrage on Wellington's forces and follow this up with a powerful cavalry charge and a final overwhelming push by the elite *Imperial Guard*, all before the Prussians came up on the left of the Duke, which Blucher had promised by mid-day. But the cannonade, scheduled to commence at 9 am, had to be postponed because of a heavy downpour. Napoleon, the supreme artillerist, needed dry ground to maneuver his guns into position and also to enhance the ricochet effect of the cannon balls which were then the most effective battle-field weapon, since the range of the musket was below 300 yards. The cannonade which commenced at 1 pm (with a 80 gun battery placed to the east of La Belle Alliance) could not be entrusted with the artillery expert **Drouot,** as he was chosen for the crucial role of leading the *Imperial Guard* in the absence of Marshal Mortier. Since there were no howitzers in the battery, the artillery barrage was ineffective against the enemy lying on the other side of the ridge. Napoleon meanwhile deployed his soldiers in battle array under Marshal Ney, while he himself oversaw the operations from **La Belle Alliance**, close by. But the tactical conduct of the battle was by Ney, whose head proved inferior to his heart on this occasion. **Reille's 2nd corps** was on the left with **Count d'Erlon's 1st corps** on the right and **Lobau's 6th corps** held in reserve, along with the *Imperial Guard*. On either side were the cavalry units under **Kellerman** and **Milhaud.**

To aggravate Wellington's worry about a threat to his right flank, 4 regiments of brother Jerome Bonaparte's division (from Reille's corps) were ordered to attack the chateau of **Hougoumont,** which was held by the British. Unfortunately, this intended diversionary tactic pulled in more and more French troops, to the detriment of the impending main attack on the ridge of **Mont St. Jean.** By the time the French cannonade commenced (1 pm), ominous movement of Prussian (Bulow's) soldiers was already seen in the woods to the northeast, on the heights around Chapelle St. Lambert. As a precautionary measure against a Prussian move against his right rear, Napoleon pulled back Lobau's reserve corps to Plancenoit.

At Waterloo, poor infantry-cavalry co-ordination ruined Napoleon's plans, but he adhered to his usual logical pattern of attack:

1) The initial barrage kept the enemy infantry fixed in *line* (the least vulnerable formation), while the French infantry advanced rapidly in *column*.
2) The French cavary charged in, forcing the enemy to form *squares* to resist them while the French infantry quickly formed *lines* to bring more firepower to bear on the enemy *squares*.
3) With the enemy in confusion, a bayonet charge scattered them.
4) The cavalry then annihilated the fugitives.

The main French assault in *columns* by **d'Erlon's** corps, was launched in the centre, around the farmhouse of **La Haye Sainte** and up the slope of Mont St. Jean, after the initial French cannonade. Arriving at the top of the ridge in massed confusion, it was repulsed by **Picton's** infantry (*in line*), which delivered a crashing volley at 40 paces. But Picton himself was killed. A charge by Kellerman's cuirassiers was met by a fierce countercharge by Lord Uxbridge's heavy cavalry which brushed aside the French horse, who were winded after the run uphill. D'Erlon's 4 infantry divisions had been so badly mauled that they could not even form *squares* to resist charges by horsemen of the Scots Greys, and 3000 were taken prisoner. But drunk with success, the Scots went on to charge the French batteries near La Belle Alliance and were well nigh annihilated.

At 1530, **Marshal Michel Ney**, "the bravest of the brave", led an attack on La Haye Sainte, followed by a charge by Milhaud's 5000 horse in the 1000 yard gap between it and Hougomont. Confined in this narrow space, they were blasted by the British batteries, but bravely pushed on past the guns to get at the English infantry, who quickly formed *squares* to resist the horsemen. Unfortunately, the French cavalry did not carry spikes and hammers to incapacitate the captured English cannon, or horses to drag them away. The guns became operational again after the horsemen retreated. Repeated French charges failed and Napoleon noted with growing concern the menacing push of **Bulow's** Prussians in his right rear. In desperation, he ordered another effort (of 10,000 cavalry) in support of Ney. Eight abortive charges were led by "Redhead" Ney, who had 4 horses killed under him. But the British infantry *squares* held firm, baffling the attempts of the French cavalry. The duke, with time on his side, retained his composure. Ney's use of infantry from Reille's corps also failed. Realising the tactical importance of **La Haye Sainte,** Napoleon now ordered Ney to take it at any cost, which was promptly done.

Desperate measures were needed. At 7 pm after sending the *Young Guard* to deal with the Prussians coming up in his rear, Napoleon personally took his *Imperial (Old and Middle) Guard* past La Belle Alliance and handed it over to Ney, who led it uphill in a final do-or-die assault. Ney moved diagonally, between Hougoumont and La Hay Sainte towards the enemy's right centre. The British cannon (loaded with grape and canister) opened up but the elite Grenadiers of the Guard came on undeterred, in two solid columns. Had they been supported by cavalry, the British infantry would have been forced to form squares and the attack might have succeeded. The British infantry (in line) now opened fire at close range and the Guard ranks were rent apart. Despite Ney's desperate efforts to rally them, the final British bayonet charge, swept the Guard downhill where they rallied briefly but soon broke up, when charged again. The impossible had happened—the Imperial Guard had been routed!

Intuitively sensing the decisive moment, Wellington, standing on the prominent mound beside the Brussels road, waved his hat and the Allied army surged forward. The Imperial Army disintegrated to cries of '*La gard recule. Sauve qui peut*'. The Young Guard, however, managed to hold back the Prussians at Plancenoit, while 3 squares of the Old Guard checked the British pursuit and escorted the Emperor safely across the border, into France. The casualties at Ligny, Quatre Bras and Waterloo (between 16th and 18th June) totaled over 100,000 of which at least 60,000 were French.

As the duke observed laconically *"It was a damned close thing"* Though he might still have been able to raise another army, Napoleon knew that he had shot his bolt politically and abdicated in favour of his little son, the King of Rome. But only a handful of Peers supported brother Lucien Bonaparte's motion to proclaim the boy, Emperor Napoleon II Desirous of avoiding a disastrous civil war Napoleon turned down Lucien's advise to disperse the Peers and carry on the war. The 2nd Treaty of Paris pushedthe boundaries of Prussia westward. England gained Malta, Mauritius and Ceylon, but more importantly, she became mistress of the seas, enforcing the *Pax Britannica* globally for a hundred years.

Predictably wary of the emperor, the Allies exiled him to the inaccessible isle of **St.Helena** in the middle of the Atlantic, where he was humiliated and ill-treated by the Governor, **Sir Hudson Lowe.** His empress, Marie-Louise, abandoned him and his only son was brought up as an Austrian prince (Duke of Reichstadt) and died young. After 6 years of cruel exile on the desolate isle, Napoleon died on 5th May 1821, probably poisoned. He was buried unceremoniously in an unmarked tomb on the island. **Nehru** observes, *"In the days of his greatness he was too much of a man of action to be a philosopher."* Marshal Michel Ney, *the bravest of brave,* was executed by a firing squad and is buried, like many other notables, at the Pierre La Chaise Cemetery, Paris.

But the Napoleonic legend grew across the world, with literary works, music and art eulogizing his multifaced achievements. His body was brought back to France and buried with full Imperial honours in the **Invalides.** His magnificent tomb, the **Arc de Triomphe** on the Champs Elysee, the bridges across the Seine commemorating his great victories and the manor of Malmaison are today among the main attractions in Paris, but his memory is undoubtedly his greatest legacy. He is bracketed with Alexander and Hannibal in a super-class of Great Commanders. **Victor Hugo** (whose father was a general of Napoleon) devotes 19 chapters of *Les Miserables* to the battle of Waterloo! The Emperor's nephew later revived the dynasty as **Napoleon III,** but was routed at Sedan by Bismarck's Prussians (commanded by Field Marshal von Moltke) in 1870 and was forced to abdicate, setting the stage for a further round of animosity between the two great Continental powers, ultimately leading to the two World Wars of the 20th century.

18

FALL OF DELHI (1857)—
JOHN NICHOLSON

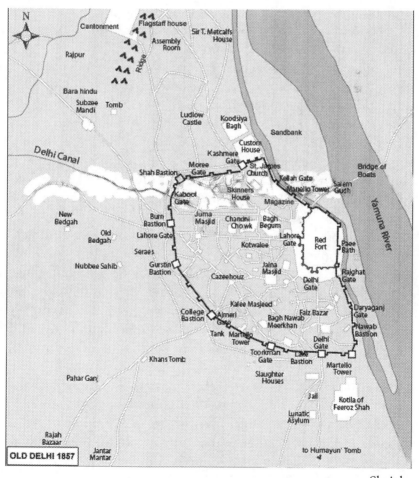

Shajahan

Delhi—1857
15

Early in 1857, the centenary year of Clive's victory over Nawab Siraj Ud Aula of Bengal, there was a subtle but perceptible movement across north India. **Dr. Gilbert Hadow** wrote to his sister in England *"the Indian papers are full of surmises . . . it is called the Chuppaty Movement"*. Chuppaties, sent to Hindu and Muslim villages alike, prove the existence of a clandestine channel of communication, certainly better than tthe Sirkar, which remained totally inactive and unresponsive during this period.

The planners of the Uprising, however, did not reckon on the sudden end of the Crimean War (1853-56), relieving the British army of its major preoccupation against Russia and fully freeing it for duty in India. The focal point of the Rising, was the sepoy army but it encompassed all classes of society—Hindu and Muslim alike.

The sepoy units of Bengal, Madras and Bombay totaling nearly 300,000, led by British officers, outnumbered the regular British units ten to one. The sepoys were specially selected from the warrior classes and Brahmin *Purabis* and were physically better built and more intelligent than their white officers. Moreover, the royal families of the sub-continent were irked by Dalhousie's Doctrine of Lapse which dispossessed the ruling families of **Jhansi, Satara** and **Nagpur** for want of a direct male heir. **Oudh** was also taken over, ostensibly because of misgovernment by Nawab Wajid Ali Shah. Though Dalhousie was replaced as Governor-General by the more sensitive (and sensible) Lord Canning, unhappiness still remained.

The South, though, remained indifferent to nationalist feeling. The abortive **Vellore mutiny** (1806) failed to restore Tippu's heirs and isolated uprisings in Kittur (**Rani Chennamma**), Sawantwadi, Kolhapur, Bijapur, Wayanad (**Pazhassi Raja**-1805), Travancore (**Velu Thampi**—1809) and Tirunelvelly (**Veerapandia Kattabomman**—1798) had been brutally put down. To make matters worse for the Uprising, the Sikhs and Gurkhas continued to loyally serve their English masters, the former having just lost the Anglo-Sikh war. In his perceptive D.D Kosambi Lecture (2007), **Sabyasachi Bhattacharya** ponders over the seminal roots of the rebellion. Was it feudal, religious, civilisational or anti-Christian? It probably meant different things to different people, he concluded, but it was indeed a passionate protest against the relentless penetration of the west and its alien culture.

The immediate spark was the introduction of cartridges greased with pork and cow fat for the new **Enfield rifles.** These had to be bitten off, which affected the religious and caste affinities of the sepoys. The disturbances commenced on 29th March in Barrackpore (Bengal) where a 27-year old sepoy **Mangal Pande**, shot 3 British officers and was tried and hanged. On **Sunday, 10th May 1857,** in a premature move, the sepoys at **Meerut**, killed their officers and dashed to Delhi, 40 miles away.

Delhi was still the symbol of empire, though the empire of the king of Delhi had shrunk to Shajahanabad (old Delhi) and its immediate environs. Nevertheless, **Bahadur Shah II**, a pensioned puppet closely watched by a British Resident (Simon Fraser), still had iconic status in the eyes of most Indians. A poet of distinction (with the nom-de-plume *"Zafar"*), he presided over a chaotic palace (the Red Fort) filled with over 2000 princes and princesses, he personally having sired 16 and 31 respectively, through various wives and concubines. Son of a Sufi, Akbar Shah, through a Rajput lady, he customarily visited temples, ate no beef and was very sensitive to the beliefs and customs of his Hindu subjects.

The ancient city itself was vibrant with art and life, with Shia music and poetry filling it in the great tradition of 14th century romancer **Amir Khusrao,** disciple of **Nizamudin Aulia. Zauq** and **Mirza Asadullah Khan** *"Ghalib"* competed fiercely for the position of leading poet, applauded by a knowledgeable, though thoroughly decadent populace. The following lines, from Ghalib, consoling a friend for the loss of his mistress, typify the hedonistic spirit of the times.

"Take a new woman each returning spring
For last year's almanac is a useless thing"

Zauq was rated on a par with the peerless Ghalib and their rival poems were bandied aloud on the lively streets of Shajahanabad, reverberating in the gullies, havelis and kebab shops around Chandni Chowk and the Jumma Masjid.

Eighty two year old Bahadur Shah was under the influence of his youngest wife **Zeenat Mahal,** who would stop at nothing to see her 16 year old son **Jawan Bhakt** anointed official heir. Since he had no claim by way of primogeniture, the British refused to acquiesce, leading to mutual recrimination and distrust. William Dalrymple's highly readable *'The Last Moghul'* paints a vivid picture of the city and its last king.

The Meerut sepoys perceived Delhi and Bahadur Shah as the vital keys for uniting Indians against the British. This 19th century descendent of medieval raiders, was quintessentially Indian and a valuable symbol of the pan-Indian empire of the great Moghuls, albeit powerless by himself. The East India company had its headquarters in Calcutta, but the seventh city of Delhi (Shajahanabad), the latest in the line of capitals after Prithviraj Chauhan's defeat by Mohamed of Ghor (Tarain,1192) and built successively by the Slave Kings, Khiljis, Tughlaks, Sayyids, Lodis and Moghuls was the last living symbol of ancient Imperial India.

The rebel *sowars* (cavalry) from Meerut dashed to Delhi crossing the bridge of boats across the Yamuna early on the 11th of May and halted on the sand-banks below the eastern wall of the Red Fort, where the emperor and Capt. Douglas of the palace guard shouted to them to go away.

Going south along the sand bank to Rajghat Gate they entered the Daryaganj area within the city, which they looted. The sowars were soon followed by a large body of sepoy infantry. **Lt. Willoughby,** in charge of the city magazine, barricaded it, seeing them crossing the Yamuna. When attacked in overwhelming force by *Jihadis* and sepoys, he blew up the largest arsenal of guns and ammunition in India. This action considerably reduced the sepoys' capability to resist the British siege which was soon to come and won Willoughby the first Victoria Cross of the war. Disregarding protocol, the sepoys stormed into the inner rooms of the Red Fort and into the very presence of the Emperor, to the great indignation of the courtiers. Killing a number of Englishmen, including Capt. Douglas, they declared their allegiance to the Great Moghul and boldly demanded supplies and money. Reluctantly, he gave them his blessings, which satisfied them for the moment. They then spread out, taking control of the city, with some random looting and killing. The surviving Englishmen (some with their families) exited the old city through the north-facing Kashmir gate towards Metcalfe house and Flagstaff house on the Ridge and on to Karnal and Ambala, where they came under the protection of the strong English force there.

In Lahore, the chief commissioner, **Sir John Lawrence,** was bold and decisive, as was Brig **John Nicholson** at Peshawar. On telegraphically getting tidings of the happenings at Meerut and Delhi, they took effective steps to prevent disaffection among their own sepoys. **Lt. William Hodson** was dispatched south with his irregular Sikh horse to establish contact with the British regiments in Meerut. Hodson sent the maulvi **Rajab Ali**, into Delhi as a spy and quickly built an espionage network in the city itself, with access to the Prime Minister Hakim Ahsamullah Khan, Zeenat Mahal and to the Emperor himself!

Within the city, it was difficult to spot any authority save that of the emperor himself, which was itself rather nebulous. Only one of his sons, the 29 year old **Mirza Moghul,** had any kind of ability—military or administrative. Hence he was nominated Commander-in-Chief, while other princes were given nominal command of various units. Zeenat Mahal, apprehensive of the victorious return of the British, kept her teenage son Jawan Bhakt away from the action. The majority of the Purabi (eastern) sepoys who had come from Meerut were Hindus and together with large numbers of Muslim Jehadis and Mewati tribesmen, the Delhi Uprising could be considered a truly secular movement.

A force was organized by Mirza Moghul to try and take Meerut, since he was unaware that Gen. Wilson was already moving from there towards Delhi, in concert with Gen. Bernard's southward thrust from Ambala. The two British forces combined at the **Hindon** river on 30th May and attacked the advancing sepoys who initially fought fiercely but suddenly turned tail and fled back to Delhi across the Yamuna. Mirza Moghul, unperturbed, set about preparing the defenses of Delhi for an attack from the north, repairing old walls and placing cannon strategically in advanced batteries on the Ridge across the Grand Trunk Road. However, when the British attacked in force on 8th June, these batteries were abandoned after a brief defense. A sepoy counterattack was beaten back by the Gurkhas at Badli-ki-serai and the rebels rushed back into the city through the north-facing Kabul and Kashmir gates. The British forces reoccupied their old cantonment on the Ridge (Delhi University) and an intense cannonade from both sides commenced on the 10th June. The Ridge commanded the 3 principal north-facing city gates, but Gen. Barnard's forces were inadequate to force an investment of the entire city or prevent entry of supplies or reinforcements for the rebels.

The British were further reinforced from Ambala, while **Bakt Khan** came into Delhi with 3500 sepoys from Bareilly as well as fakirs from Hissar and 5000 jehadis from the Nawab of Tonk (in Rajasthan). Bakt Khan, an experienced non-commissioned officer related to the Oudh royal family, was appointed Commander-in-Chief on 4th July by Zafar. He planned and executed some successful night attacks on the rear of the British positions on the Ridge and Flagstaff House and Hindu Rao's House which faced the north-western Kabul Gate of the city. But Bakt Khan became a victim of palace intrigue and was dismissed from his command, citing his insufferable arrogance. The artillery barrage continued and 24 pounder cannonballs often hit the Red Fort itself, to the great terror of the inmates. Soon there was severe shortage of food and violent squabbling in the city, often between Hindus and Muslims. The Emperor, truly secular, imposed a ban on cow-slaughter to reduce tensions among his subjects, setting an example by sacrificing a sheep for Eid. But dissensions continued and Zafar in deep melancholy, wrote, *"Clothed in my burial sheet I shall spend my remaining days in the seclusion of some garden"* Gujar mobs roamed the countryside, robbing refugees fleeing the doomed city. The prevailing scenario is lucidly depicted in Surendranath Sen's authoritative *"1857",* which has a forward by Maulana Abul Kalam Azad.

The stalemate continued but with the onset of the monsoons, cholera hit both the armies. The British lost generals Anson and Barnard, apart from Reed, who retired sick. The arrival of **Brigadier John Nicholson** with 1000 British, 3000 Sikhs and 600 Punjabi irregular horsemen on 14th August, caused a sea change in the situation since he became de facto commander, though General Wilson was nominally still in charge. Of gigantic stature, Nicholson towered over the others in all respects and totally dominated the siege activities. He had a visceral hatred towards Indians, displaying extreme cruelty even to his own servants whom he personally thrashed regularly. Ensign Wilberforce observed, *"He did not like Indians, detesting sepoys with a hatred no words can describe".* But he was decisive, proactive and a competent field commander. On 24th August, in a clever ruse, Bakt Khan led his Bareilly soldiers and the Nimach brigade west-wards out of the Lahore and Ajmer Gates, apparently withdrawing towards Jaipur, but with the intention of turning north near Najafgarh to take the British encampment in the rear. Watching through spy-glasses from the Ridge, Nicholson saw through Bakt Khan's subterfuge and himself led a 3000-strong mobile force southwest-wards to take the marching sepoys by surprise, routing them in the marshy fields near Najafgarh.

But capturing the ancient city itself was a different proposition since it was surrounded by an impassable moat and massive walls with 14 huge gates—Nigambodh, Kashmir, Moree, Kabul, Lahore, Ajmer, Turkman, Delhi etc—and sundry bastions. The stalemate was broken on 4th September when a siege-train of elephants reached the Ridge from the Punjab with 30 heavy howitzers, accompanied by sappers and 800 Baluchi horsemen. Four powerful batteries were set up opposite the northern wall and heavy cannonade was directed at the northeast stretch of wall between the Water Bastion and the Kashmir Gate, causing extensive damage and opening breaches. The resourceful prince, **Mirza Moghul,** managed to put up barricades of broken masonry and sandbags to block the openings, but the British guns destroyed them and silenced the Indian guns by 12ᵗʰ September. In preparation for the final assault eight thousand men in 5 columns, under Nicholson's overall command, were given blessings at Flagstaff House at midnight, along with detailed operational instructions.

The assault began at 3 am on the 13ᵗʰ September. The first column, led by Nicholson himself, entered the city through the breach near the Kashmir Gate and gathered in the compound of St.James Church, while Col.Jones' 2ⁿᵈ column to its left, penetrated into the city via the breach near the Water Bastion and joined the first column. Col. Campbell's 3ʳᵈ column crossed the moat and entered through the Kashmir Gate itself, blowing it up with bags of gunpowder, despite coming under heavy fire. After intense hand to hand fighting, they went west along the wall, to open the Kabul Gate for Maj. Reid's 4ᵗʰ column to enter. The 5ᵗʰ column under Brig. Longfield was held in reserve. The assault went according to Nicholson's plan, except in the west where Reid's column was pushed back to Sabzi Mandi by the sepoy counterattack. Nicholson was isolated and mortally wounded while recklessly leading a charge (along what is now, Nicholson Road) towards the Lahore Gate, which was manned by Bakt Khan's Bareilly troops. He was carried in a *dooly* to the Kabul Gate and back to the Ridge, in great pain. But he had achieved his main objective. The Union Jack was hoisted over the Kashmir Gate and the entire northern wall from the Water Bastion in the east to the Kabul Gate in the west was entirely in British hands.

However, further advance into the city was fiercely resisted and without Nicholson, the British forces were indecisively led. Pushing out from the Lahore Gate towards Hindu Rao, Bakt Khan' soldiers threatened to encircle the attackers. At that stage, the nervous Gen. Wilson even considered a complete withdrawal from the city! Indiscipline was rife as the troops got drunk, looted and killed civilians, indiscriminately.

The Skinner Haveli, Lahore Gate, Salimgarh Fort and Jumma Masjid fell only after desperate resistance lasting several days. The gates of the Red Fort were blown open, but the Emperor and the imperial family had already fled to Humayun's Tomb, 5 miles to the south. After he, Zeenat Mahal and Jawan Bakt were brought back on 21ˢᵗ September, Lt. Hodson, with 50 cavalrymen, returned to pick up the other imperial princes—**Mirza Moghul, Khizr Sultan** and **Abu Bakr** (Zafar's grandson). Though surrounded by a hostile crowd, Hodson cruelly butchered the defenseless captives. Shortly afterwards, 21 Mughal princes were hanged as were many others of noble birth like the honorable Nawab of Jajjar and the innocent young Raja of Ballabgarh. Many were exiled to the Andamans. Mirza Ghalib was picked up, questioned and was fortunate to be released as a harmless eccentric. Prize agents entered native havelis and tortured wealthy citizens (Hindu and Muslim alike) to extort hidden treasure!

Despite Sir John Lawrence's best efforts, looting and massacres continued for weeks in the city, led by the sadistic **Theo Metcalfe,** who had lost several close relatives in what the British termed the Great Mutiny. The Governor-General Lord "Clemency" Canning was constrained to protest *"Your bloody, off-hand measures are not the cure for this sort of disease. Don't mistake violence for vigour."* But the conquerors' blood lust cannot be curbed by logic and Delhi was indeed lucky to escape the horrible fate of Carthage or Vijaynagar—general massacre, genocide, vandalism and destruction!

Zafar was tried in the Diwan-I Khas by a military court and sentenced to be transported for life to Rangoon. Zeenat Mahal and Jawan Bakt accompanied him to Rangoon, where the Emperor died in utter destitution on 7th November, 1862 at the age of 87. Ironically, in 1885, **Thi Baw**, the last King of Burma was exiled to India (Ratnagiri), where he too died miserably, as depicted vividly in Amitav Ghosh's *"The Glass Palace."* Emperor **Bahadur Shah,** the last Moghul, was forgotten, but the lyrics of **Zafar**, the poet, survived to be heard by future generations in Mohamed Rafi's mellifluous voice.

"I am the light of nobody's eye,
I am the companion of nobody's soul"

In 2008, **Vice-President Hameed Ansari**, in belated national recognition of the last King of Delhi, visited the burial site in Rangoon, but his grave could not be located amidst the thick grass in the garden of the humble abode where he had lived out his last days.

Elsewhere, the uprisings took different shapes, being small and isolated at Dacca, Chittagong, Jalpaiguri, Indore and Mhow. In Lucknow, the British were besieged in the Residency by sepoys allied to **Begum Hazrat Mahal** of Oudh (which had been annexed in 1856). **Nana Sahib**

(Dondu Pant), adopted son of the last Peshwa of the Marathas, Baji Rao II, was living in exile at Bithur, near Kanpur. With his able henchman **Tantia Topi** (Ramchandra Yevelekar), he organized the local sepoys in an attack on the British in Kanpur, which unwittingly led to the gruesome and totally uncalled for Bibighar massacre of British women and children.

Rani Lakshmibai, widow of Gangadhar Rao, the late ruler of Jhansi, aligned herself with the sepoys and was besieged in Jhansi Fort (21st March,1858) by **Gen. Sir Hugh Rose**, advancing from Sagar. Tantia Topi, who arrived with 20,000 men to relieve Jhansi, was driven off by **Gen. Rose**. In the early hours of 4th April, the British stormed Jhansi, killing over 5000 non-combatents and taking the palace, room by room. The intrepid Rani, in male attire, cut her way out of the burning stables and escaped on her horse Badal with her adopted son, to join Tantia, the Nawab of Banda and Kunwar Singh of Jagdishpur at the strategic **Kalpi Fort**. Marching on Gwalior, they induced Maharaja Jayaji Rao Scindia's soldiers to join them but then had to face the formidable **Sir Hugh Rose** at Kotah-ki-serai near Gwalior on 17th June, 1857. The Rani, holding the reins in her mouth and wielding the sword with both hands, was mortally wounded. Cornet Combe wrote admiringly, *"She is a wonderful woman, very brave and determined."* Tantia along with Rao Saheb (Nana's nephew) fled across the Chambal to Rajputana, bringing to an end the phase of set-piece battles against the British.

Tantia proved himself a talented guerilla leader, leading several British armies in a catch-me-if-you-can chase around what are now the States of Rajasthan, Madhya Pradesh, Uttar Pradesh, Gujarat and Maharashtra. Accompanied by the fugitive Moghul Prince **Feroze Shah,** this elusive pimpernel was successively sighted at Tonk, Jaipur, Bundi, Banswara, Jhalawar, Baroda, Nagpur, Chote Udaipur and Gwalior. A true *karmayogi* in the tradition of the *Bhagwat Gita,* Tantia Tope soldiered on, helped by local sympathizers, despite losing skirmishes regularly.

Finally, betrayed by Man Singh of Narwar, he was captured and hanged at Sipri on 18th April 1859, practically ending the War of Independence, since Hazrat Mahal and Nana Sahib had earlier disappeared into the jungles of Nepal. Manohar Malgaonkar's *The Devil's Wind* gives an account of the Nana's doings. Rao Saheb, too, was betrayed and hanged, while Feroze Shah fled overseas and took refuge in Mecca.

In retrospect, the freedom struggle of 1857 failed because many prominent rulers remained neutral or supported the British, though their people were sympathetic to the national cause. V D Savarkar called it a *"truly national revolt"* and Nehru *"a popular rebellion"*. But historian R C Majumdar opined that it was *"not the first, national, nor a war of independence"*. The **Nizam** of Hyderabad would have brought in his formidable army but for the malignant influence of his Anglophile minister, **Salar Jung I** and the sustained activity of the British Resident Major Cuthbert Davidson. Though the war of Independence was lost, it led to several positive developments for Indians, the most important being the takeover of the administration by the **Crown** from the corrupt and venal **Company** officials. Queen Victoria became Empress of India, with the Governor-General, Lord Canning, being appointed the first **Viceroy of India**.

Mushirul Hasan writes *"Maulana Azad, Minister of Education in Free India and sponsor of an official history of the 1857 Rebellion, referred to the two communities standing shoulder to shoulder to liberate themselves from the British yoke. Probably, he wanted to record the regret that the British swept away the late Mughals' pluralistic and philosophically composite nationalism and to bemoan that the common action by Hindus and Muslims would not be easily accomplished in future."*

For Indians, **1857** was an important symbol representing the genesis of the Freedom Struggle, culminating 90 years later in complete independence.

19

ROBERT LEE, GETTYSBURG (1863)

The details of wars waged in pre-Columbian America are beyond our ken, but several commanders have distinguished themselves in the new continent after 1492. Spanish Conquistadors Hernando **Cortez** and Francisco **Pizarro,** and the great liberators **George Washington, Simon Bolivar** and **San Martin** would figure in any list of outstanding military leaders. But **Robert Lee,** General of the Confederate Army of Virginia, was arguably the greatest ever strategist from the Americas, just as his defeat by Lincoln's Union Army of the Potomac at Gettysburg, was the most decisive battle ever fought on the new Continent.

Before his defeat, Lee had fought and overcome a succession of **Union Generals**—Pope at Bull Run, McClellan at Antietem, Burnside at Fredericksburg and finally, Hooker at Chancellorsville in May 1863, where the South was unlucky to lose its most brilliant tactical leader, **"Stonewall" Jackson** to *"friendly-fire"* at the moment of victory. The hands-on opportunism of Jackson complemented the strategic genius of Lee, whose laissez-faire style of functioning gave ample leeway to his proactive deputy to function independently. Lee said *"I plan and work with all my might to bring the troops to the right place at the right time. With that I have done my duty"*. He was never quite the same commander after the death of the charismatic Jackson, with no other subordinate capable of understanding his grand strategic plans and implementing them at the tactical level!

One more major Confederate victory would have brought inordinate political pressure on **President Lincoln** to agree to split the nation. The North-South political divide was more about economic issues as it was about slavery. The Lancashire mills were dependent on cotton from the Southern states and English opinion was therefore blatantly pro-Confederacy. It was suggested by the Confederate President **Jefferson Davis** that Lee go west with his victorious army to undertake the relief of Vicksburg on the Mississippi, which was in danger of falling to the Union general **U.S Grant.** But Lee with remarkable perspicacity decided to unsettle Lincoln by threatening Washington itself. He readied himself for an invasion of the North, by reorganizing his **70,000**-strong army into 3 corps under the experienced **James Longstreet** (Ist Corps) and 2 newly promoted Lt. Generals—the methodical **Richard Ewell,** who had already lost a leg (IInd Corps), and the pugnacious **A.P. Hill** (IIIrd Corps). Though Lee's army was inferior in numbers and equipment, the rebel soldiers were highly motivated and they (and President Davis), had full faith in Lee's abilities as war leader. Lee, the grand strategist, expected that a quick victory would destroy the Army of the Potomac, relieve pressure on **Vicksburg** in the west and also induce wavering foreign powers to formally recognize the Confederacy.

Yet, at the commencement of hostilities (1861), it would have been difficult to gauge where Lee's loyalties lay. He was the son of **Gen. "Light Horse" Harry Lee,** whose eulogy to George Washington is widely remembered—"*First in War, First in Peace, First in the hearts of his Countrymen,*" and had married the daughter of George Washington's adopted son. Graduating from West Point with perfect scores in infantry, cavalry and artillery studies, he served in the **U.S. Army** for 31 years, distinguishing himself in the Mexican War (1846-48). He had mentored awhole generation of officers, as Superintendent at West Point and had put down the Abolitionist uprising at Harper's Ferry, led by John Brown. By his own account, he had wept "*tears of blood*" when Virginia joined the Secessionist States.

On 18th April 1861, **President Lincoln** offered him command of the US Army of the Potomac, which he turned down. Though he had freed his own slaves, calling slavery "*a moral and political evil*", and believed that individual states had no right to secede from the Union, he had been reared to accept that his first loyalty lay with the State of **Virginia.** He had therefore moved to Richmond, the Confederate capital, to offer his services to President Davis.

On 3rd June 1863, Lee's victorious army, which was South of the Rappahannock River, moved west towards Culpeper and then swung north led by **Ewell's Corps,** with Longstreet's and Hill's following. Crossing the Shenandoah River, Ewell defeated a strong Union force and took Winchester on 15th June. Gen. Hooker marched parallel to the Confederates, cleverly keeping himself between them and the Union capital, Washington. **Lee** sent his 5000 strong cavalry under the dashing **J.E.B. Stuart** to go northeast as a mobile screen. But leaving just 2 brigades for this vital purpose, Stuart inexplicably went off northwards with 3000 horsemen, crossing the Potomac and even passing between Hooker and Washington (which was however too strong to be attacked). For 8 critical days, from 25th June, he was totally out of touch with **Lee,** depriving the latter of his "eyes". While Lee's 3 corps were strung out and marching, he received news that **Lincoln** had suddenly replaced Hooker with **Gen. Meade,** whose 7 corps were now led as follows:

Ist Corps: **Reynolds**	Divisions under Wadsworth, Doubleday (inventor of baseball), Robinson
IInd Corps: **Hancock**	Divisions under Caldwell, Gibbon, Hays
IIIrd Corps: **Sickles**	Divisions under Birney, Humphreys
Vth Corps: **Sykes**	Divisions under Barnes, Ayces, Crawford
VIth Corps: **Sedgewick**	Divisions under Wright, Howe, Newton
XIth Corps: **Howard**	Divisions under Barlow, Steinwehhr, Schuriz
XIIth Corps: **Slocum**	Divisions under Williams, Gravy

Meade was the least glamorous of the Civil War Generals, looking more like *"a learned pundit than a soldier",* according to a contemporary journalist. But indecisiveness was not one of his shortcomings. Instead of continuing with Hooker's plans of a westward strike at Lee's supply line, he moved north to cover Lee's prospective swinging strike at Baltimore and Washington. Against Meade's 7 Corps, Lee had just 3 corps and 275 guns. Lee's distribution divisionally was:

Ist Corps: **Longstreet**	Divisional Commanders McLaws, Pickett, Hood
IInd Corps: **Ewell**	Divisional Commanders Early, Johnson., Rodes
IIIrd Corps: **AP Hill**	Divisional Commanders Anderson, Heth, Pender

Hearing that the Union forces had concentrated at Frederick and were moving north east to Westminster, **Lee** moved to a position west of **Gettysburg,** but had no accurate idea of the enemy's whereabouts, in the absence of Stuart's cavalry. On 30th July, Heth asked permission from **Gen.A.P.Hill** to move into Gettysburg "to obtain some shoes stored there" and unexpectedly ran into 2 brigades of Buford's Union cavalry, who soon got additional support from infantry from Reynold's Corps.

Roads radiated in all directions from **Gettysburg.** Two north—south ridges were located south of the small college town—Seminary Ridge on the west and Cemetery Ridge to its east. The latter had Cemetery Hill on its northern extremity, with Culps Hill east of it; at the southern end of this ridge were the Big and Little Round Tops. West of the Tops was a boulder strewn area known as Devil's Den. Since supremos Lee and Meade were both keen on battle, the rival armies percolating through very many country roads were sucked into the gathering maelstrom.

Wadsworth's division led the Union attack on Heth but the corps commander, Gen.Reynolds, was killed early, as Pender came up in support of Heth, on Hill's orders. Supremos Lee and Meade were both initially unaware of the fighting in the northern sector but they soon sent in Pender's division and Hancock's corps, respectively, to reinforce the rival combatants. By the evening of 1st July, the 4 Union corps of **Hancock, Howard, Reynolds** and **Slocum** were up on the north end of Cemetery Ridge, facing the 2 Confederate corps of **AP Hill** (along Seminary Ridge) and **Ewell** (in front of Gettysburg). The fighting so far, had gone in favour of the Confederates and had Lee's orders to Ewell to attack with **Jubal Early's division** at 5:00 p.m. been promptly carried out, the grey-clad Rebels could have clinched the issue on the 1 st of July. **Longstreet** who had now arrived, suggested a swing attack south around the left of the enemy and on to his rear. But Lee with no idea of Meade's actual dispositions (in the absence of Jeb Stuart's cavalry), demurred. **Ewell** suggested that he would attack **Culp's Hill** on the 2nd, while **Hill** would attack **Cemetery Hill** simultaneously from the West. Unfortunately, **Culp's Hill** was found to be too strongly held by the Union forces. Instead, **Gen. Longstreet** was now ordered to attack the southern end of **Cemetery Ridge** from Seminary Ridge to the west with his 3 divisions., Probably sulking because his suggestion of the previous evening was not accepted by Lee, he was tardy in executing this. In any case, the division led by Pickett was still some 10 miles away. On the Union side, against Gen. Meade's express orders, Sickles now aggressively moved his corps west into the **Peach Orchard** and was badly mauled there by the Rebels under Mc Laws, with Sickles himself, losing a leg in the action. The critical battle area now was the South end of the Cemetery Ridge. **Hood's** division fought its way east through the **Devils Den** and up **Little Round Top** but were ultimately repulsed by strong Union forces ensconced there.

The attacks continued all around on 3rd July. Finally, in a desperate throw of the dice, Lee flung in the fresh division of George Picket (of Longstreet's Corps) against the Union centre, just south of Cemetery

Hill. It was one of the most famous infantry charges in military history, but it was doomed to fail, just like the heroic cavalry charge of the Light Brigade in the Crimean War, a decade before. Pickett's Virginians were augmented by Trimble's and Pettigrew's brigades. The 12000 strong force moved forward at13.25, after a heavy preparatory bombardment by the Confederate gunners, who had placed their guns in concealed positions. But the Union casualties were few as the bluecoats were protected by the slope and crouched behind stone walls. The rebel greys moved due east from Lee's command post towards a clump of umbrella shaped trees on Cemetery Ridge. The dapper **George Pickett**, mounted on his black warhorse, led from the front, his black felt hat upraised on his swordpoint. But as they desended from Seminary Hill, it was into a veritable valley of death.

Though devastated by Union artillery and infantry fire from all along the west slope of Cemetery Ridge, focussed entirely on them, they boldly traversed the valley and went up the **Cemetery Ridge,** crossing a low wall. There they encountered **Hancock's** men who were bolstered by a reserve force of Vermonters. After bitter hand to hand fighting, the gallant Rebels, with a loss of over 9000 men, were finally pushed back, gaining *"nothing but glory"*. The conflict was not renewed on the following day (4th July). Had Lee pulled off a victory through Pickett's charge, it would have been an astounding feat—attacking across an open valley and then uphill against a well-entrenched and numerically superior force. Though Lee blamed himself for setting Pickett an impossible task, he was cheered by the ragged but gallant survivors as they straggled in after their bloody repulse!

Lee began his strategic retreat south, with **Jeb Stuart's** newly-arrived horsemen screening it ably from the Union army. Had Stuart been available during the crucial phase of the battle, Lee would have won the battle, with 3 just corps against Meade's 7 corps. The latter failed to follow up his advantage and was promptly sacked by Lincoln. In this bloody clash, though Lee lost only 20,000 to Meade's 26000 men, the South had shot its bolt and had no means of replacing its loss of manpower.

On the same day, (4th **July**), **Vicksburg** in the west, fell to **Gen. U S Grant** and defeat stared the Confederacy in the face, a fate that was delayed for 2 years by the skilful generalship of **Robert Lee** and the courage, skill and tenacity of the Southerners. They won with vastly inferior forces at Cold Harbour, Wilderness and Deep Bottom. But the superb **Army of Virginia** was never quite the same again. Just as all roads once led to Gettysburg, now all roads led to the **Court-house** at **Appomattox**, where Lee finally surrendered on 9th **April, 1865.** Five days later, **President Lincoln** was assassinated by a crazed actor, John Wilkes Booth, while watching a play, but only after "*the fearful trip was done*" and his great mission accomplished. The **Union** was saved and **Emancipation** was finally accepted throughout the nation.

Respected internationally as a great commander and a true gentleman, **Robert Lee** passed his final days quietly as President of the Washington and Lee College, Virginia. British historian Lord Acton wrote to him "*You were fighting battles for our liberty, our progress and our civilisation*". Petty opponents in the US government however, contrived to legally confiscate his grand mansion and 1100 acres of prime plantation overlooking Washington and converted it into the Arlington War Cemetery.

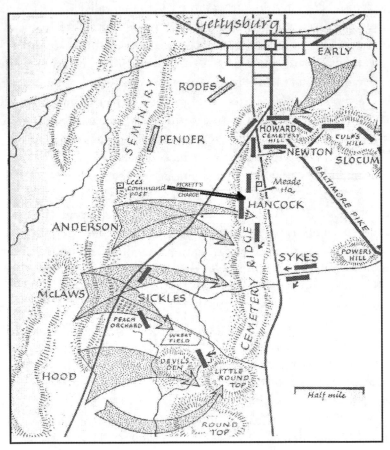

Shajahan

Gettysburg (Battle Plan)—1863
16

President Lincoln's empathy and sense of history were unmatched. There was no hint of triumphalism in his sober, conciliatory and philosophic address delivered on 19th November, 1863 at the inauguration of the Gettysburg Cemetery. Beginning, *"Four score and seven years ago—"* it has been memorized by millions of students all over the world. He then fittingly dedicated the war cemetery to the memory of **all** those who fought there. There is hardly anyone who has not heard the concluding words, *"the government of the people, by the people and for the people shall not perish from this earth!"*

20

WORLD WAR I & STRATEGIC/TACTICAL DEVELOPMENTS BEFORE WWII

Three men, all named Charles, revolutionized the *course of thinking* in the 19th century. While the contributions of Charles Darwin and Karl Marx are widely recognized, less well known to the general public is the equally radical work of **Carl von Clausewitz.** Warfare after **Napoleon** was greatly influenced by Clausewitz' treatise **"On War",** which drew strategic lessons not only from the **Emperor's campaigns** but also went back to the battles of **Frederick the Great.** But Clausewitz, a Prussian general who had fought against Napoleon at Waterloo, was not a simple writer to understand and subsequent theoreticians and practitioners often picked up the wrong lessons from his writings. Clausewitz considered War as an *"extension of policy"* and as a *"province of social life. Therefore the leading outlines of a war are determined by a political body—the Cabinet"* While the battles of the Civil War (Ch.19) were being fought in North America, in Europe, the second half of the 19th century saw the rapid **rise of Prussia** and the long-awaited **unification of Germany**, leading to its inevitable confrontation with **Napoleon III's France.** Gen. Ducrot described the situation," *Nous sommes dans un pot du chambre!"*, after the humiliating defeat of the French at Sedan, in 1870, entailing the **loss** of **Alsace-Lorraine**. It was now not a question of *whether*, but *when*, the next round of hostilities would take place.

A shot fired by a terrorist in **Serajevo** killed the heir to the Austrian throne and set in motion the process leading to **World War I** in **1914**. Although the Germans unveiled the mobile **Schlieffen Plan** which featured a powerful **right swing** through Holland and Belgium, they were soon bogged down in static war in northern France because of the Allies' **defensive tactics** supported by trenches, barbed wire, artillery and well-placed machine-guns—an impenetrable combination. Heavy artillery barrages against such defensive systems were self-defeating as they created muddy death-holes through which no attacking infantry could advance, as at Passchendaele and the Ypres salient. In fact, nothing could move through the swampy waste and attacks floundered even before they reached the barbed wire. And the strategically placed firepower of the defense decimated the hapless attackers, quickly leading to a static war along the entire western front! Elsewhere, in Mespotamia, Palestine, East Africa and Churchill's disastrous Gallipoli venture in Turkey, the conflict was more fluid. On the Eastern front, the Hindenberg-Ludendorf duo crafted a massive Cannae-type victory over the Russians at the Masurian lakes (Tannenberg). One million Indians fought in World War I, of whom over 75,000 laid down their lives for the Empire.

To break the stalemate in the west, English military thinkers harked back 20 centuries to the campaigns of the Carthagenian genius Hannibal to find a solution to crack open these impenetrable defences. He had, in his campaign against Rome, transported elephants across the Pyrenees, the Rhone and the Alps (218 BC), to use them as mobile bastions to bolster his attacking tactics. Though their unpredictable nature sometimes rendered them equally dangerous to friend and foe, they could crash through masses of defenders with ease, when properly handled.

Leonardo Da Vinci, the supreme genius, had made sketches of **tanks**, 400 yearsago, but the only energy source available until the 19th century was animal power, which was not suitable for the purpose of driving heavy armoured vehicles at high speed. The harnessing of steam power and the invention of the IC engine changed that. The experimental use of rudimentary petrol-driven **tracked tanks** by the British in World War I at **Arras** in April 1917, was badly bungled. But in October, because of the enthusiasm of **Gen. J F C Fuller**, a better-planned stealth attack with 470 tanks, at **Cambrai,** was more successful, although full integration with the infantry or the newly-formed air force could still not be effected. **Ludendorff,** the German Chief of Staff, who had previously underplayed the tank threat, now blamed his subordinates for failing to hold their defences. Though the tactical use of tanks in defense was yet to be, a new offensive weapon with a combination of enhanced mobility and firepower, well protected by armour, was born. Overall development was rapid. Use of diesel, instead of petrol, reduced fire hazard; tracks ensured rapid movement irrespective of ground conditions; gyroscopes gave stability to the gunners and sloping armour deflected missiles effectively. The sudden end of World War I, precluded further large scale use of tanks in actual combat but the adversaries had already recognized the potential of the new weapon.

After the war, the British, French, Americans, Russians and even the Japanese, pushed rapidly ahead with R&D, the defeated **Germans** being precluded by the **Treaty of Versailles** from developing or even possessing this radical offensive weapon. Light and heavy tanks of all types were designed and tested—with varying degrees of defensive armament, firepower, speed, maneuverability etc. to suit different situations and terrain—desert, marshy land, hills, snow-covered areas, forests etc. While **Maj. Gen. JFC Fuller** and **Capt. Liddell Hart** enthusiastically promoted the tank doctrine in **England**, **Col. Charles de Gaulle (France)** and **Col. Chaffee** (USA), also pioneered it in their countries. After 1930, **Heinz Guderian** championed tank development for Germany, linking up in Russia's **Kazan Tank School** with the brilliant young **Marshal Tukhachevsky**, who was unfortunately liquidated by a paranoiac Stalin. In 1936, in the **Spanish Civil War,** German (von Thoma) and Russian (Malinovski and Koniev) generals fought on opposite sides, using tanks and air-craft in a dress-rehearsal, learning the valuable lesson that tanks should not be expended piece-meal, but concentrated in bulk to be really effective. In 1938, **Japan** tried out its new tanks against the **Russians** in the East near Vladivostock, but neither side used them as the principal weapon.

In every army, advocates of this new weapon faced stiff opposition from the traditionalists who continued to put their faith in the power of the infantry and horse cavalry, supported by heavy artillery. In pioneering Britain, however, the Tank Corps had come into existence early in WW I. After the war, **Gen. Fuller's** "Plan 1919" outlined a tank offensive in 3 distinct phases—Infiltration, Disintegration (Breakthrough) and Pursuit. Fuller, who believed that a tank's speed was a more important factor than its guns and armour, was technically supported by his superior, Gen. Hugh Elles, and deputy, Capt. Basil Liddell Hart. Unfortunately, even before field trials could take place on Salisbury Plain to prove the claimed superiority of '*a fast runner, albeit with a thin skin*', both Fuller and Liddell Hart were pushed out of the British army by vested interests in the infantry and cavalry. However, the duo continued to wield tremendous worldwide influence on military strategy, advocating the use of armour through their prolific books and articles. Their ideas were analysed and implemented by the rising generation of German tank commanders. During World War II, Liddell Hart was military advisor to

Prime Minister Winston Churchill. Later, as mentor to several military leaders (mainly Israeli), he was given the sobriquet *"the Captain who taught Generals"*. In Germany, the Versailles clauses restricted the over-all strength of the armed forces to 100,000, which resulted in the fortuitous creation of a high-quality standing professional core with the expertise to subsequently train and bolster a much larger army. The limitation on its numbers also forced the German leadership to adopt *defence by mobility,* since the system of lining an endless fixed barrier was no longer feasible. **Heinz Guderian** fought to keep all tanks (successively Mark I, II, III and IV) concentrated in the 3 Panzer divisions which were created in 1935, as detailed in his treatise *"Achtung Panzer"*, after Hitler repudiated the Treaty of Versailles. Pz I had an air-cooled Krupp engine and just 2 machine guns; Pz II had a water-cooled Maybach Mercedes engine with a 20 mm gun. Pz III (Panther) and Pz IV (Tiger) were even bigger, better and more powerful.

Von Thoma, Guderian and **Manstein** were the most gifted and energetic of the young panzer leaders, and their innovative ideas were strongly supported by the **Fuhrer**, who not only had a fresh and open mind on these issues but also wanted to undermine the senior German generals. *"As is usual in war, it was the losing side which learnt most"* as Fuller sagely observed. However, the Germans were initially constrained to practice field manoeuvres with motor cars—they had real tanks only by 1934, after Hitler unilaterally broke the treaty terms. The legendary Panzer leader, **Erwin Rommel** was initially an infantry commander and teacher, with training assignments at the Dresden, Potsdam and Theresian Academies, but he soon started preaching the efficacy of the tanks. Given command of the 7th **Panzer Division ('Ghost Div.')** in May, 1940, his tanks sped on recklessly towards the coast, inviting a dangerous flank attack by the 2 tank battalions of the British Expeditionary Force, which his exposed infantry beat off with 88mm guns. Less familiar with tank tactics, initially, than his compatriots, **Rommel** made up for this with his amazing audacity, intuition and risk-taking ability, invariably leading from the front. His memorable tank duels with Montgomery in the North African Desert are collated in the **"Rommel Papers"**, edited after his tragic death, by Sir Basil Liddell Hart.

The older German generals like Beck and von Fritsch were reluctant to put all eggs in the Panzer basket and hence (as a compromise), the horse cavalry divisions were upgraded to become motorized reconnaissance forces equipped with non-tracked armoured cars. To further placate the traditionalists, the infantry was strengthened with anti-tank guns and 4 infantry divisions were motorized to link up with the Panzer units—altogether a happy arrangement, since Germany based its integrated tank strategy and tactics on the teachings of Liddell Hart and Fuller and De Gaulle's theories (in his path-breaking *"Vers l'Armee de Metier" (The Army of the Future")*. As put in practice by the Germans, blitzkrieg involved lightning manoevre, focus on a *schwerpunkt*, breakthrough, pursuit and destruction of pockets of resistance. Close support by dive bombers was an essential feature, particularly during the early period of the war when the Luftwaffe dominated the air. It is surprising that the Allies had no answer to this, since the Germans only implemented what the pioneers like Fuller and Lidell Hart had been preaching for years!

Blitzkrieg—Integrated Attack

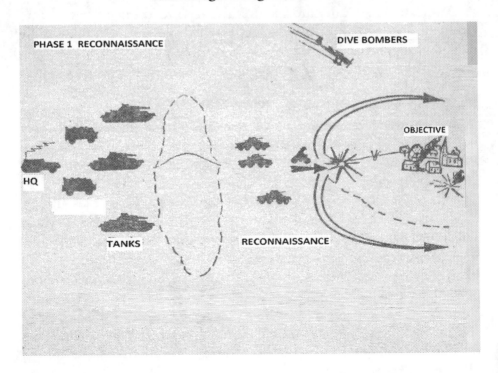

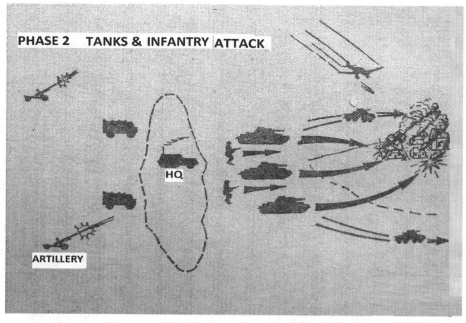

Shajahan

Blitzkreig—1940
17

De Gaulle's aggressive strategic thinking was not palatable to the pacifist French Government (3rd Republic) which gave priority to fortifying the **Maginot Line** (a massive pile of steel-and-concrete forts) along its border with Germany. The totally unprotected Belgian frontier was forgotten! **France** soon lagged behind in the new offensive tactics because of an inbuilt defensive mindset (induced by the massive blood-letting of World War I), quite unlike that of the great French armies of the past. Napoleon's axiomatic *"the side which remains within its fortifications is beaten"* was given a go by. **Paul Reynaud,** who supported De Gaulle, was the only French politician to understand the potential of armour, with all the others rooting for the traditional methods—mass conscription, numbers, static defense, artillery and infantry. But Reynaud became Prime Minister only after the German Blitz was launched on 10th May, 1940, too late to make a difference to the outcome!

The car manufacturer **Renault,** played a leading technical role in tank design and manufacture in France, as did **Vickers** in England and **Mercedes** and **Krupp** in Germany. All nations developed light, medium and heavy tanks in differing proportions, depending on their tactical and strategic perceptions and available industrial infrastructure. The British automobile industry was adapted to producing tracked vehicles but by 1938 was at least a year behind the Germans in tank technology and production. French heavy tanks were slow but powerful in combat,. Unfortunately, they were bogged down in action by the over-all defensive strategy which relegated them to an infantry-support role. The **Russian T-34s**, simple and reliable, suffered very few breakdowns even in the sub-zero conditions in which they fought the German Panthers and Tigers.

After Hitler occupied the Rhineland, annexed Austria and invaded Czechoslovakia, it was clear that his next aggressive move would force Britain and France to declare war. After the hammering that the panzers gave the Allied forces in the Blitzkrieg of May-June 1940, a British Army report recomended.

1) Tank **armour** to be increased to between 40mm and 80mm and to develop a larger 57mm gun.

2) Improved tank **reliability**, since 75% failure was experienced on the battle-field.

3) **Higher road speed** to enable tanks to switch quickly from one front to another.

4) An end to light tanks, which had **insufficient armour** and were also routiely **out-gunned** by the panzers.

5) Armoured units to be **homogenous** and controlled solely by **tank experts.**

Tank development was speeded up by both the Allies and the Axis Powers and the vehicles were tailor-made for different conditions and every conceivable situation—snowy Russian expanses, sandy deserts of North Africa, swamps and marshes, mountain and jungle terrain and amphibious craft of the Pacific. The world was now embarking on what would truly be a world-wide war.

21

WORLD WAR II, PANZER LEADERS: ROMMEL, MANSTEIN, GUDERIAN & THE BLITZKRIEG (1940)

Hitler provocatively sent military forces into the **Rhineland** (1936) and the occupation of **Austria** and **Czecho-Slovakia** followed. France and Britain failed to go to the aid of the Czechs who had a strong army and the second largest armaments industry in the world. He was emboldened (on 1ˢᵗ Sept. 1 939) to strike at **Poland,** annexation of which would strengthen Germany geographically by fully integrating **East Prussia** with the rest of the Germany. **Poland** was extremely vulnerable after the fall of **Czechoslavakia**, sharing 1750 miles of border with Germany and Czechoslovakia and was exposed to German attack from the North, West and South. It also offered extensive plains for a mobile invader, although lacking roads and being interspersed with lakes and forests. The Poles would have done well militarily, to withdraw east to *defensive positions* behind the Vistula and San rivers, but were reluctant to abandon the valuable Silesian coal-fields located close to the border with Germany. The Poles also expected early support from their Western allies, unrealistically, as it turned out.

Their extreme *forward concentration* precluded any chance of fighting a series of delaying actions since their *foot-marching army* could not withdraw fast enough after losing the initial border clashes. Germany's 14 swift armoured, mechanized and semi-mechanized divisions therefore did far more damage than its 40 infantry divisions. A third of the Polish army was caught in a massive 'double envelopment' and the *Luftwaffe* dominated the skies! In the north, Bock's Army Group ((Kuchler's 3ʳᵈ Army and Kluge's 4th) struck east, with Kuchler later swinging south to join Kluge in a pincer movement. In the south, the more powerful Runstedt's Army Group (Blaskowitz' 8ᵗʰ Army, Reichenau's 10ᵗʰ and List's 14ᵗʰ) captured Lodz, Poznan, Cracow and the Carpathians, isolating the Poles and smothering their counter-attacks. On 3ʳᵈ September, France and Britain declared war on Germany but by the 8th, Reichenau's panzers were at the gates of Warsaw, while **Guderian's** armoured corps (of Kuchler's 3rd Army) was already to the rear (east) of **Warsaw**! Though the Poles fought bravely, they were enveloped by multiple German pincers and a belated retreat was ordered into south-eastern Poland. The situation became untenable, on September 17th, when Poland was treacherously attacked from the east by communist Russia whose incongruous (temporary) partnership with fascist Germany was sealed by the partition of unhappy Poland. Thousands of the elite of eastern Poland who opposed the Soviets, were secretly butchered in the remote **Katyn** forest 70 years ago. **President Lech Kaczynski** was on his way to pay tribute to these honoured dead when he was killed in a plane crash. The Germans targeted Jews, clergy, the nobility and the intelligentsia as they tightened their grip on their half of Poland.

The belated **French** effort in the west, after mobilization on the 17th of September, had no impact on the Germans. Only a 90 mile stretch of Germany's western border was accessible, unless the French violated the neutrality of Belgium and Luxembourg; and even this small stretch was protected by mine-fields and the strong defences of the German Siegfried Line. Consequently, Europe entered a 1-year period of *Phoney War,* with the antagonists watching and waiting, while preparing for the inevitable major clash of nations. **Hitler** utilized this interregnum to occupy Denmark and Norway. He did not trust **Stalin** in the east, and hoped that a quick victory over France would make the western front safe, enablimg him to deal conclusively with the Russian bear. There was nothing he feared more, strategically, than a simultaneous war on two fronts as Germany had been confronted with, in the First World War.

In *Blitzkrieg*, **Len Deighton** describes the organizational details of the German army. The Division, headed by a general, was the smallest unit which could fight independently, with infantry, cavalry and artillery combining effectively. Divisional HQ organized transport, maintenance, rations, ammo, medical care, religious services, pay etc and even administered captured territory! A Panzer Division's composition was even more complex and versatile, being mixed right down to its basic constituent units (battle groups). These groups had *"plug-in capability"* and typically consisted of a panzer regiment, a rifle regiment, engineers, signals, and an artillery battalion. The non-Panzer elements had half-track armoured vehicles and reconnaissance motorcycle units reported to divisional headquarters. A typical panzer division comprised @ 3000 vehicles and 14000 men, compared to 17000 men in an infantry division. Movement of a panzer division by rail or road was slow, conspicuous and vulnerable to air attack. Panzers were supported by aircraft (Stork for reconnaissance, Junker transports and Stuka divebombers) and Bofors Anti Aircraft guns. Tanks communicated by visual signals and radio-telephone, allowing commanders to be in the thick of battle. High speeds made concentration easy and tanks advanced in echelon, 60 yards apart, using available cover, avoiding enemy tanks, bypassing and infiltrating, converging in pincers and then diverging to avoid congestion. Air support supplanted artillery as tank groups leap-frogged ahead along parallel roads. Strategy and tactics were supplemented by logistics and administration. Map-reading, terrain knowledge, 2-D graphs of advance against time were among the critical skills that led to victory.

As a recipe for a swift victory in the west, the German General Staff produced practically a copy of the **World War I Schlieffen Plan**, with the main attack through **Belgium** by **Bock's Army Group B in the north**, while **Runsdtedt's Army Group A in the south** would launch a secondary attack through the hilly **Ardennes forests** of south Belgium and Luxembourg. A static situation was planned in the southern-most sector, where the French Maginot Line and the German Siegefried Line were both almost impenetrable.

Runsdtedt's brilliant young Chief of Staff, **Erich von Manstein**, found the repeat plan too obvious and also likely to lead to an early clash with the tough, well-equipped **British forces**. After confirming with **Guderian** (who had trekked in the region) that the **Ardennes** could be penetrated by **panzers**, he suggested **reversing** the roles of the 2 Army Groups—the major attack by **Runsdtedt** in the south and the secondary northern attack with lesser forces to be assigned to **Bock**. He sold the idea to his own chief Rundstedt, and despite strong opposition by the High Command, to **Hitler** himself, in February, 1940. The latter, soon deluded himself that it was his own plan and observed," *Of all the generals I talked to about the new plan in the west, Manstein was the only one who understood me!"*

Because of the antipathy of the senior generals, **Manstein** was relegated to head an infantry unit, far away from the frenetic action to come. He later distinguished himself in Russia, in the great armoured battles against the 30 tonne T-34 tanks, arguably the best in the world. There, he proved himself a master of mobile defense, managing despite heavy odds, to keep the German eastern front from crumbling, but was ignominiously dismissed for undertaking necessary strategic retreats, against Hitler's express orders of "*no retreat, no surrender*".

Heinz Guderian (1888-1954) was a passionate advocate of the mobile tank warfare doctrine preached by Fuller, Liddell Hart and De Gaulle. After WW I, he was part of the 100,000 strong Reichswehr and copied British war games, using "mock-ups" of tanks. Equally fluent in English and French, he wrote the brilliant treatise "*Achtung Panzer*" in 1937 to explain his theories of blitzkrieg, by integrating tanks, infantry, air power and artillery in the operations. His passage of the Ardennes and the Meuse in May 1940, were executed with verve and dash, ensuring that Manstein's novel plan succeeded on the ground. Though he led competently in Russia where he was posted next, he was dismissed in 1941, recalled for duty in 1943 and sacked again in March 1945, following a tremendous row with Hitler. World War I had been the first major war where the senior army commanders of both sides were not within range of hostile fire. But tank warfare changed that, as the commanders were right up in front.

On the day (**10**[th] **May,1940**) that Hitler launched his attack in the west, the farsighted and charismatic **Winston Churchill** appropriately replaced the colourless and ineffective Neville Chamberlain as Prime Minister of Great Britain. On the 13th, **Guderian's panzer corps (Rundstedt's Army Group A)** reached the **Meuse River** at **Sedan**, after dashing through the supposedly impenetrable **Ardennes** forest. He struck at the weak extension of the **Maginot Line** which was also the hinge connecting the **British Expeditionary Force** and the **French Army**. Guderian continued deep penetration with his tanks, despite being repeatedly cautioned by his superiors about the risk of losing his **line of communication**. He was even temporarily removed from his command for disobedience, though later reinstated. His superb execution of **Manstein's** original idea led to results comparable with other disruptive **military innovations**—use of *the horse, the long spear, oblique order in battle, the horse-archer, the phalanx, longbow, cannon, musket, bayonet and organization of the army into divisions.*

Hitler's armies were actually inferior to those opposing them. According to **Liddell Hart**, "*Although his armoured attacks proved decisive, he had fewer and less powerful tanks than his opponents. Only in airpower had he a clear superiority*". The German initiative achieved success on the secondary right flank **(Bock),** on 10th May itself, against key points in neutral Holland and Belgium, spearheaded by **airborne** troops. This diverted Allied attention from the main German thrust (**Rundstedt**) through the **Ardennes** into the heart of France. The Ardennes being a classic example of a *natural hilly barrier backed by a sizeable water barrier* (River Meuse) was not strongly held by the Allies. Marshal Petain of France asserted strongly *"It is impenetrable"*.

The Allies logically expected a repetition of the Schlieffen Plan of WW I and were fooled into thinking that the right flank (northern) attack was the major thrust. In this northern sector, while paratroopers attacked the **Hague** and the communications hub at **Rotterdam**, **Goering's Luftwaffe** created overall confusion. At the same time, 100 miles to the east, **Bock's Army Group B** attacked the **Dutch** frontier. Panzers raced west through the Dutch frontier defences to link up with the 4000 paratroopers led by **Gen. Student,** at Rotterdam. Bock's invasion of **Belgium** (led by Reichenau's 6th Army) was also sensationally successful. The ultra-modern fort of **Eben Emael** and 2 strategic bridges across the Albert Canal were captured by paratroops landing on them (Hitler's brainwave), enabling 2 Panzer divisions to push through rapidly.

Mobile Franco-British forces were quickly brought in from the south to bolster the Belgian defense, but were pulled out and rushed back south on the 13th to meet the armoured threat that suddenly loomed up on the weakest part of the French frontier, just north of the impregnable **Maginot Line**. For the mechanized spearhead, (2 armoured and 1 motorized division), consisting of the **19th panzer corps** led by **Guderian**—part of **Rundstedt's Army Group A (Kliest's Army),** had driven through the wooded but lightly defended hills of the southern Ardennes (South Belgium and Luxembourg) to reach the River Meuse at **Sedan** on 14th May.

To Kliest's right, Hoth's 15th panzer corps and Reinhardt's 41st panzer corps had also driven through the **northern Ardennes** to the Meuse to cross at **Dinant**. A total of **50 divisions**, including **7 panzer divisions** had crowded through the forest, brushing aside some **French Light Cavalry Divisions**, including horsed units. But once they crossed the river, using rafts and improvised bridges, supported by massive German air cover, there was ample room to maneuver. **Guderian's 3 panzer divisions (XIX Panzer Corps)** beat off French counter attacks and dashed west. His cautious superior (Kleist), reluctantly allowed him just 24 hours, to widen the bridgehead. **Reinhardt's 2 panzer divisions (XLI Panzer Corps)** and **Hoth's 2 panzer divisions (XV Panzer**

Corps) joined the sweep into the empty space behind the Allied lines, on towards the English Channel, reaching the Oise at a depth of 50 miles by 16th May. **Guderian** was halted by his cautious High Command, then allowed to carry on "strong reconnaissance", which he interpreted as permission to again race westwards, pulling the whole German army after him! Both the French and German top brass had expected that any assault on the **Meuse** would come only on **Day 9,** whereas by then **(20th June) Guderian** had reached the Channel itself! Only the new French Premier **Paul Reynaud** (a tank enthusiast) foresaw this turn of events, as he immediately replaced the incompetent C-in-C Gen. Gamelin with Weygand, who was flown in from Syria. The Allies invariably did things too late, or did the wrong thing. But as his panzers were poised to take **Dunkirk**, the only available port of escape for the British Expeditionary Force, **Hitler**, unaccountably, held them back for 3 days, enabling the miracle of **Dunkirk**.

    Lord Gort, C-in-C of the BEF, had already pulled it back west from Brussels, but even this withdrawn position was jeopardized by the presence of **Guderian** astride **Gort's line of communication** with the coast. On 21st May, **Gort** made a riposte to the south from **Arras** with his **2 (Matilda) tank battalions** and **2 infantry battalions** to hit **Rommel's** **7th panzer division** in the flank. Since the Rommel's tanks were far advanced, the British had a fair chance against his trailing infantry. But they were scared off by 88mm guns and German Stuka dive bombers, since the French (except **de Gaulle's 4th DCR**) failed to co-operate with Gort's move. Yet, even this little **British counter with armour** had a profound, negative psychological effect on the German High Command, and even on the Fuhrer himself. It is interesting to speculate what would have happened if the **BEF** had been equipped with 2-3 armoured divisions instead of just 2 tank battalions. Fortunately for the British, the increasing pressure from Bock's Army Group B, pushed the BEF in the right direction—towards the coast—instead of south as the French would have them move. The French were already cracking up and despite Churchill's passionate appeal, **King Leopold of Belgium** surrendered on 25th May, deciding to stay on with his defeated people.

    The British retreat became a race to the coast (**Dunkirk**), before the German trap closed, even as frantic preparations were made in **England** to mobilize all types of boats (over 900) to evacuate the **BEF. Operation Dynamo** commenced on 26th June, under Admiral Ramsay, and almost the entire **BEF (245,000)** was saved along with **90,000 Allies**. There is a theory that **Hitler** permitted the escape of the BEF from Dunkirk as a conciliatory gesture to the British, whom he wanted on his side in his future war on communist Russia. Or that he wanted to demonstrate the stand-alone power of the **Luftwaffe,** by keeping the panzers out of the final action, at the behest of air chief **Hermann Goering**. Perhaps Hitler thought he could win cheaply using just airpower, without losing any tanks. In any event, thanks to his bizarre decision, Britain's main forces were evacuated along with some French units and survived to fight another day!

For defending the new French line along the Somme and Aisne, **Weygand** collected **49 divisions**, strangely leaving **17** divisions to hold the already outflanked **Maginot Line**. On 5th June, the Germans brought in **10 panzer** and **130 infantry divisions** in **multiple pincers**, west of the Maginot Line and penetrated deep to the south, despite some French resistance. Rommel crossed the Somme, while Guderian's panzers swept southeast to the Swiss border, trapping the 17 French divisions still manning the Maginot Line. Once the Germans entered **Paris** on 14th June, the war was practically over. The aged hero of WWI, **Marshal Petain** took over as **Premier** from Reynaud. An armistice was signed on **25th June 1940** in the same railway coach in the forest of Compiegne where defeated Germany's envoys had signed the humiliating armistice of 1918! German troops occupied most of France while the puppet **Vichy** government was set up in the southern part of the country.

The Axis powers seemed invincible. Britain was pulverized by wave after wave of Luftwaffe bombers but survived, bruised but not beaten, in what is famously called the **Battle of Britain**. Germany swiftly overran the **Balkans** and **Greece** in a pre-emptive move to protect the oil-fields in **Rumania**. The capture of the island of **Crete** was the result of a massive operation with 15,000 paratroops. Finding the time ripe, Germany then turned on **Russia** with the brilliantly conceived *Operation Barbarossa,* with Manstein and von Rundstedt facing off against Marshals Timoshenko and Zhukov. Hitler also assisted Mussolini to salvage his misadventure in North Africa by sending the dashing Desert Fox **Erwin Rommel** and the **Afrika corps. Rommel's tank** clashes in the desert with **O'Connor, Wavell** and **Montgomery** are the stuff of legend.

Victory there finally went to the British, with their far superior resources of men and material and Rommel's supply lines overextended as he neared Egypt. Not to be outdone, Axis ally **Japan** attacked the **US**

Pacific fleet at **Pearl Harbour** on 7th Dec. 1941 and overran Indo-China, Malaya, Singapore, Burma, Philipines and the Dutch East Indies.

The **Axis** reversal was slow, but steady. With over 100 divisions involved on the eastern front, the war of attrition in **Russia** wore out German resources, despite the outstanding **management of materials**, by Armaments Minister, **Albert Speer** (described in his *"Inside the Third Reich"*). The **Allies** opened new European fronts in **Sicily (Italy)** and in **June, 1944,** in **Normandy (France)**. **Rommel,** who was now put in charge of defending the French coast, had innovatively strengthened the coastal defensive system, with mines, steel hedgehogs and anti-tank ditches though his real forte was mobility, not static defense. Rommel was badly wounded in the initial Allied bombing which preceeded *Operation Overlord*. The Allied landings on **D-Day** and breakthrough from the landing beaches were effected under massive air cover. But it took nearly a year of further hard fighting before Germany succumbed to the Allied pressure on multiple fronts, with Hitler committing suicide as the Russians entered Berlin from the east. The senior surviving German leaders were put on trial at **Nuremburg** as war criminals. Italy's Fascist *Duce* **Benito Mussolini** was lynched by a mob. The story of Japan's (the third Axis power) rapid expansion, desperate resistance and ultimate surrender is recounted in the next chapter.

22

WORLD WAR II, YAMASHITA, SAMURAI WARRIOR—MALAYSIA, SINGAPORE

The active phase of the 2nd World War opened in September 1939 with Germany's blitzkrieg on Poland, with the collaboration of Stalin who swallowed the eastern half of the hapless nation. Hitler, already the master of Austria Czechoslovakia and Sudetanland, aimed at creating a Pan European 1000-year German Reich. After a period of relative quiet, a blitzkrieg was launched on arch-enemy France on 10th May 1940. In a mirror reversal of the Schlieffen Plan of 1914, this time it was the powerful left wing of the Wehrmacht which swung into action, while the right made strong diversionary attacks in the north. Panzer divisions under Gen. Guderian traversed the seemingly impassible Ardennes forests and the Meuse at Sedan to punch into the French army near its junction with the British Expeditionary Force. This led to the collapse of France. Continental Europe was soon almost wholly under German control. But Hitler fell out with Stalin and attacked Russia, meanwhile bolstering Italy's Duce, Benito Mussolini in his reckless North African adventure. The 3rd member of the Axis, Japan, now launched a massive preemptive strike on the US Pacific fleet at the naval base at Pearl Harbour (Hawaii) on 7th December,1941, quickly transforming the conflict into a veritable World War which touched every continent.

As part of its own expansionist policy, **Japan,** which had already occupied much of China, decided to take over British and Dutch colonies in the Far East, as well as the Philippines. The Japanese could move freely through ostensibly neutral Thailand and Vichy-held French Indo-China. Malaya offered huge rewards, producing 40% of the rubber and 60% of the world's tin, both of which were invaluable materials in war. But the truly glittering prize was the island harbour of Singapore (The Gibraltar of the East) which was considered impregnable by military experts. For these formidable tasks, Gen. Tomoyuki Yamashita was given the 25th Army (3 divisions) of 80,000 soldiers, supported by 400 planes, against

160 aircraft available with the RAF. Six engineer regiments were also allotted to Yamashita, to ensure rapid crossing of the numerous rivers of Malaya (Malaysia).

The British in Malaya, under Gen. Dobbie, had planned a pre-emptive strike on the Japanese through Siam (Thailand) but Yamashita's own attack through French Indo-China on 8th December, the day after Pearl Harbour, caught them completely on the wrong foot. Fifty seven year-old **Tomoyuki Yamashita,** who hailed from Kochi in the island of Shikoku, had passed out from the Imperial Japanese Army Academy in 1905, seen active service in China and also served as Japan's Military Attache in Switzerland, Germany and Austria. Despite his excellent track record, he was distrusted by the ruling Tojo faction because he strongly advocated peace with China and the U S. He was however fortunate to have the able **Gen. Susuku Suzuki** as his chief of staff and also the valuable services of **Col. Tsuji**, who had done pioneering work on jungle warfare at the "Taiwan Research Station. Japanese officers belonging to the samurai class had imbibed the Bushido code of 17th century duelist Musashi's classic *"Book of the 5 Rings"* and the essence of Sun Tzu's ancient but unorthodox theories from the *"Art of War"*. The Japanese plan was to move quickly down the west coast of Malaya, using bicycles and 228 Mitsubishi light tanks. Meanwhile, they distracted the enemy with amphibious flank attacks on the east coast, in the most innovative series of battles of the 2nd World War. Yamashita was a true disciple of Sun Tzu "The way of war is a way of deception. When able, feign inability; when deploying troops, appear not to be; when near, appear far; when far, appear near; lure with bait;strike with chaos!"

The Japanese strategy of *indirect engagement* on such a massive scale—launching a powerful blow at an unexpected point, while unsettling the enemy with multiple threats elsewhere—would normally have required the aggressor to have 3:1 superiority, at the very least. But superb leadership, better weapons, innovative tactics, relevant terrain training, superior discipline and fanatic commitment made up for Yamashita's paucity of numbers. He creatively unleashed the ideas propounded in 17th century samurai Miyamoto Musashi's Fire Book, *"create confusion and uncertainty to keep the enemy off balance"*. Audacious attacks were launched along the east coast (Patani, Kotah Baru, Kuantan) to divert attention from the main thrust along the west coast (Jitra, Penang, Selangor). The great British warships HMS *Prince of Wales* and HMS *Repulse* were sunk by *kami kazi* dive-bombers, depriving the retreating

British soldiers of sorely-needed naval support. Soaked by incessant rain and untrained in jungle fighting, the dispirited and hungry British soldiers continually fell back south to fresh defensive positons.

The British made a belated effort to mobilize the anti-Japanese Malayan Chinese as a guerilla force under **Col. John Dalley**, but they were too poorly trained and ill-armed to be effective. This "Dalforce", 4000 strong, played a role later, in the defence of Singapore, patrolling mangrove swamps where Japanese landings could be made. They, still later, formed the nucleus of the 7000 strong Malayan anti-Japanese guerilla army. This, in turn, snowballed into the communist force that fought against the British from 1948-60, finally precipitating independence for Malaysia—such are the ironies, fortunes and ups and downs of world history!

After decisive Japanese victories at Jitra and on the river Slim (8th January1942), **Kuala Lumpur** fell on 11th January 1942. There was then a disorganized British flight southwards, to the supposed safety of the island-fortress of Singapore. With the fall of Johore at the southern extremity of Malaya (31st Jan), only the narrow straits (less than 1000 yards broad) separated Yamashita's men from their ultimate target— Singapore. They had miraculously advanced 500 miles in 8 weeks braving bad weather and hostile terrain, against resistance, albeit of poor quality. Displaying a totally defeatist mindset, the local British commanders contemplated destroying the stores and ammunition in Singapore to prevent their falling into enemy hands. However, the indomitable **Prime Minister Sir Winston Churchill** defiantly ordered, in these dark days of despair, *"the obvious method is to fire the ammunition at the enemy!"*

Yamashita audaciously set up his HQ in the exposed 5-storey palace of the Sultan of Johore, overlooking the partially destroyed **Causeway** to Singapore Island. **General Arthur Perceval** who had only recently taken charge in this theatre of operations, was essentially a staff officer, lacking both combat experience as well as charisma. Not having a clue where the main attack would come, he spread out his British, Australian, Indian and Malay soldiers, 85,000 in all, to protect the entire island (32kms by 16kms). The western defence, including the mouths of the Kranji and Jurang rivers and the **RAF base at Tengah,** was the responsibility of the 8th Australian division. Perceval's best soldiers, the British 18th division, were surprisingly placed on the north-eastern side, with the 17th Indians between them and the Aussies, occupying the naval base. The least endangered southern part of the island, was held by the 12th Indian infantry and Malay battalions. Many of the big guns still faced seaward and had armour-piercing shells (to destroy ships) instead of facing north with high explosive ones, since only a sea attack, from the south or east, had earlier been anticipated.

Gen. Perceval goofed up badly, in anticipating an attack on the north-eastern side of the island. He put his best soldiers, the British, there, since Yamashita bamboozled him by undertaking feint landings on **Pulao Ubin Island** and then shelling **Changi** Fort, in the East, from there. The Japanese effectively numbered only 35,000 in the final stage of the Singapore operation. Gen.Perceval, surprisingly, still harboured a poor opinion of Japanese fighting ability, despite their brilliant performance in Malaya. He felt that they were only suited for jungle fighting, and lacked the organization, equipment and guts to undertake a massive direct assault! The fog of war had totally enveloped the unfortunate general and he had no idea about his enemies' capabilities, intentions or indeed, movements. Yamashita, on the other hand, had studied his enemy and the terrain and had perfected his logistics—*SWOT Analysis* at its best!

Yamashita focused his real assault on the area west of the **Kranji river**, which was defended by the **22nd Australian** division. After a heavy bombardment on 9th February, 15,000 men of the **5th & 18th Japanese** divisions crossed the Johore Straits in 300 craft, led by armoured vessels. The assault was spearheaded by 4,000 battle-hardened veterans of the war in China. Since the straits were only 700 yards broad at this point, Japanese air superiority assured quick success for the assault. Perceval brought in the 44th Indian brigade to try and plug the gaps thus created in his defences, but at sunset on the same day, Yamashita himself boldly crossed over by raft and set up his tent near the Tengah airfield, which the Japanese had just captured. That night, the crack Japanese **Imperial Guards** crossed the repaired Causeway to attack the 27th Australian brigade. Unengaged soldiers from the **British 18th division** were hurriedly brought west, as Perceval reacted predictably to each Japanese move. But even these fresh troops could not check the Japanese momentum as they pushed on south to take the **MacRitchie Reservoir** in the centre of the island, on which the city depended for its water supply.

Yamashita called for the British to surrender on 11th February, but Perceval did not reply and started evacuating valuable personnel—3000 nurses and officers—to Java by sea, in any vessel available. The Japanese artillery placed on the heights then blasted the hapless city, totally destroying the great harbour. Even the pugnacious Churchill realised the hopelessness of the situation. Through Gen.Wavell in India, he finally permitted Perceval to capitulate in order to save the non-combatants from the rigours of a full-scale Japanese assault on the city.

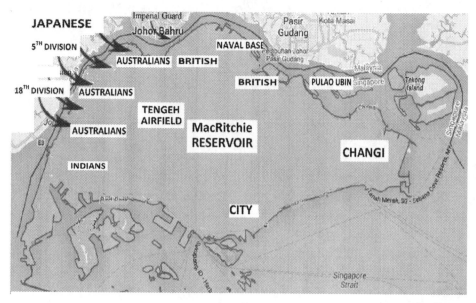

Stalin

Fall of Singapore—1942
18

On 15th February 1942, Gen. Arthur Perceval surrendered unconditionally, going into a long, hard captivity. 90,000 prisoners (half of them British and Australian) were captured. Many of these unfortunates were lodged in the notorious Changi prison camp, the site of the present airport. Thousands more were transported to do slave labour on the military railways being built in Burma—depicted vividly in the Oscar-winning *"The Bridge on the River Kwai"*. Over 20,000 Indian soldiers opted to serve in the INA (Indian National Army) under **Subash Chandra Bose**, and fight alongside the Japanese. The latter lost less than 10,000 killed and wounded in this overwhelming victory which brought Japan to the zenith of her power, with the successive capture of the Dutch East Indies (Indonesia), the Philippines and Burma too, into India. Even Australia was threatened with invasion!

But the seeds of Japan's ultimate defeat were already sprouting—they had unfortunately awakened and set in motion the dormant American giant. But at that juncture (15th February 1942), the loss of Malaya-Singapore was certainly considered an unmitigated catastrophe for the Allies. Even the indomitable Churchill accounted it *"the worst disaster and largest capitulation in British history"*. It is indeed a paradox that the Allied disaster at Dunkirk in May1940 is considered heroic while the Singapore episode is deemed shameful and ignominious! Perhaps the contemptuous Japanese attitude towards those who surrendered (instead of "bravely" committing *seppuku*) has much to do with this general perception.

The victor of Singapore, **Gen.Yamashita,** was shabbily treated by the Japanese Government, being relegated to the back-waters of Manchuria by the inimical Prime Minister **Hideki Tojo.** Tojo, always wary of his victorious generals, similarly sidelined Shojiro Iida (victor of Burma) and Masaharu Homma (conqueror of the Philippines). In 1944 when the situation had turned critical for Japan, Yamashita was sent on a desperate mission to command the 265,000 soldiers in the Philippines. He ably managed a strategic retreat from Manila into the Luzon Mountains, when confronted by overwhelming American forces. Later, after Japan's capitulation, he emerged from the jungle on 2nd Sept 1945 to surrender to US troops, Perceval, his ex-prisoner, making it a point to be present. Unlike most senior officers, Yamashita had eschewed the option of ritual Japanese suicide (*seppuku*), since he did not want his subordinates to shoulder responsibility for any of his actions. Although he was not personally involved, as C-in-C he was accused of abetting the Alexandra Hospital massacre in Singapore and of atrocities committed in Manila by **sailors** who were not even under his command! After a trial which still evokes extreme judicial controversy, he was held guilty of '*command responsibility,*' even though he had publicly apologized and also ordered the immediate execution of the Japanese officers and men actually involved in the war crimes. Although the '*Yamashita Standard,*' under which he was convicted, was deemed to be against the principles of equity even by the great US Supreme Court Justice, **William O Douglas,** Gen. Yamashita was hanged on 23rd February 1946 at the age of 60, at Manila—a tragic fate for a brilliantly innovative warrior and a true samurai.

EPILOGUE

"Defeat into Victory" is the remarkable story of General **Sir William Slim,** who was air lifted in February 1942, all the way from Iraq, to try and stem the surging Japanese tide in Burma. Taking charge of the 17th Indian Division (trained and equipped only for desert war) and the newly recruited (and totally untrained) 1st Burmese, Slim staged a cleverly conducted strategic retreat across the mountains and rivers of Burma, into India. A British diversionary counter-attack in the Akyab peninsula having failed, Slim's forces were pursued all the way north across Burma by determined Japanese troops led by the dashing **Col. Tanahashi** who even improved on Yamashita's Malayan tactics—frontal assaults mixed with flank attacks and road-blocks in the rear. The tide, however finally turned as Slim brilliantly managed the twin battles of Imphal and Kohima in India, while the strong Japanese diversionary thrust westward on strategic Chittagong Port in Bengal was repulsed.

It was now the turn of the Japanese to be pushed south down the Arakan Yoma and east of the Irrawady River, as Slim's British 14th Army with the help of Gen. Vinegar Joe Stillwell's Americans and Chiang Kai-shek's Chinese forces, integrated air power and jungle tactics effectively. Useful in these mountains and dense forests were elephants, 17 tonne Valentine Bridging Tanks and other unconventional and improvised means of transport. **Brig. Orde Wingate** and his British/Gurkha "Chindits" became legendary as jungle fighters par excellence, though Burma, a low priority war theatre for the Allies, had to make do with minimal material support from the newly appointed Supreme Commander, Admiral Lord Louis Mountbatten.

Slim then feinted at Mandalay in the north, while actually striking in strength, deep at the vital transportation hub of Meiktila, where his tough Gurkhas actually out-performed the tenacious Japanese jungle fighters. **Gen. Kimura's** defense of Burma with 3 small Armies (25000 each) was masterly, but he was up against a grand master! While these battles were raging in northern Burma, an eastward sea-borne assault from India (Operation Dracula) resulted in the Japanese surrendering Rangoon itself. Both Kimura and Slim participated in the surrender ceremony at Singapore on 12th Sept. 1945. The former was hanged for alleged war crimes, while the latter went on to become Chief of the Imperial General Staff and Governor-General of Australia, as **Field Marshal Viscount Slim.**

Despite desperately defending every position, Japan eventually lost the entire Pacific to the "island-hopping isolation strategy" of **Douglas MacArthur's** American troops, the final surrender being precipitated by the horrendous nuclear attacks on Hiroshima and Nagasaki in August, 1945. A factor that greatly contributed to the ultimate victory of the Allies was their naval and air superiority in all theatres of the War which prevented adequate logistical support to the Axis war machine, whereas neither the German U-boats nor the Japanese *kamikaze* pilots could effectively curb Allied shipping movements.

It is significant that, despite inferior resources, Germany and Japan not only struck first, but also acted innovatively, setting a scorching pace in all theatres of World War II. Germany's synergized Blitzkrieg of tanks, planes, artillery and infantry stunned its enemies by presenting an assortment of high tech weaponry coupled with appropriate strategy and tactics. This was borrowed from the ideas of 19th century military thinker, **Clausewitz,** as adapted by 20th century "tank" theorists like **Fuller** and **Liddell Hart.** Even after being caught, ultimately, in a war on multiple fronts, Germany was able to keep its enemies at bay through mobile defensive tactics and intelligent counter-attacks.

Japan's methods were radically different but equally appropriate to the conditions obtaining in its own theatres of war, drawing ideas from the oriental masters like Chinese war guru **Sun Tzu** (circa 350 BC) and the 17th century Japanese duelist, **Miyamoto Mushashi.** Many valuable strategic and tactical lessons can be learnt from Japan's conduct of the war, especially the all-out offensive operations with inferior resources during the early stages of the conflict. Even the defensive operations towards the fag end of the war were brilliantly executed and one wonders how much longer the war would have lasted, but for the holocausts at Hiroshima and Nagasaki. The third Axis member, Italy, was largely irrelevant, with its Fascist government (led by showman Benito Mussolini) in shambles and its ill-trained, poorly equipped, badly led and de-motivated troops often providing only cannon fodder on the battlefield.

Two million Indians fought for the British in Burma, Egypt, Ethiopia, Libya, Tunisia and Italy, of whom nearly 50,000 laid down their lives. Over 40,000 joined Bose's INA and fought alongside the Japanese, primarily in Burma. The post-war trial in the Red Fort of Shah Nawaz Khan and other INA leaders (who were defended by Nehru and Congress lawyers) became a huge emotive issue for Indians, as the country was entering the final lap of Freedom Struggle.

23

CONFLICTS AFTER WORLD WAR II

Although nothing approaching the scale of WWII has occurred since 1945, wars continued to be waged, newer weapons were developed and fresh strategies and appropriate tactics evolved in the subsequent years. Fear of a nuclear holocaust ensured that the visceral antipathy between the political systems led by the USA and Soviet Russia did not precipitate a shooting war but remained a Cold War, despite the relentless arms race and intermittent periods of extreme tension and irrational leadership. While NATO and Warsaw Pact forces confronted each other across the Iron Curtain in Western Europe, CENTO and SEATO tie-ups ensured containment of the Soviets in the south and east, a policy formulated by the aggressive and uncompromising Eisenhower-Dulles duo.

When the young President John F Kennedy assumed office in January 1961, Nikita Khruschev decided to counter this global US strategy by arming Fidel Castro's Cuba with nuclear weapons pointing at the soft underbelly of America, in the wake of an abortive invasion by Cuban émigrés supported by the CIA. Eyeball to eyeball confrontation, threats and counter threats followed before the issue was resolved. Similar situations arose worldwide, often instigated by the 2 main protagonists, sometimes leading to proxy shooting wars, but generally without their direct involvement in the actual fighting.

The major wars, post-World War II, can be logically grouped into the **Indo-Pak** Wars, wars in the **Middle East** and those in the **Far East.** One conflict from each category will be examined to understand the art and practice of war, as obtaining in the latter half of the 20th century. In all the three cases—**Moshe Dayan** in the Sinai (1956), **Vo Nguyen Giap** at Dien Bien Phu (1954) and **Manekshaw** in East Pakistan (1971)—the victors achieved all their major objectives, including capture of territory and capitulation of the entire enemy force!

A—VIET NAM

Gen. Giap & The Fall Of Dien Bien Phu (1954)

The uprising in northern Indo-China (1946-54) against the French occupiers was the precursor to the war later successfully waged in the south by the Vietnamese, against the Americans and their local proxies, culminating in the fall of Saigon (1975). The victors were led in both these bitter conflicts by the remarkable **Gen. Vo Nguyen Giap** (1911-2013), called "the general of generals". "The Red Napoleon" was arguably the greatest guerilla commander in history, bleeding his enemies with a thousand cuts. He was ruthless in action and was prepared to suffer heavy casualties to achieve his objectives. Allied with the sharp political skills of **Ho Chi Minh**, the leftist duo formed a powerful combination which successfully endured for over 4 decades of unrelenting war against the colonial powers.

After studying law and political science at Hue and Hanoi, Giap taught in the University of Hanoi while imbibing the essence of the classics in military history, revering Sun Tzu and Napoleon, in particular. It was said that he could sketch the detailed plan of any the latter's numerous battles, from memory! He fled to China in 1939 to escape arrest by the French for his revolutionary activities, but his father, wife and daughter were tortured and killed. Returning to Indo-China in 1944 to resist the Japanese invaders, he joined Ho Chi Minh's Provisional Government in August 1945 as Interior Minister in the new Republic of Viet Nam. After liberation from the Japanese, sporadic fighting against the French turned into a full-scale war in 1946, with the nationalists using weapons supplied by the Allies during WW II. French dissidents led by Jean Paul Sartre, strongly supported the freedom-fighters politically, making the repressive war highly unpopular in the mother country, France.

A succession of eminent French Commanders, including **Jean de Tassigny** and **Raoul Salan**, failed to find a military solution and by 1953, the Viet Minh fighters had over-run vast swathes of territory extending even into the Kingdom of Laos to the West. In desperation, in May 1953, French Premier Rene Mayer, appointed **Gen. Henri Navarre** over-all commander of the French forces in Indo-China, hoping *"to create an honourable political solution"*. This was indeed a formidable task considering Viet Nam's long borders with Communist China in

174

the north, a difficult terrain of tropical forests and steep mountains and a totally alienated and hostile population. Coming out of the trauma of World War II and the horrors of Nazi occupation, the French people were opposed to continued bloodletting in a distant land to prop up puppet **Emperor Bao Dai** and an unpopular regime.

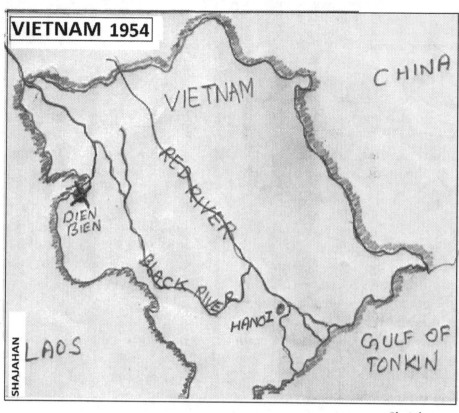

Shajahan

Dien Bien Phu—Location Map—1954
19

The French forces in Viet Nam (150,000 strong) were a heterogeneous mix of French regular troops along with soldiers from Morocco, Algeria, Tunisia, Laos and local ethnic minorities, bolstered by elite French Foreign Legionaries. **General Navarre**, an obstinate cavalryman, saw previous French strategy as *"reactive on a day to day basis"* and wanted to be more proactive and aggressive. His confidant, **Col. Berteuil,** formulated the *"hedgehog"* concept of creating an advanced airhead, based on the successful French experience at Na Sai in December 1952, when they had repeatedly beaten back Giap's attacks, inflicting heavy losses on the Vietnamese. The French Govt. followed a laissez faire policy, failing to monitor or supervise Navarre's bizarre strategic plans. Giap, the consummate guerilla leader, wisely refused to directly confront the French forces, except on his own terms and skirmishes invariably went in favour of the native freedom fighters.

With vastly inferior numbers, the French should have stood on the defensive. Instead of keeping his force intact, the exasperated Navarre went on the offensive in a piece meal manner. With *"Operation Castor"*, he set about establishing an army complex at remote **Dien Bien Phu**, (which had an old Japanese air strip), 200 miles to the west of Hanoi, close to the Laos border. The objective was apparently to prevent rebel infiltration from across the border and also to lure Giap into fighting a conventional battle, albeit under the most adverse conditions for the French!

But the garrison of 5 battalions (11,000 men) was too small to hold the 30 mile perimeter against the 5 divisions (50,000 men) with which **Giap** soon surrounded the camp. Using bicycles, Giap moved in artillery which was then pulled up by hand (24 nos of 105mm howitzers) onto the hills around Dien Bien Phu. This deterred French air attacks and pinned down the garrison, which was holed up in 7 strong points. Fellow cavalryman **Col. De Castries**, whom Navarre in Saigon selected to command the Dien Bien Phu garrison, was totally unsuited, by training, experience and temperament, for such a defensive role. The 7 strong points were reputedly named after de Castries' mistresses and *"Isabelle"*, the southern-most, was dangerously isolated from the rest. Further depleting the overall force (150,000) at his disposal, Gen. Navarre simultaneously initiated *"Operation Atlante"* with 25,000 troops, in South Viet Nam!

Giap's circumvallation tactics at Dien Bien Phu were implemented meticulously, with trenches being dug inwards in a zigzag manner to pin down the garrison, much like Julius Caesar's tactics against **Vercingtorix'** Gauls penned up in Alesia, 2000 years before. Unlike the ancient Gauls who sent strong forces to try and relieve Alesia, with synchronised counter-attacks by the besieged garrison, Navarre made no serious relief effort from outside. De Castries himself remained totally inert in his tent, leaving his subordinates to make the best of a hopeless cause. The desolate situation is described in Bertrand Fall's *Hell is a Very Small Place*.

For delivering the *coup de grace*, Giap shifted his own HQ to Dien Bien Phu in March and commenced mass human wave attacks against the demoralised garrison while Viet Minh guns tore up the runway preventing any further operation of the airfield. **Gen. Gilles** was paradropped to replace the incompetent De Castries, but it was too late. The US was pressured to make a tactical nukestrike, but wisely refused to oblige, despite its implicit belief in the Domino Theory that the fall of Viet Nam would lead to a serial toppling of other governments in the vicinity—Laos, Cambodia, Thailand, Malaya, Burma. But the US did give substantial financial and material assistance to the French to carry on the conflict, even lending 40 pilots to support the air-borne operations. Despite this, the garrison laid down arms on 7th May, 1954, after several strong points fell, ending a siege lasting 209 days, since it was impossible to sustain adequate food and other supplies through air-dropping alone. Creating history, a full battalion of the elite French Foreign Legion surrendered to the enemy! Just 70 of the garrison escaped south, while the 11000 prisoners were marched north to distant camps where many died, despite the best efforts of the Red Cross.

Ho Chi Minh and Giap now controlled **North Viet Nam** and Hanoi, with a uniquely liberal brand of communism which was popular and successful. But they had to wait patiently before taking the **South** (Saigon and the Mekong delta) and unifying the country—a dream they achieved only after 20 years and another bitter war, this time against the Americans. In 1968, Giap's attempt to replicate his 1954 DBP success, failed at Khe San against American troops, but his long-term strategy of attrition eventually paid off in 1975. Giap's strategy and tactics were impeccable, but the defeat at Dien Bien Phu was largely because of Gen. Navarre's confused strategy, aggravated by the the flawed implementation of tactics by the French field commanders.

a) Navarre had no clear objectives for *"Operation Castor"*. Even blocking the Laos route was not a feasible proposition since several alternative routes were available for would-be infiltrators.

b) Why occupy an inaccessible valley, apparently useless, so deep in enemy-controlled territory?

c) Gen. Navarre did get his desired full-scale clash with the elusive enemy, but he and his subordinates had not learnt anything tactically from the earlier French experiences in Indo-China and the innovative Giap always had new surprises ready for him.

d) Cavalry commander **De Castries'** appointment at Dien Bien Phu implies that Navarre expected some sort of mobile conflict whereas actually, the French were soon embroiled in static trench warfare of the World War I type.

e) No overland line of supply was available for the 11,000 French troops trapped at Dien Bien Phu, with total reliance on replenishment by air.

f) In spite of the increasingly parlous situation, no serious effort was ever made by the garrison to break out of the encampment or by Navarre to relieve it.

Giap, on the other hand, had clear objectives, primarily to encircle and neutralise the enemy. He analysed the flaws in **Navarre's** strategy, *"The French have to either extend their strong points and spread themelves thin, laying themselves open to attack. Or reduce the number of strong points, freeing territory for us!"* Giap dictated the time, place and terms of engagement. He neutralized French air power effectively with tactically placed guns on the hills surrounding Dien Bien Phu. Always systematic and patient, he slowly strangled the enemy and launched mass attacks on the demoralized garrison only after 12th March, with overwhelming force and no publicity or forewarning. Symbolically, it was a great victory of East over West! After the defeat of the French and their puppet emperor Bao Dai, it was the turn of the US to try to turn the tide in South Vietnam, albeit at a cost of 50,000 American lives. Viet Nam was finally unified in 1975, with its capital at Hanoi. Saigon, the southern metropolis, was appropriately renamed Ho Chi Minh City. Vietnamese and their erstwhile foes, the Americans are now the best of friends and trading partners.

> *"What war could ravish, commerce could bestow*
> *And he returned a friend, who came a foe"*—Alexander Pope

For India too, Vietnam today is potentially a key ally in the strategy to contain Chinese aggression. Hence, China is over-reacting even to innocuous commercial activity like ONGC's tie-up for oil exploration jointly with Vietnam. Probably China is apprehensive that India too will implement the policy of making the enemy's neighbour (enemy) one's friend!

B—ARAB-ISRAEL WAR (1956)

Moshe Dayan's Sinai Campaign

The post-World War I decision to resettle members of the Jewish diaspora in Palestine has resulted in almost continuous conflict with the Arabs living there, directly causing 5 major wars. But militarily, it is **Gen. Moshe Dayan's** 7-day Sinai campaign in 1956 that is considered truly remarkable for its strategic conception and tactical brilliance.

The son of Ukrainian Jews who settled in Palestine, Dayan joined the underground Jewish Army, '*Haganah*', in 1929 at the age of 14. He then fought alongside British forces under Brig. Orde Wingate, future leader of the Chindits in Burma, to counter Arab raids on Jewish settlements.

Later, fighting alongside the British against the pro-German Vichy French in Syria (1941), he lost his left eye and thenceforward wore his trademark eye patch. In 1948, while fighting the Arabs for the nascent state of Israel, he commanded a mechanized unit in the battles in the Jordan Valley, distinguishing himself in the raids on Lod and Ramleh before taking charge in Jerusalem. He attended the Senior Officers' School in England in 1952 before becoming Israel's Chief of Staff and was considerably influenced by the ideas of Sir Basil Liddell Hart, (*"the Captain who taught Generals"*), who had been a pioneer in advocating tank warfare.

Dayan's 7-day Sinai campaign is an example of textbook strategy formulation followed by impeccable execution and impromptu reaction to ground realities and battlefield variances as and when they occurred. The integrated plan fully took into account Israel's grand strategy and political objectives. He was able to conduct the war as a practical extension of national policy, since many of the Israeli field commanders were members of the *Knesset* and alternatively held top-level civilian posts in the government! Most of them were Ashkenazi Jews of European stock.

In July 1956, Egypt's President Nasser, upset by the West's unwillingness to provide funds for the prestigious Aswan Dam on the Nile, nationalized the Suez Canal and also blocked the entry of Israeli shipping into the Gulf of Aqaba and the Straits of Tiran. Faced with a critical situation, Israel, in concert with Britain and France, resolved to mount a pre-emptive offensive. For Israel, the major objectives were to neutralize the strong Egyptian Army and to capture **Sharm el-Sheikh.** This resort town at the southern tip of the Sinai peninsula, overlooked the entrance to the Gulf of Aqaba which led to the strategic Israeli port of **Eilat.** However, the only serviceable road to the town ran along the west (not east) coast of the Sinai Peninsula, the whole of which would therefore have to be brought under Israeli control to secure the town. Dayan readied 100,000 troops for his *Operation Kadesh,* supported by the dare-devil pilots of the Israeli Air Force. Ironically, the original Kadesh Operation featured an attack by the Egytian Pharoah Ramesses II on Palestine in 1274 BC!

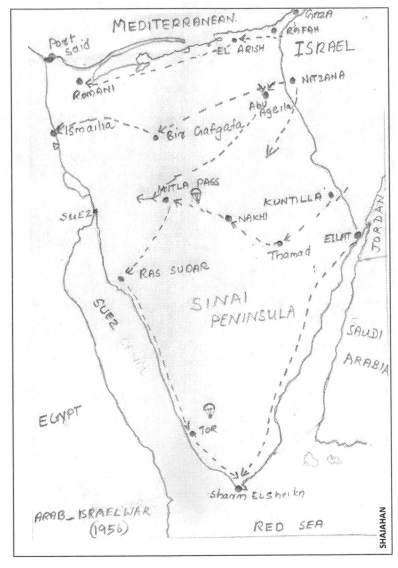

Sinai Map—1956
20

Imaginative improvisation was the hallmark of the Israeli forces at all levels, in all the wars which they fought. On 29th October, 4 Mustang fighters, flying at an altitude of just 10 feet, daringly severed vital Egyptian telephone lines in the Sinai. Then, 400 paratroopers dropped from low-flying Dakotas, captured the eastern end of the **Mitla Pass,** 30 miles east of the Suez Canal. In the centre, Colonel (later Premier) **Ariel Sharon** thrust through the Negev Desert to Kuntilla and forward to Thawad and Nakhi to support the paratroopers fighting at the Mitla Pass. They were also aided by armoured brigades from Nitzana, from where tanks were also dispatched due west to take Abu Agheila and Bir Gafgafa. Disobeying explicit orders from Dayan (who wanted this attack to be only a diversionary tactic), Sharon riskily thrust further east to take Ismailia on the Suez Canal itself (31st October). Israeli unit commanders invariably acted with great initiative, but like the German Panzer leaders—Guderian, Rommel and Manstein—had a penchant for exceeding their brief, if they sensed an opportunity!

Though central Sinai was now secured, the bulk of the Egyptian army was stationed in the north along the Mediterranean coast from **Gaza** and Rafah to El Arish. Separate Israeli tank attacks were launched eastwards on these positions. Strongly fortified earthen mounds at Rafah were bypassed and isolated, in tactics reminiscent of MacArthur's island-hopping operations in the Pacific. By now, Sharm el Sheikh in the extreme south, was totally cut off and ready to fall. Along the arid wastes of the east coast of the Sinai Peninsula, 2000 Israelis in 200 vehicles advanced southwards from Eilat to reach the town on 4th November. In support of this operation, tanks came down the west coast from the Mitla Pass and paratroopers were also dropped to secure various strategic points. The town surrendered on the 5th of November. All the major objectives of Dayan's "Operation Kadesh" were thus achieved within 7 days, with minimum casualties on either side, since Dayan's intention was to secure strategic territory, without suffering or even inflicting much damage to personnel. Though Israel was later forced, during negotiations, to give up her extensive territorial gains (including Sharm el Shaikh), she secured guaranteed access to the Gulf of Aqaba, her prime goal in this short but decisive war.

The Egyptian forces were under the overall command of **Gen. Al-Hakem Amer,** Deputy Supreme Commander, who was one of the leading lights of the revolution which had overthrown King Farouk. A conventionally competent soldier, he was, however, no match for the unpredictable Dayan, just as the professionally well-trained Egyptian army was no match for the innovative Israelis. After Egypt suffered another catastrophic defeat in the 6-day war of 1967, the unfortunate Amer was disgraced and forced to commit suicide.

The victor of the war of 1956, Moshe Dayan, was a multifaceted personality who later served as a war correspondent in Viet Nam, besides organizing archeological digs in the Middle East. He was Defence Minister during the 1967 and 1973 Arab-Israeli Wars. In 1979, as Foreign Minister, he negotiated the momentous peace treaty with Egypt, which led to Egypt's **Anwar Sadat** and Israel's **Menachim Begin** both receiving the Nobel Peace Prize. Though the vexed question of **Palestine** is still unresolved, the success of the treaty is demonstrated by the fact that there has been no Egypt-Israel War since. **Sadat** and his successor **Hosni Mubarak** (both secular but dictatorial rulers), consistently refused to undertake any overt anti-Israel move, despite the strong feelings of support among the Egyptian public towards their fellow-Arabs in the Gaza strip. In fact, the assassination of the former and the overthrow of the latter, can be largely attributed to their desire to coexist peacefully with the Jewish State. **Morsi**, the Muslim Brotherhood leader who took over from Mubarak, has himself been deposed by the Army, which has imposed a state of emergency.

C—PAKISTAN CUT TO SIZE

Sam Manekshaw and the Fall of Dacca (1971)

Of all the wars fought between India and Pakistan, the one in December, 1971 was the most important. It is also the most significant international conflict after 1945, resulting as it did, in the creation of a major nation, **Bangladesh**. The surrender en bloc of 93,000 Pakistani soldiers, and the liberation of East Pakistan and its 100 million people, effectively cut Pakistan down to size.

However, in hindsight, it was an event just waiting to happen, after decades of oppression of the Bengalis of East Pakistan by the aggressive Punjabis and Pathans—racially different peoples, with alien cultures and languages. Only 15 % of the national budget was allocated to East Pakistan, despite having over 50% of the population and only 5% of the officers in the Army were from the East!

The total neglect of the East after the horrendous cyclone of 1970, when 400,000 Bengalis lost their lives, was the last straw! The Pakistan election of 1970 saw **Mujib-ur Rahman's** Awami League winning 167 out of 169 seats in East Pakistan and out of 313 seats overall, with Bhutto's PPP securing just 88 seats, all in the West. With this clear majority, Sheik Mujib should have become Prime Minister of Pakistan, instead of which, he was thrown into jail and a reign of terror unleashed in the East. In the past too, Prime Ministers like Suhrawardy and Kwaja Nazimudin had been forced out because they were from East Pakistan. The crackdown in Dacca and elsewhere on 25th March, 1971 led to an influx of 10 million refugees into India. **Prime Minister Indira Gandhi** openly came out in support of Mujibur Rahman, and there was general international sympathy for the oppressed Bengalis of East Pakistan. The East Pakistan Rifles and the East Bengal Regiment mutinied to form the bulk of the revolutionary **Mukti Bahini.** To counter the pro-Pakistani vigilantes of the **Razakar Bahini**, the 50,000-strong nationalist **Mukti Bahini** was backed by India and given weapons and training.

The Pakistani leadership, including **President Yahya Khan** and **Gen Tikka Khan** (Martial Law Administrator), wanted to force India to fight the war mainly in the West. On 3rd December 1971, sorties were made on 8 Indian airfields in a not very successful pre-emptive strike. The war had begun in earnest. Pakistan was backed by USA, led by the virulently anti-Indian duo of President Nixon and Henry Kissinger. China too, was an open supporter of the Pakistani aggression.

The Indo-Soviet Treaty signed in August, 1971, proved a great source of strength for India. **Mrs. Gandhi's** core group of advisers included Defence Minister Jagjivan Ram, Defence Secretary K B Lall, P N Haksar, D P Dhar, T N Kaul and R N Kao (R&AW). The Navy was commanded by Admiral Nanda and the IAF by Air Chief Marshal P C Lal, both very competent professionals, but it was the iconic **Army Chief, Gen. Manekshaw,** who dominated the military operations and captured the public imagination!

"Sam" Manekshaw belonged to the tiny (but elite) Parsi community which produced greats like Phirozesha Mehta, Dadabhai Naoroji, Cricketers Polly Umrigar, Nari Contractor and Farokh Engineer, Homi Babha, conductor Zubin Mehta, Jurists Nani Palkiwala, S. H. Kapadia, Soli Sorabji and Fali Nariman, the Tatas, the Wadias and the Godrej family. Descendents of refugees from Persia, they have managed to retain their religion (Zoroastrianism), ethnicity, culture and identity over generations of exile. Manekshaw, after schooling at Sherwood, passed out in the first batch from the Indian Military Academy, Dehra Dun.

Sam Bahadur (as he was known) distinguished himself fighting the Japanese in Burma in 1942, winning the coveted Military Cross but was seriously wounded. When his unit (the Frontier Force) was transferred to the new Pakistan Army in 1947, he joined the Gurkha regiment of the Indian Army and had hands-on experience in Kashmir and the North-East, besides heading the Infantry School (Mhow) and (as Lt. General), the Defense Staff College (Wellington) in 1963. He was awarded the Padma Bhushan in 1968 and succeeded Gen. Kumaramangalam as Chief of Army Staff in 1969, proving himself a very popular, caring, professional and charismatic leader.

Extremely provocative action in March 1971 by **Tikka Khan**, *"the Butcher of Bengal"*, would have elicited an immediate punitive response from India, but Manekshaw convinced Indira Gandhi to wait till the winter snows in the Himalayas precluded any possible move by the Chinese, in support of Pakistan. Gen. Tikka's *"Operation Searchlight"* in March 1971 was not only focused against the minority Hindus, but also hit out at all **Bengali** speakers, drawing local support from the Urdu-speaking Bihari refugees who formed violent squads of vigilantes. They concentrated on hunting down Bengali intellectuals—teachers, writers, doctors, engineers, lawyers. **Maj.Gen. Rao Farman Ali** who led the operation asserted that Bengalis were not pure Muslims, because of undue Hindu influence. It was genocide at its worst as the lumpen elements raped, pillaged and murdered the hapless people of East Pakistan. According to **Haroon Habib,** Liberation fighter and author, 3 million Bengalis were butchered and hundreds of thousands of women molested during the next 9 months!

On 27th March, **"Bangladesh"** formally declared its independence from Pakistan through a radio broadcast. The Mukti Bahini strengthened by Bengali deserters from the armed forces attacked convoys, blew up bridges, sank ships and derailed trains, driving the Pakistanis out of Mymensing, Khulna, Rangpur and the northern Districts. The Bahini and its leaders—**Col. Osmani, Major (later President) Zia-Ur-Rahman** and **Mushtaq Mohamed**—were trained and guided by the dashing **Maj. Gen. Shabeg Singh** of the Indian Army. Gen Singh was ironically to die alongside Jarnail Singh **Bindranwale** in the Golden Temple on 6th June, 1984, resisting the Indian Army assault. There is indeed nothing more terrible than a fratricidal conflict!

Pakistan based its overall strategy on Israel's brilliant execution of the 6-day war in 1967 but the Bengal terrain was marshy and full of water bodies and paddy fields, inhibiting mobility and curtailing the use of US-supplied heavy armour. Eventually, Pakistan's **GOC (East) Lt.Gen. AAK Niazi** had to settle for holding on desperately to **Dacca** and sundry isolated strong points, with the **Mukti Bahini** moving freely around the rest of the country. In alliance with the Indian forces which now moved into East Bengal, they were now known as the **Mitro Bahini.** From West Pakistan, 3 powerful land attacks were launched eastwards across the border after the heavy Pakistani bombing of 8 Indian airfields on 3rd December, like the Israelis had done in the war of 1967. But learning the right lessons from that war, India had widely dispersed its Air Force planes in airfields away from the border and the pre-emptive strike achieved nothing. However, in the Pak land attack on the lightly held Chamb sector, India lost **Munawar Tawi** as strong enemy forces punched through the defences. J&K's land-link with India was threatened, but not severed and Yahya's plan of prising off that state failed. In the **Dras-Kargil** sector in the extreme north, India made valuable strategic gains occupying several high altitude points, which advantage Pakistan later sought to nullify in the next conflict in 1998! In the south, the Pakistani armoured assaults around **Longowal** were handicapped by the absence of specialist Bengali technicians. Moreover, lacking air support, they suffered heavy losses in men, material and territory.

Thus, Pakistan's attempt to shift the focus of the fighting to the Western sector, failed and the war was to be won, or lost, in Bengal by **Lt.Gen.AAK Niazi, Pakistan's GOC (East)** and his army of 93,000 West Pakistanis. Niazi's opponent in the eastern theatre was **Lt. Gen Jasjit Singh Arora, India's GOC (East)** and he termed the conflict in Sonar Bengal, *"the Battle of the Obstacles".* This would turn out to be an engineers' war since all bridges across the numerous rivers of the Ganges-Brahmaputra delta had been destroyed either by the Mukti Bahini or the retreating Pakistanis. India formulated an effective grand strategy in advance and the Joint Chiefs of Staff Committee had clear plans and objectives and enough time to prepare for the conflict. This enabled India to provide proper training for the patriots of the Mukti Bahini, a decisive factor in the coming conflict. The grand strategy spelt out the roles of the Navy and Air Force to provide synergy to the operations. The disastrous defeat of 1962 against China was now a closed chapter, followed as it was by the thumping victory over Pakistan in 1965. The morale of the Indian

Army was high and the soldiers firmly believed that they were fighting a just war to liberate the oppressed and downtrodden kindred people of Bangladesh from a cruel and tyrannical enemy.

Arjun A

Bangladesh—1971
21

As the IAF pounded Dacca's runways on 4th December, Gen. Arora ordered his multi-pronged forces to move into East Pakistan. From the West, **Lt. Gen. Raina's** 2nd Corps attacked in 3 columns—the northern column from Jibbanagar striking at Darsana; another due east from Royra to **Jessore**; the third, in the south, towards **Khulna.** From the northwest, 33 Corps thrusting from Balurghat, by-passed many Pak-held points and got behind **Dinajpur.** The bulk of the fighting in the north was undertaken by the native Mukti Bahini. **Gen Sagat Singh's** 4 Corps in the north-east, thrust at **Maulvi Bazar** in the Sylhet sector. The major thrust from Agartala was 3-pronged, all aiming west at strategic ferry-crossings on the **Meghna River,** which winds around Dacca on the southern and eastern sides, forming a strong defensive curtain.

Meanwhile, East Bengal was sealed off from the rest of the world by the Indian Air Force and Navy. IAF planes destroyed 14 Dacca-based Sabrejets. Against PAF's F86 Sabrejets and F 104 Starfighters, the IAF deployed Hunters, Gnat fighters and the Russian made MIG 21 and Sukhoi fighter bomber. Dive bombing created huge craters, rendering Pak airfields unusable. Air and heli borne support facilitated Indian army's aggressive operations. The aircraft-carrier *INS Vikrant* proved its worth with its planes striking the ports of **Chittagong** and **Cox's Bazar.** The Pakistan Navy's pride, the submarine *PNS Ghazi* (gifted by the US) was destroyed as it snooped around Vishakpatnam, by well-placed depth-charges dropped by the *INS Rajput*. India's Western Fleet created mayhem. Four missile boats and 2 warships bombarded **Karachi Harbour** at close range, after sinking the warship *PNS Khaibar*, the minesweeper *PNS Muhafiz* and several merchant vessels, besides crippling the *PNS Shah Jahan*. The only Indian loss was the frigate *INS Kukri* in the West, torpedoed by a Pak submarine. **Capt Mulla**, who posthumously received the Maha Veer Chakra for his valour, went down with his command, honorably refusing to abandon his ship.

On 6th December, India formally recognized Bangladesh. The noose tightened around Dacca as Indian paratroopers were dropped to take strategic points around it. Unconventional methods were used by the Indian army engineers to thrust rapidly forward. At **Jhenida** near Jessore, tanks crossed a 20-mile marshy stretch, using duckboards, to get behind the enemy! Some garrisons were bypassed and others surrendered, often without firing a shot. But the Pakistani forces were still entrenched strongly in Chittagong, Khushtia, Rangpur, Dinajpur and Rajshahi, apart from their main stronghold, Dacca.

President Nixon sent in the aircraft carrier *USS Enterprise threateningly*, but the US was warned off by the Soviets. The Indian columns converged rapidly on Dacca, crossing the waterways protecting the city. After Government House was attacked by planes of the IAF led by **S K Kaul** (later Air Chief) on 12th December, **Dr. Malik,** Governor of East Pakistan, resigned. The Pak army then moved into civilian areas, with Niazi's HQ positioned in the Dacca University buildings. The general himself enquired on 15th December, through the US Embassy, about the possibility of a ceasefire. In reply, Gen Manekshaw insisted that all Pakistani forces surrender **unconditionally** to the advancing Indians. **Maj.Gen.Jacob** was sent to Dacca with a draft "surrender instrument". On its acceptance by Niazi, Gen. Arora himself flew into Dacca accompanied by **Air Marshal Dhawan, Vice Admiral Krishnan** and **Maj. Khondkar** of the Mukti Bahini.

At 4.30 pm on Thursday, !6th December, 1971, Gen. Niazi signed the surrender papers and handed them over to Gen. J S Arora, along with his revolver, at the packed Race Course Maidan. A total of 93,000 Pakistanis surrendered, the largest capitulation since World War II. The Pakistani soldiers were apprehensive of reprisals if they were captured by the Mukti Bahini, since they had continued the massacre of civilians even on the 15th! They were therefore genuinely relieved to become prisoners of the Indian Army, which would treat them honourably, as per the Geneva Convention.

On 10th January 1972, **Mujib-ur-rahman,** released from a West Pakistan jail returned to a tumultuous welcome in Dacca. India secured a friendly neighbor, albeit briefly, for the secular Shaikh Mujib was assassinated by pro-Pakistan jihadi elements in 1975, heralding a succession of unfriendly regimes in Dacca like that of Khalida Zia and Gen. Ershad. Mujib's daughter, Shaikh Hasina, won the elections in 2008 with a massive mandate and the extremists and jihadis have been ousted. Interestingly, Tagore's *"Sonar Bengal"* was adopted as the national anthem for Bangladesh, in symbolic re-unification of Bengal, rectifying the sinister partitions of 1905 and 1947! It is indeed a matter of national pride that Tagore also scripted the anthem of Sri Lanka, apart from *"Jana Gana Mana"*! Bilateral talks during Prime Minister **Manmohan Singh's** state visit in September, 2011 have helped to resolve several issues. But the contentious Teesta riparian dispute could not be taken up because of **Chief Minister Mamata Banerji's** stiff opposition. The problem of 102 Indian enclaves in Bangladesh and 92 Bangladesh enclaves in India was also unresolved. Legend has it that these pockets were wagered by the Raja of Coochbehar and the Nawab of Rangpur, when they played chess! During the Partition in 1947, the former's kingdom joined India, while the latter's territories were absorbed into East Pakistan.

Pro-Pakistan elements are currently being tried for their complicity in the atrocities and genocide in 1971. In January, 2014 the *pro-jihadi* parties led by the **BNP** and **Jamaat,** boycotted the national elections, enabling the Awami League to continue in power but leaving the future uncertain.

24

EPILOGUE—THE INDIAN OCEAN SCENARIO—2014 AD

With the collapse of the Soviet Union and the breakdown of the bi-polar system, the USA became undisputed top dog in the global scheme, militarily and economically. But matters have not panned out quite as the US expected. Guerilla warfare and terror hits nullified the gains made by American military success in Iraq and Afghanistan, given the superpower's reluctance to maintain "boots on the ground" and suffer consequential casualties. It continues to need allies to assist in enforcing its global political agenda. Since the pendulum has clearly swung east, India, the world's largest democracy, is an obvious choice. Most analysts agree that the South/East China Seas and the lands east of the Caspian Sea are the two potential "super-hot spots" of the world, with India placed plumb in the middle.

America's gun boat style diplomacy, enforced through its 11 active air-craft carriers, necessitates a strong presence in the 74 million sq km Indian Ocean which straddles these spots. With 8 choke points and numerous regional hot spots, the Ocean is the most unstable area in the world. Add to this, the presence of pirates, especially at the eastern and western extremities, and you have a boiling cauldron of troubles. Through this passes 50% of the world's energy trade and 100,000 ships, annually. Jointly with Britain, the US has a presence through bases in **Diego Garcia, Seychelles, Oman** and **Singapore**, but the major participant in the region has to be India.

China's *"string of pearls"* policy threatens the status quo and can result in its attaining dominance. China's participation in the development of **Gwadar** (Pakistan), **Chittagong** (Bangladesh), **Cocos Island** (Myanmar) and **Hambantota** (Srilanka) ports plus acquisition of its first aircraft carrier, *Liaoning*, signal the initiation of its new **Blue Ocean** ie **open sea** strategy. China's PLA Navy has 3 commands—North, Central and South with an abundance of traditional **closed sea** forces—submarines, frigates, minesweepers. Its proposed Blue Ocean strategy involves the use of 3 Aircraft Carriers, Amphibious Transport Docks and Troop Landing Craft. China, under **Kublai Khan** in the 13th century, started looking west after its Hakata Bay invasions of Japan failed. Consequently, it developed trade and a significant presence in the "western ocean". **Marco Polo**, escorting a Mongol bride for the Shah of Persia, began his return journey to Europe in 1292, from Xanadu (Shengdu). He travelled with a small fleet of junks via Malacca to Jaffna and visited the court of Jatavarman Sundara **Pandyan** at **Madurai,** before proceeding across the Arabian Sea. Chinese involvement in the "Western Ocean" reached its apotheosis under the great **Admiral Cheng Ho** whose voyages (1405-33) criss-crossed the waters—Andamans, Bengal, Srilanka, Quilon, Cochin, Maldives, Aden, East Africa. However, when the Chinese homeland was threatened by nomadic raiders from across the Great Wall, they abandoned their ambitious Western Ocean plans. Pressure from Portuguese, Dutch and English sea power thereafter, kept them confined to their own shores. Currently, there is a revival of expansionist marine activity after 500 years, based on altered strategic perceptions. Symptomatic of this outreach is the new interest of Chinese scholars in the ceramic collection from the **Pattanam** excavations in Kerala to link up with the voyages and settlements of the past.

Aggressive posturing in land disputes with neighbours has been a consistent feature of China's foreign policy. The recent disputes with **Japan** over suzerainty of islands in the East China Sea, ADIZ (Air Defence Identification Zone) monitoring and buzzing of non-Chinese ships and planes are symptomatic of China's new awareness of the importance of sea power as propounded by **Admiral Mahan**. China's next obvious major step will be into the Indian Ocean on some pretext like fighting pirates or assisting an ally!

While it may not be feasible for India to directly flex its muscles in the Yellow Sea or the South and East China Seas, we are strengthening ties with Vietnam, Taiwan, South Korea, Malaysia, Singapore, Brunei, Philippines, Thailand and most importantly, **Japan.** The Japanese refer to India as *Tenjiku* (the Heavenly Country) and their cultural heritage, religion and even language owe much to the ancient Indian connection. Japan's victory in the Russo-Japanese War (1904-5) was seen by Indians as a triumph of the East over the West and spurred on our Freedom Movement. During the 2nd World War Subash Chandra Bose and the INA fought alongside the Japanese Imperial forces. The recent visit of **Emperor Akihito** and **Empress Machiko**, 50 years after their honeymoon trip, was a watershed in bilateral relations. Despite the emperor's age and poor health, the imperial couple acceded to a pressing request from **Prime Minister Shinzo Abe**, a clear signal that India is a vital ally on economic, strategic, diplomatic and other fronts. Significantly, Shinzo Abe was the Chief Guest at India's Republic Day function in 2014, leading to an agreement to promote investment in the politically sensitive North-Eastern States, parts of which China terms "disputed territoty". Closer ties in the nuclear industry are also in the offing. Japan is already a critical technology provider and India's largest source of aid, especially in infrastructure building.

Western Freight Corridor, Delhi-Mumbai and Chennai-Bangalore Industrial Corridors, several Metro Rail Projects and Nalanda University. The two countries have entered into a $ 50 billion currency swap agreement to ease foreign exchange problems. For energy-poor Japan, keeping the Indian Ocean traffic hassle-free is a top priority. The interests of India and Japan are obviously congruent and their strengths are complementary. Japan's Maritime Self Defence Force, the largest navy in Asia, could keep PLAN tied down to its home waters and thwart China's aggressive designs in the Indian Ocean.

India astutely planned its Indian Ocean response early, with a 3 aircraft carrier strategy. Unfortunate delays in the commissioning of the *INS Vikramaditya* (formerly *Admiral Gorshkov*) have held up execution of India's **grand strategy,** which includes empowering the army and air force suitably. While ensuring procurement of the highest quality, India should not forget the consistent support provided by the Soviet Union and its successor state, **Russia,** while sourcing defense equipment from abroad. The 45,000 tonne supership, equipped with a variety of helicopters and 45 MIG-29K planes, will be based out of *INS Kadamba* (Karwar). A force multiplier in attack, it can be vulnerable to surface ships, submarines, torpedoes and air attack, unless screened by an appropriate fleet. Any failure of this protective cover could be disastrous considering its cost of $ 3 billion! India's longterm plans include acquisition of a nuclear-powered carrier, *INS Vishal*. India's focus has always been on the Pakistan and China land borders, with deserts, plains and mountain warfare as terrain options. Our new holistic strategy will involve developing **amphibious** divisions and other relevant additions to our army and air force to help the navy sustain its superiority out in the Indian Ocean. The sheltered peninsula of South India is rapidly gaining importance in defence matters as it now hosts not only increasing air and naval power through bases, but also important production and training facilities.

It is clear that India's future security hinges on integrated and synergistic action by the three armed forces. The proposed appointment of a **Chief of Defence Staff** to formulate, coordinate and implement **grand strategy** will be a major step forward. While retaining relative autonomy in technical matters like choice of equipment or details of operational tactics, the **strategy level** decisions of the defence forces should be fully complemented by symbiosis with the supervisory **political system**. Keeping a **firewall** between civil and military matters/authority was an integral part of the British system, a fine democratic tradition which India rightly adopted and maintained despite frictions and provocations on both sides.

The recent spate of submarine accidents has put these relationships under great stress Frictions have to be amicably resolved. Leakage of the apparently adverse Henderson Brooks Report has also put the political leadership on the defensive. IDSA guru Subrahmanyam however opined in a 1970 paper that we lost in 1962 because we fought the wrong kind of war with our "Forward Policy", much like the failed French "hedgehog "strategy in Viet Nam for territory domination, but with very small posts. This reckless policy was spurred by jingoistic pressure from sections of the Indian polity.

But the ultimate decision to **make war** or negotiate **peace** can and should rest only with the representatives of the people. As **Carl Clausewitz** elegantly put it 200 years ago, *"war is an extension of policy"* and further that *"the outlines of a war are determined by a political body— the* **Cabinet***".*

Arvind Gupta, Director—general of IDSA (Institute for Defence Studies and Analysis) stresses the need for India to refocus on the interface between "the Siamese twins" ie defence and diplomacy, in our dealings with foreign powers to ensure synergy between the efforts of the Defence and External Affairs ministries. This is detailed in IDSA'sTask Force Reports-*Deliberations of a Working Group on Military and Diplomacy*, available on *www.idsa.in.* It is not enough that a few IFS officers like G Parthasarathy have a military background; all MEA officers should receive defence orientation, especially since the top post of NSA appears to be exclusively earmarked for the IFS cadre.

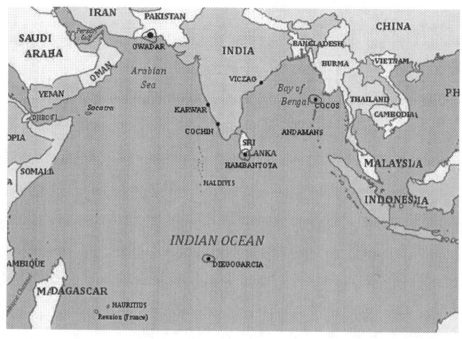

Jaya A

Indian Ocean—2014
22

India has several significant advantages over most countries. Though noisy and fractious, our truly democratic form of government represents the genuine will of the people. Like SPQR, "**Senate and People of Rome**", (Ch. 4, page 37) of Republican Rome, we often err in decision-making and are rather slow to act, but our policies reflect the real aspirations of our people.

Apart from aspects of *hard power* discussed above, India has greater potential for using its *soft power* thanks to affinities in culture, language, ethnicity, religion, economics and a long and uninterrupted historical engagement with the peoples of the **islands** and littoral lands of the Indian Ocean. This invisible sphere of influence covers the vast land arc from South Africa all the way to Australia and includes the island nations—Madagascar, Seychelles. Mauritius, Maldives, Srilanka. India is a **full member** of the **Indian Ocean Rim Association,** an organization for regional cooperation, with China being only a dialogue partner.

In our dealings with other association members, we should not allow national policy to be sacrificed at the altar of sectoral interests and opinions of individual states and regions, as is happening in our dealings with Bangladesh and Srilanka.

Holistic bonding through increased political, economic, cultural, trade, industrial, academic and technological interaction is an imperative, apart from the obvious defense tie-ups. Special relationships have to be entered into wherever deemed essential. Only then can we hope to create a truly **Indian Ocean** at our door-step, as a zone of security, peace and cooperation for us, and for all others!

SELECT BIBLIOGRAPHY

Arrian—*Anabasis of Alexander*

Aurelius, Marcus—*Thoughts*

Bahl, Raghav—*Superpower*

Barnett, Corelli—(1) *The Swordbearers* (2) *Britain and her Army* 3) *Marlborough*

Banerji, A.N.—*Great Commanders*

Barry, James—*Business War Games*

Bhargava, P.L.—*Chandragupta*

Baigent, Michael et al.—*Holy Blood, Holy Grail*

Berne, Eric—*Games People Play*

Barrow, G.W.S.—*Robert Bruce*

Bhonsle, Prince Tulajendra—*Serfoji II & a History of Thanjavur Marathas*

Bhutto, Z A—*If I am Assassinated*

Blake, Robert—*Management Grid for Situational Leadership*

Bray, Warwick—*Penguin Dictionary of Archaeology*

Brecht, Berthold—*Mother Courage*

Brown, Dan—*Da Vinci Code*

Buchan, John—*Montrose*

Bury, A.J.—*The History of Greece*

Burne, A—*Agincourt War*

Byron, Lord-*The Destruction of Sennacherib (poem)*

Cam, Helen—*England before Elizabeth*

Calvocoressi, P.—*Total War*

Carell, Paul—*Scorched Earth*

Chanakya/Kautilya (tr by R Shamasastri)—*Arthasastra*

Clammer, D.—*Zulu War*

Churchill, Sir Winston—(1) *Marlborough* (2) *Frontiers and Wars* (3) *History of the English Speaking People*

Choudhary, N.C.—*Clive of India*

Cottrell, Leonard—*Enemy of Rome*

Creasy, Sir Edward—*15 Decisive Battles*

Clausewitz, Carl von—*On War*

Clavell, James—*Shogun*

Dalrymple, William—*The Last Mughal*

Das, Gurcharan—*India Unbound*

De Gaulle, Charles—*The Army of the Future*

Daumas, Maurice—*A History of Technology*

Debray, Regis—*1) Revolution in the Revolution 2) Che's Guerilla War*

Deanesly, M—*History of Early Medieval Europe*

Deighton, Len—*Blitzkrieg*

Downs, Robert—*Books that changed the world*

Drucker, Peter—(1) *The Effective Executive* (2) *Management*

Dumas, Alexandre—*1) The Three Musketeers 2) Twenty Years After*

Edward, E I S—*The Pyramids of Egypt*

Eliot, T S—*Little Gidding*

Fall, Bertrand—*Hell is a very small place*

Fayol, Henry—*Industrial and General Administration*

Fisher, H A L—*A History of Europe*

Fitzgerald, C P-*1) History of East Asia 2) Birth of Communist China*

Fuller, J.F.C—(1) *Grant and Lee* (2) *Decisive Battles of the Western World* (3) *Plan 1919* (4) *Instructions for Tank Commanders*

Fletcher, Sir Bannister—*A History of Architecture*

Fletcher, G.R.L.—*Gustavus Adolphus*

Fraser, Lady Antonia—*Mary, Queen of Scots*

Fry, P S—*The Zebra Bookof Castles*

Gandhi, M K—*Discourses on the Gita*

Ghosh, Amitav—*The Glass Palace*

Gladwell, Malcolm—*1) Blink, 2) Outliers*

Gleig, G.R.—*Wellington*

Goldratt, Elihu—*Goal*

Green, H.—*Great Military Battles*

Guderian, Field Marshal Heinz—*Panzer Leader*

Hacket, Gen. Sir John—(1) *World War III* (2) *Popski's Private Army* (3) *I was a stranger*

Henty, G.A.—1) *The Young Carthagenian* 2) *With Clive in India*

Heyer, G.—*The Conqueror*

Hibbert, Christopher—(1) *The Great Indian Mutiny* (2) *Waterloo* (3) *Corunna* (4) *Anzio*

Hitti, Prof Philip—1) *History of the Arabs* 2) *Makers of Arab History* 3) *The Near East in History*

Hohne, H and Zolling H—*The General was a Spy*

Horne, Alistair—1) *Napoleon* 2) *To Lose a Battle*

Hough, Richard—*Mountbatten*

Hugo, Victor—*Les Miserables*

Itasaka, Gen—*Gates to Japan*

Jarman, T.L.—*Rise and Fall of Nazi Germany*

Jewel, D.—*Alamein* Kingsley, Charles—*Hereward the Wake*

Kinross, John—*Discovering Castles in England and Wales*

Kodansha International—*Japan*

Kondo, Prof Yoshio—*Human Motivation*

Kosambi, D.D.—*Ancient India*

Kulkarni, U.S—*Solstice at Paniput*

Lawrence, T.E—*The Seven Pillars of Wisdom*

Lewis, Bernard—*The World of Islam*

Liddell Heart, Sir Basil—(1) *Rommel Papers* (2) *Greater than Napoleon* (3) *The Other Side of the Hill* (4) *T.E. Lawrence* (5) *World War I* (6) *World War II* 7) *Strategy of the Indirect Approach*

Livesy, A—*Battles of the Great Commanders*

Lockhart, J.E.—*Napoleon*

Ludwig, Emil—*Napoleon*

Lytton, Lord—*The Last of the Barons*

Macaulay, Lord—*History of England*

Macksey, K.—(1) *Tank Warfare* (2) *Africa Corps*

Mahingoda, P—*Monarchs of Lanka*

Majumdar, R.C.—*Advanced History of India*

Malgaokar, Manohar—(1) *The Sea Hawk* (2) *The Devil's Wind*

Man, John—*Genghis Khan*

Markham, Felix—*Napoleon*

Mattingley, Gerard—*Renaissance Diplomacy*

Maule, Henry—*Battles of World War II*

Miers, E.S.—*Robert Lee*

Mitford, Nancy—*The Sun King*

Mordal, J.—*25 Centuries of Sea Warfare*

Montgomery, Field Marshal B.L.—*Memoirs*

Melenthin, F. von—*Panzer Battles*

McGregor, Douglas—*The Human Side of Enterprise*

McClelland, David—*Achievement Motivation*

Moorehead, Allan—*Montgomery*

Morita, Akio—*Made in Japan*

Mosely, Leonard—*Marshall, Organizer of Victory*

Motley, J.F.—*The Dutch Republic*

Musashi, Miyamoto—*The Book of the Five Rings*

Naisbitt, John—*Megatrends*

Nehru, Jawaharlal—(1) *Glimpses of World History* (2) *The Discovery of India*

Nutting, Anthony—*The Arabs*

Oblonsky, Dimitri—*The Byzantine Commonwealth*

Ohmae, Keneichi—*The Mind of the Strategist*

Oman, C.W.C.—1) *A History of Greece* 2) *Wellington's Army*

O'Neill, S J—*Castles of England and Wales*

Pamuk, Orhan—1) *Istanbul* 2) *My Name is Red*

Perroy, Edouard Prof—*The Hundred Years War* (tr. By David Douglas)

Petrie, Sir Charles—*The Jacobite Movement*

Porter, Jane—*The Scottish Chiefs*

Prakash, Dr. Budhi—*The History of Porus*

Ramaswamy, N S—*House of God*

Redford, Donald—*Wars of Thothmes in Syria/Palestine*

Revans, Prof Reg—*Action Learning*

Ritter, E.A.—*Shaka Zulu*

Runciman, Sir Stephen—*The Crusades*

Scot, Sir Walter—*Ivanhoe* 2) *Talisman*

Seymour, William—*Battles in Britain*

Sen, Amartya—*The Argumentative Indian*

Sewell, Robert—*The Forgotten Empire*

Shakespeare, William—*1) Henry IV, Parts 1&2 2) Henry V 3) Macbeth 3) Julius Caesar*

Shastri, K.A. Neelakanta—*Comprehensive History of India*

Shaw, George Bernard—*St. Joan*

Sheoray, I.—*Tantia Tope*

Shirer, William—1) *The Rise and Fall of the Third Reich* 3) *Collapse of the 3rd Republic*

Slim, Field Marshal Viscount—*Defeat into Victory*

Speer, Albert—*Inside the Third Reich*

Summerton, Oswald—*Transactional Analysis*

Sun, Tzu—*The Art of War*

Sutcliffe, R—*Simon*

Taylor, A.J.P.—(1) *Bismarck* (2) *Churchill* (3) *The Origins of World War II*

Thapar, Romila—*A History of India*

Tolstoy, Count Leo—*War and Peace*

Tolstoy, Nikolai—*Night of the Long Knives*

Tout, T F—*The Empire and the Papacy*

Toy, Sidney—*The Castles of Great Britain*

Toynbee, A J—*A Study of History*

Tranter, Nigel—*1) Black Douglas 2) Lords of Misrule*

Trevelyan, G.M.—*History of England*

Tuchman, Barbara—1) *The Zimmerman Telegram 2) Stilwell and American Experience in Chna*

Verrier, Anthony—*The Bomber Offensive*

Vidal, Gore—*Julian*

Vroom, Victor—*Leadership and Decisionmaking*

Vyasa (tr by C Rajagoplachari)—*Mahabharata*

Warner, Rex—*World Mythology*

Wells, H.G.—*Outlines of World History*

Waugh, Elizabeth—*Simon Bolivar*

WebsterSmith—Sieges from Troy to Kut

Wedgewood C V—*The King's War*

Wheatcroft, Andrew—*The World Atlas of Revolutions*

Wilkinson, Frederick—*Arms and Armour*

Williams, John—*The Ides of May*

Wilson, W S—*The Lone Samurai*

Xenophon—*The Retreat of the Ten Thousand*

Yonge, C—*A Book of Golden Deeds*

Young, Desmond—*Rommel*

Zubrzycki, John—*The Last Nizam*

Bryson, Bill—*A Short History Of Nearly Everything*

Misra, Jayasree—*Rani*